IN GLORIOUS TECHNICOLOR

Also by Francine Stock

A Foreign Country
Man-Made Fibre

IN GLORIOUS TECHNICOLOR

A Century of Film and How it Has Shaped Us

Francine Stock

with Stephen Hughes

Chatto & Windus
LONDON

Published by Chatto & Windus 2011

2 4 6 8 10 9 7 5 3 1

Copyright © Francine Stock 2011

Francine Stock has asserted her right under the Copyright, Designs and
Patents Act 1988 to be identified as the author of this work.

'Nanook' song on page 60, words by John Milton Hagen and Herb Crooker,
music by Victor Nurnberg, copyright 1922 Cameo Music Publishing Co..
'Remember My Forgotten Man' from *Gold Diggers of 1933*, quoted on page 92, by
Harry Warren and Al Dubin, copyright Warner Communications, Inc., 2004.

Every effort has been made to trace or contact all copyright holders, and the
publishers will be pleased to correct any omissions brought to their notice
at the earliest convenience.

First published in Great Britain in 2011 by
Chatto & Windus
Random House, 20 Vauxhall Bridge Road,
London SW1V 2SA

www.randomhouse.co.uk

Addresses for companies within The Random House Group Limited can be
found at: www.randomhouse.co.uk/offices.htm

The Random House Group Limited Reg. No. 954009

A CIP catalogue record for this book
is available from the British Library

ISBN 9780701183950

The Random House Group Limited supports The Forest Stewardship
Council, the leading international forest certification organisation.
Our books carrying the FSC label are printed on FSC certified paper.
FSC is the only forest certification scheme endorsed by the leading
environmental organisations, including Greenpeace. Our paper

CONTENTS

· · · · · · · · · · · ·

I stir the blood. I quicken the pulses. I encourage the imagination, I stimulate the young. I comfort and I solace the old and sorrowing . . .

I show more of travel than all the books penned by all the writers of the world. I preach sermons to congregations, greater than the combined flocks of the pulpits of all lands . . .

I am history, written for generations to come in a tongue that every race and sect and creed can understand. I preserve heroes for posterity. I give centuries more of life to the arts and sciences. I am man's greatest and noblest invention.

I am the Motion Picture.

Arthur James, distributed by Metro Pictures to theatres throughout the US in the spring of 1916

PROLOGUE

· · · · · · · · · · · · · · · · ·

When I was small I was taken to see *My Fair Lady*. Excited enough by the business of being there – plush seats, promise of an ice cream – I knew that a story of the 'long ago' type with lovely dresses and singing would unfold. Nothing though prepared me for the titles. Huge blooms filled the screen; flowers so large and lustrous that I thought my head would burst. I realised later their connection to Eliza Doolittle's occupation but at that moment they were inexplicable and nothing in the film, not even Rex Harrison's barking or Audrey Hepburn's frocks, came anywhere near that first overwhelming combination of florescence and melody. At once terrifying and rapturous, it was a glimpse into a world infinitely more intense than the one outside. We were living in Australia at the time where the gardens were bursting with exotic flora yet those Technicolor flowers were suddenly, startlingly authentic while the real thing faded to pale imitation. When, decades later, I peered into universes created by Max Ophuls, Vincente Minnelli or Martin Scorsese, that dizziness returned.

For years simply recalling the monolith in *2001: A Space Odyssey* would send a bolt of adrenaline through my system. Later, at secondary school in England, if rain prevented sport, we might be corralled into the hall where the projector would spool through either a gruesome natural history film or one of three old and oddly assorted features. There was the 1958 *A Tale of Two Cities* – meant I think to be inspirational, as Dirk Bogarde spent time gazing onscreen at Dorothy Tutin, who was, incidentally, an Old Girl. The other two (far less popular, except with me) were Kosintsev's *Hamlet* and Kurosawa's *Throne of Blood*, always referred to by the teachers as the Japanese *Macbeth* (they really knew how to sell their entertainment). These were strange sights, particularly through the fog of steam rising from a hundred heads of damp hair. The subtitles were wobbly and puzzling or silly but that was incidental; what was compelling, although it was hardly cool to say so, was the restless camera in Elsinore and the horrors rising out at the samurai from the mists around Cobweb Castle (the subtitles always did their best to spoil the drama).

My memories are punctuated and intertwined with film. As far as I can see from records, the summer of 1970 was meteorologically unremarkable yet coloured for me by repeated visits with my friend Ali to see *Butch Cassidy and the Sundance Kid*. Bicycles or horses, it hardly mattered – we were both the outlaws and simultaneously Katharine Ross, and the summer holidays were tinted with the dusty gold of that film's ready-made nostalgia, a sentiment we were too young to recognise.

As an only child, I had felt that I lived in books until the cinema revealed to me an almost physical presence that literature, though incomparably better in other ways – could not achieve. Books I appropriated, the characters belonged to me insofar as I knew them intimately, but I was haunted by films. They kept their independence and left me sometimes with a feeling of being incomplete. It was not so much a case of being in love with a screen idol as with the whole contents of the screen itself. Even a mundane location, a kitchen or corridor, took on a profundity that belied its two dimensions.

It could even displace reality. At sixteen, I was watching *Chinatown* in a local cinema; Jack Nicholson's nose had just been sliced by Roman Polanski's blade when suddenly a policeman clambered up in front of the screen and told us to leave the cinema as quickly and as calmly as we could. IRA terrorists had detonated a bomb in an adjacent pub and a second blast was anticipated. Even as we sheltered outside in the blue flashing lights, I was still in 1930s Los Angeles. Something of the film's confusion and guilt clung to me even in that emergency.

As a student, the first film I reviewed was Werner Herzog's *Stroszek*, in which the central character was played by Bruno S. He was not a trained actor; this was only his second film and the script, written for him by Herzog, had aspects that mirrored his own life. Was he even acting? I emerged from the cinema in a kind of uneasy stupor, suddenly displaced in a familiar street. If Bruno S was wandering America in a state of genuine amazement, was I also the lead actor in my own feature? Later I read Jean Cocteau's observation that film was not so much the account of a dream 'as a dream in which we all participate together through a kind of hypnosis'.

Film's influence was also a knowing joke. I fell for a man who could nail James Mason's distinctive voice and later for a Francophone with an irresistible Jean-Paul Belmondo grin. There were many more important reasons to love them but that connection gave them a secret familiarity. In some small way, we had met before.

Like a shape behind the curtain, film was continually a presence. Reporting for the BBC from the Bush–Gorbachev summit in Washington in 1990, my friend Margaret and I went after work to a late-night screening of the Ridley Scott thriller *Black Rain*, set in Tokyo. When Michael Douglas despatched his first Japanese opponent shouts and whoops erupted from the theatre, shocking us out of our jetlag. Our daytime challenge was to interpret the Russian and American presidents' careful proclamations about the 'New World Order' that would succeed Cold War aggression. Here, though, both onscreen and in the audience around us, was something more immediate, visceral and disturbing – another glimpse of geopolitics.

Time and time again, this parallel view of the world has cut across my experience in a way that is constantly intriguing. When I started working on arts programmes and spent an increasing amount of time in the dark gazing at a screen, I began to wonder more about film's effect beyond the traditional parameters of film criticism and film history. Discussions and disagreements over the years working with Stephen Hughes, on BBC Radio 4's *The Film Programme*, with his encyclopaedic knowledge, search-engine curiosity and philosopher's logic, raised all kinds of new areas of interest. How could something as patently artificial as film seem so real? We all know that what we see on screen is not real and yet we experience it so intensely that it provokes a physical response. Might there be particular effects on our behaviour – both public and private? Ways in which we had become indoctrinated by this most seductive medium? Researching for a series on film some years ago, we hunted in vain for a book that tackled these ideas.

For a hundred years, in ways entertaining, mysterious and occasionally sinister, film – this thing of our own creation – has framed our view of the world. Increasingly, our reference points tend to be situations, characters and lines not from books but cinema. Yet this looking-glass world does not simply reflect back to us directly our experiences, aspirations and fears. Advertising can do that. Film, by contrast, regularly distorts or obscures; we may even for a while not recognise ourselves at all. Our relationship with the screen is not so much cause and effect as a counterpoint of real events with a range of refracted invisibles like ambition, regret, pride, neurosis and euphoria.

This book is neither a comprehensive history of cinema nor an attempt to extend the sometimes daunting territory of film studies. It is an impressionistic map of the way film has entered our lives, criss-crossing with our experience and permeating our values. The films selected here may not necessarily be the best of their kind or even personal favourites, although many are. Rather, they are films that exert a particular power – whether, for example, to forge national identity or set ideals for romantic love or even persuade the fashionable male to abandon the vest. Such effects may not be confined to a particular decade nor are these films the exclusive examples, but they are for one reason or another outstanding.

The reason for taking this idiosyncratic journey through a century of film is precisely to provoke argument and further exploration. It is easier now than ever to get hold of films from earlier decades and different continents: everyone will add their own suggestions. This selection is necessarily skewed towards the American film because, like it or not, Hollywood has for nearly a hundred years dominated cinema viewing in the English-speaking world and often beyond. The journey would take another route if this book were written in China, Russia or India, or in the second half of the twenty-first century. For now, though, from here, this is the view.

Good films don't submit to a single interpretation; they may spring from a particular era but they refuse to be anchored there. That vitality and variety has provoked a thousand conversations between screen and audience. It can travel with us as we leave the cinema, arguing over what we've seen, as we make our way home and then over dinner that night; it can lodge in our memories, emerging at unexpected moments, slowly changing our view of the world around us. This book is an attempt to record snatches of the conversation that has been taking place between us and film for the past hundred years. It is also a very personal contribution to that discussion.

1910s
....

THE FACE IN THE CROWD

The mass entertainment that aspired to dominate continents and decades began with a small, involuntary paroxysm. In 1894, twenty-two years before Arthur James's grandiose eulogy, Thomas Edison registered the first copyrighted motion picture in America. Recorded in a New Jersey studio, it comprised a five-second performance by Fred Ott, a photographic assistant. For the *Edison Kinetoscopic Record of a Sneeze* he negotiated a pinch of snuff above his fine handlebar moustache and sneezed heartily, holding a handkerchief for dramatic rather than practical effect. Like a number of the diversions developed by Edison in collaboration with photographer W.K.L. Dickson, the *Record of a Sneeze* had few pretensions. The Kinetoscope was a box to be set up at showgrounds and other entertainments; the film was operated on a small mechanism and viewed by one or two people at a time, and the whole exercise was simply a gimmick, a sideshow that might relieve the crowds of a cent or two.

Yet the filmed sneeze was also – in a tiny, absurd way – an analysis of an enigma. Travelling at thirty-five to forty miles an hour, a sneeze eluded scrutiny, especially by the sneezer. This everyday puzzle could now be observed in all its comic violence. Everyone would understand at once what they were seeing and yet they were fascinated: perhaps something hitherto unknown might be revealed.

Was it simply the motion that was so compelling? A device called the Zoetrope, whereby the spectator gazed through a small gap at a revolving frieze of images, had amused children and adults alike since the second century and was still a popular parlour entertainment in the mid-nineteenth century. Yet by the century's final decade and Edison's snippets of flickering marvels – the boxing cats, bucking broncos and bulging strongmen – the attraction may have lain partly in pinning down the evanescent, in mysteries captured. Edison did not at first believe that film would have a mass appeal and fill theatres to bursting but the selection of subjects suggests that, even in the most apparently banal, there was a riddle that tugged at people's understanding of reality. In a world of laws and logic there are phenomena too fast or too curious not to make us wonder.

Moving pictures themselves had been recorded a few years before in 1888, when an English family had staggered for a handful of seconds in a garden, captured on paper film with a single lens camera by Louis Le Prince, a Frenchman living in Leeds. William Friese Greene, an Englishman, patented a celluloid process the following year. Their work was the logical technical development of sequential photographs of cantering horses, lumbering buffalo or bathing girls taken a decade earlier by Eadweard Muybridge with multiple cameras. He had placed twenty-four cameras side by side along a racetrack in response to a wager as to whether a horse ever kept all four hooves off the ground at once. By 1879 the hand-cranked Zoopraxiscope allowed spectators to see the photographs in sequence. If they glimpsed all twenty-four images within a second the eye and the brain believed there was no interruption. That ratio came to be the standard exposure speed for film. In 1960 the French New Wave director Jean-Luc Godard had a character in *Le Petit Soldat* state that if photography were truth, then film was truth twenty-four times a second . . . Nearly forty years later, however, in *The Matrix*, the Wachowski Brothers would use a similar – if far more elaborate – setup to Muybridge's to create a surreal effect that questioned the apparent veracity of each frame. With a circular arrangement of cameras, they appeared to capture the movement of bullets in slow motion as the hero Keanu Reeves bent backwards to dodge them, an effect known as 'bullet time', as a composition of images created an illusion, fragments of truth combined to create a fiction.

The shift from nineteenth to twentieth century must at times have seemed like science fiction in its unprecedented haste and movement. New methods and inventions from the second industrial revolution, the technological innovations of applied electricity and the diesel engine, of phonograph and radio, aeroplanes and automobiles, had transformed life and work for people in developed areas.

Increasingly, the population shifted from the country to towns and cities; they might travel on railways that transformed trade and warfare alike, from coast to coast in the United States, crossing the Omaha prairies, as well as English moors and Italian plains. Bold planners considered laying iron tracks across Africa or the Middle East. There were trials of flying machines and floating dirigibles. The world was at once shrinking and becoming more populous: the global tally of one billion in 1825 doubled within the next hundred years. Crowds were now an unremarkable feature of urban life. Pavements were daily used by more individuals than most people had ever glimpsed on market days in their childhoods. Telegraph and newspaper carried information about yet more unknown individuals. The old networks of kith and kin were stretched and disturbed.

A series of World's Fairs from London's 1851 Great Exhibition onwards celebrated not only innovation and achievement but also scale. The 1889

Paris Exposition Universelle attracted more than thirty-two million visitors over six months and Chicago's World's Fair in 1893 twenty-seven million. The Chicago Fair was also the first to honour the increasing presence of women in the workforce. By now, two-thirds of teachers were women as were a third of factory workers; soon they would become enthusiastic consumers of film and even the earliest filmmakers recognised the importance of providing women onscreen whom they could relate to or admire.

The fairs were spectacular showcases of new technology where ideas could be exchanged or purloined. At the 1889 Paris Exposition, Thomas Edison could have glimpsed French and German film devices; by the 1900 fair, Auguste and Louis Lumière had erected a huge screen on which their short films were projected. The brothers, who worked in their father's photographic business, first screened in public a film of workers leaving their factory in Lyons in December 1895, having patented the *cinématographe* the previous February.

Over the next few years, even sceptics realised that the penny diversion of moving pictures had mass appeal. It was no longer a question of a minor attraction on a variety bill but an entertainment in itself. British and French production companies were formed, including Gaumont in 1895 and Pathé in 1896. The Lumières travelled the world from Moscow to Shanghai, New York to Buenos Aires showing their glimpses of factory workers, oncoming trains and sea-bathing. Many of the early films in all countries were documentary, such as state occasions, panoramic views or tableaux vivants on historical or literary themes. One of the earliest from the Edison stable, *The Execution of Mary Queen of Scots* (1895), employs the first recorded special effect, with the camera stopped and a dummy inserted for the fall of the axe. However basic the effect, it is plausible and even horrible: the decapitation still jolts. Contemporary audiences might well have believed at the very least that the actress had been harmed in the making of the twenty-second picture.

Filmmakers even experimented with sound and colour until practicalities forced them to put those to one side. Edison's studio had worked on coordinating the technologies of Kinetoscope and phonograph and a French cylinder-based system was shown at the 1900 Exposition but, as with other methods, these early talking pictures were hampered by insufficient amplification and the crucial difficulty of synchronising sound to picture. Pictures might be hand-painted or stencilled, tinted or toned – often in sections to emphasise a rosy or crepuscular mood – but colour was not central to the experience.

As Arthur James rhapsodised in 1916, travel had become instantly possible simply by a visit to a vaudeville show, where film might be one of the many acts, or to a dedicated movie theatre. Mexico City, for example, had sixteen film salons by 1906. A wildly popular attraction, Hale's Tours and Scenes of the World, shown in old railway carriages, first appeared at the St Louis Exposition of 1904 – by the end of the decade, there had been five hundred appearances in locations as widely spread as Germany, Australia, South Africa and Hong Kong. Spectators sat inside the converted carriage while travelling views of scenic wonders were projected on to screens in the windows, giving the participants a virtual journey through the Rocky Mountains or Utah. Effects – whistles, clanking and steam – were provided, the whole being billed as 'the last word in the practical use of the animated picture as an educative entertainment'.

Pathé opened an office in the United States in 1904 and within four years was established as the major supplier of film there, demonstrating the industrial principles of direct integration that would be taken up later by American studios. While the French company soon had offices all around the world, London, capital of a great shipping and broking nation, served as the clearing house for the international film market.

Out of Europe arose many of the genres that would later dominate the medium. The French excelled in comedies, and in magician Georges Méliès, with his fairy and absurdist tales and *A Trip to the Moon* (1902), they produced a master of the fantastical image whose dreamscapes would continue to influence a century later. The French were also early producers of screen villains or fiendish anti-heroes. The young Jean-Paul Sartre, born in 1905, spent formative childhood years with his mother visiting Boulevard cinemas in Paris, to the disapproval of his grandfather. As he recalled in his memoir, *Words*, published in 1964, 'In the egalitarian discomfort of the local halls, I had realised that this new art was mine, was everyone's. We had the same mental age: I was seven and could read; it was twelve and could not speak. They said it was just starting and would improve; I thought we would grow up together.' There the undoubtedly excitable, if not over-stimulated, youth saw the exploits of the criminals *Zigomar* (1911) and *Fantomas* (1913), early examples of almost instant page to screen adaptation. The British also favoured clowning, documentary and early detective stories like *Rescued by Rover* (1905). The Scandinavians were masters of the intense melodrama, dwelling on the darker side of the psyche. These films were not set in palaces or hovels, but often in comfortable parlours and kitchens; the protagonists might be artists or doctors or teachers, like Magda in *Afgrunden* – great tragedy played out among the middle classes. The Italians launched the epic with tales of early Rome, shot on location among the ruins.

Until the end of the nineteenth century, Europe had led the world in population growth; seventy million Europeans had emigrated in the previous hundred years, mostly to the United States and to British colonies. These movements and resettlements disturbed national identities and created a need for new, cohesive histories. Now the medium had arrived to portray them.

Romanticism in the nineteenth century had reawakened interest in national characteristics and tradition, with the nation state an expression of that notional communal will. Italian unification was largely achieved by 1871, with the establishment of the capital in Rome. Civil war in America had ended only in 1865 and reconstruction of the united federal republic continued for over a decade. Forty years later, in different ways, both

America and Italy were still young and in need of popular ways of celebrating their creation and identity. Film could illustrate history – larger than life and, in James's words again, 'in a tongue that every race and sect and creed can understand' – not only preserving but sometimes creating heroes.

In Australia, the world's first feature-length film, the hour-long *Story of the Kelly Gang* (1906), shot in the Melbourne suburbs, portrayed Ned Kelly as 'the last of the Bushrangers', an emblem of the national trait of hardy independence. In Brazil, *O Guarani* (1912) commemorated the foundation of Rio de Janeiro. In Soviet Russia, after the 1917 Bolshevik Revolution, David Kaufman, the filmmaker who operated under the pseudonym Dziga Vertov, or Spinning Top, screened rousing documentary footage with sound accompaniment to carriages of children and adults on Kalinin's agitprop train.

Artists, writers and aesthetes began to acknowledge the new art form. James Joyce, for example, had watched films in Europe from 1902. Towards the end of the decade, he persuaded a Trieste film syndicate to set up the Cinematograph Volta in Mary Street, Dublin, with him as manager. The cinema opened in December 1909 with a selection of European films, including a dramatic rendition of the sixteenth-century Cenci murder plot. Joyce lasted little more than six months before moving on, apparently frustrated that audiences wanted American films which the syndicate had not booked.

Commerce would always provide the impetus for change and in the United States business interests would drive a crucial movement of the film industry from east to west coast. A patent war over the tools of production such as cameras and projectors resulted in a restrictive arrangement in 1908, the Motion Picture Patents Company – also known as the Edison Trust – by which the leading American film companies, distributor and film supplier established a monopoly. It did not hold for long. In 1910 the director D.W. Griffith made several successful films for the American Mutoscope and Biograph Company in California. Within a couple of years, many smaller independent companies moved west where the locations were plentiful and varied, the light favourable – and the judiciary more relaxed about patent enforcement.

Around the same time, in a parallel industry, a former employee of Thomas Edison at the Edison Illuminating Company, Henry Ford, introduced the Model T automobile. Franchises of local dealers followed to sell the cars. When Ford introduced the first moving assembly line in 1913, he became head of one of the first vertically integrated industrial processes which would prove a model in many ways for the emerging film industry. Within ten years, the movie business in America would be dominated by five similarly structured movie giants with control of all stages of the business, from filmsets to popcorn.

There was another significant shift, however, beyond industrial practices, beginning in 1914. Since Reconstruction and the strengthening of its internal market, America's foreign trade had increased, most markedly in a dramatic growth of its exports abroad. For the film producers, this began to show itself in an accelerated way after the outbreak of war in Europe. A detailed analysis by Kristin Thompson, in *Exporting Entertainment*, suggests that it was not only the effect of war on production in France and Italy that reversed the flow of films from Europe to the United States. London had long been a prime distribution centre with American sales into Europe passing through the capital for onward shipping. With the outbreak of war, not only was the merchant fleet inhibited by the threat of German attack but new tariffs were introduced, including a tax on luxury imports such as foreign films, to raise money for the war effort. More than that, a fear that nitrate cellulose might fall into enemy hands – film and explosives being close cousins – restricted the transport of cans of film.

The American studios were quick to exploit the situation and grasp control of international distribution, neatly replacing French, Italian, Swedish and Danish films with home-grown products. By the second half of 1915, Hollywood, the relative newcomer, was on its way to establishing commercial dominance; it was also, by virtue of one film, D.W. Griffith's *The Birth of a Nation*, the most commercially successful film of the silent era, about to forge an artistic template which has affected international filmmaking ever since.

During the conflict itself, audiences in Europe in particular became accustomed to seeing events recorded in motion through early newsreels, many of them produced by Pathé and Gaumont. Wartime newsreels did not at that stage have the immediacy of later photojournalism. They were usually supervised by governments and confined to generic and encouraging shots of marching troops or even the restaging of battlefield incidents. Even under those controlled conditions, however, they still gave Germans, for example, a glimpse of the desolation of defeat that would leave two and a half million dead from a population of forty-five million. The Weimar Republic was formed in a fractured and traumatised country with a collapsed economy, further disturbed internally by the Spartacist uprising of January 1919. Inflation and the devaluation of the currency made German films after the war easier to export, leading to the wider dissemination abroad of stylistic masterpieces such as *The Golem* and *The Cabinet of Dr Caligari*. The nightmare vision of *Dr Caligari* in particular, came to be regarded as a prism of national anguish.

Through all this change and upheaval, film, the first mass entertainment, communicated to individuals about direct experience. The circumstances and settings might vary but the emotions and reactions were recognisable. Characters onscreen gazed straight into the eyes of each separate person in the crowd. What were they like for the audience, those first confrontations with men and women just like their own neighbours whom they watched thronging out of the Lumière factory gates, crossing in front of each other, forming a weave of humanity, offset by an elegant mongrel that passed nonchalantly in the foreground as if seeking out an assignation? The audience may have felt disoriented; they might have entered the darkened hall for some kind of dramatic performance but were instead ambushed by lives much like their own, only larger and transformed, more luminous.

Soon that audience would be represented by screen avatars, nameless actors at first, sometimes in different costumes or settings but always with a reliably recognisable persona. In time the simple street or domestic scenes would become more complex and impressive. The audience would be dazzled and amazed, like young Charity Royall, heroine of Edith Wharton's 1917 novel *Summer*, the country girl from the Mountain who goes to the Fourth of July festivities in the local town. There, intoxicated by the charms of a young architect and her first taste of wine, she is persuaded into a glittering place

> . . . where they passed, between immense pictures of yellow-haired beauties stabbing villains in evening dress, into a velvet-curtained auditorium packed with spectators to the last limit of compression. After that, for a while, everything was merged in her brain in swimming circles of heat and blinding alternations of light and darkness. All the world has to show seemed to pass before her in a chaos of palms and minarets, charging cavalry regiments, roaring lions, comic policemen and scowling murderers; and the crowd around her, the hundreds of hot sallow candy-munching faces, young, old, middle-aged, but all kindled with the same contagious excitement, became part of the spectacle, and danced on the screen with the rest.

During the 1910s, the vital duality of the audience's relationship with film was established: they felt at once a blend of admiration and excitement, of sympathy and judgement; the blood stirred, the pulse quickened. They, too, in an extension of Arthur James's eulogy, were the Motion Picture. Like the precocious John-Paul Sartre sitting with his mother at the matinee, each could for a spell of an hour or so be utterly bound to the film characters whether in adventure, comedy or melodrama, '. . . *that was not me,* that young widow crying on the screen, yet she and I had but one soul'.

AFGRUNDEN (THE ABYSS) (1910)

Denmark
Director: Urban Gad
Cast: Asta Nielsen, Robert Dinesen, Poul Reumert
Black and white, silent

A slim young woman boards a tram on a sunny day in Copenhagen. Riding in the open at the back of the streetcar, gazing out at the tree-lined boulevards, she meets a well-dressed, polite young man. Magda (Nielsen) and Knud (Dinesen) exchange pleasantries. She alights and sets off at a determined pace through the park. Knud follows, as he is destined to do all the way through this story of an independent woman's fall from grace.

Magda works as a piano teacher. She is delighted when Knud invites her to spend the summer with his parents in the country but their stifling conventionality soon bores her. The arrival of the Circus Fortuna brings fatal excitement – to Knud's embarrassment Magda wants to dance alongside a gypsy girl but, even worse, she has caught the eye of a handsome gaucho rider Rudolf (Reumert). With admirable economy – the film is just thirty-seven minutes long – she elopes with him, is abused by him, considers reconciliation with Knud and then turns back to a path of resentful passion which can only have a tragic ending.

The sequence that made *Afgrunden* a sensation occurs whilst Magda is living the bohemian life and performing onstage with Rudolf. Angry at his repeated dalliances with other *artistes*, she infuses their act with her desire and rage in a notorious dance. Wearing only a silky shift with a shredded hem, she is clearly not corseted and her dark, curly hair is free. Her dress is loosely belted with a rope at her waist which she employs as a lasso to pull and bind her wayward lover. She advances on him, as he stands trapped in the centre of the stage; gyrating her pelvis to a Latin rhythm she grinds against him, rubbing her buttocks into his groin. At the end of the dance, she suddenly forces him to his knees, pushing his head back and appears to bite his neck.

This is not just a salacious interlude or a cinematic peepshow: the dance goes on for a full three minutes and is steeped in character. For a moment, Magda has Rudolf exactly where she wants him and he does not seem entirely unhappy about the turn of events either. This is the precarious climax of a psychosexual drama. Inevitably, it is about to go even more horribly awry.

This was Asta Nielsen's first screen appearance. She was twenty-nine, an actress from a working-class family who had studied at the drama school of the Royal Theatre of Copenhagen. While still a teenager she had given birth to a daughter but never identified the father. As a stage actress she was striking to look at but otherwise unremarkable; in a 1928 interview looking back on her career, she described her frustration in 1910 at her failure to land good roles. When the New Theatre where she worked turned to operetta to bring in audiences, Nielsen opted to take part in the film, *Afgrunden*, which was directed by Urban Gad, formerly a painter. Her theatre colleagues were disdainful: cinema was little more than the circus attraction featured in the film itself. Onscreen, however, Nielsen proved extraordinary – candid, natural, expressive; having nothing to lose, she found a way to be noticed. It seemed that she was not so much depicting stylised reality as simply being.

The theatrical establishment of Copenhagen was duly impressed and began to revise its lofty opinion. Nineteenth-century theatre had been moving towards greater realism onstage with ever more elaborate sets; Scandinavian cinema in particular drew on the modernist psychology of dramatists such as Ibsen and Strindberg. Banned for two decades, Strindberg's *Miss Julie* was first performed in Stockholm in 1906 with a kitchen set that from contemporary photographs looks decidedly functional for all the frying and simmering that the drama requires. In 1912, this same stage production formed the basis of a film.

After the success of *Afgrunden*, Urban Gad, Nielsen's husband for a short while, argued the advantages of this new art form over stage drama in an interview with *Masken* theatre review, cited by Ron Mottram in his study of early Danish cinema. Film did away with tedious and artificial speeches, he maintained, 'the tiring lines, so destructive to the imagination' and cumbersome explanations (*Afgrunden's* intertitles – the printed captions that provide dialogue or plot detail in a silent film – are a model of distilled precision) or unwieldy introductions of new characters. Instead, its impact was increased by 'the rapid changes from place to place in the development of the drama, the almost simultaneous contemplation of and identification with the different situations created by the development of the conflict'. Best of all, it allowed a direct view of 'often excellent facial expressions' which could promote 'an intense feeling of personally and closely taking part in the course of the action'.

The dance ensured that *Afgrunden* became notorious. Nielsen turned down offers from music halls across Europe to repeat the performance on their stages. In the United States, somewhat cut for the sake of decency, it was released under the title *The Woman Always Pays*. After this blatant display of eroticism, though, the narrative does indeed descend into a more conventional moralistic tale whereby the free spirit must suffer for her passionate ways. Gad was not a particularly inspired director; there is little in the way of camera movement or significant intercutting (despite his boast of rapid changes). The budget was low – the film was shot on available light only (as later Danes would in the Dogme movement) and there are fascinating glimpses of Danish streets and countryside and sociological details of bourgeois life and manners, as well as a few set pieces of the period, including the obligatory train pulling into a station. Above all, the film is still compelling for the way Nielsen moves with an unselfconscious fluidity and apparent lack of vanity. In one scene, she is at home wearing simply a sleeveless top that might even be underwear and skirt when Rudolf barges back in and drags her into an impromptu rehearsal while his latest paramour accompanies them on the piano. Nielsen's clothes are disorganised and sometimes revealing but the effect is never coy.

As was the norm in film all over the world, the actors were given no credit in the titles, let alone their names in lights above the entrance as they might in live theatre. The early studios were reluctant to pay big salaries (Nielsen received two hundred Danish crowns – around $40 at the time – for *Afgrunden*) but actors accepted the anonymity for as long as film was considered a lesser art. Audiences were so enthusiastic about Nielsen's performance, however, particularly in Germany, that journalists soon discovered her identity. Within a year or two, enterprising marketers had labelled Asta merchandise from cigarettes to confectionery to lingerie, and it is said that she was a pin-up for the soldiers on both sides in the trenches during the First World War. The German studio that had helped finance *Afgrunden* now put her on contract.

Nielsen may be acknowledged as the first international filmstar but her appearance in the firmament was solely on the strength of what audiences saw onscreen. She was in some ways the accidental star. The star system as a commercial stratagem was launched in the United States by the founder of Universal Pictures, Carl Laemmle. A young Canadian actress, Florence Lawrence, had been appearing in short films since 1906 for the Edison and then Biograph Studios. By 1910 she had a hundred and thirty film credits and audiences were said to like her face, yet she was anonymous and apparently interchangeable with others. When Laemmle hired her for his Independent Moving Pictures (IMP), he promised to give her billing. First, though, he organised a stunt, telling newspapers that one of his best actresses (and here she was named for the first time) had been killed in a streetcar accident. He promptly followed this up with advertisements in magazines, dismissing the story as a rumour spread by a rival. At the opening of her next film, Florence Lawrence, hitherto unknown, was mobbed. Audiences now not only knew her name but that, miraculously, she had escaped death.

Lawrence's brief appeal – with a certain irony, her career in effect ended after an accident in 1914 – was that of the girl next door. The first stars had an approachable quality; the gods and goddesses would come later. Her replacement at IMP was another Canadian, Mary Pickford, whose earthy daring was summed up by *Photoplay* magazine: 'luminous tenderness in a steel band of gutter ferocity'. The first recurring screen character, as opposed to named star, was arguably Max the Dandy, created by French music-hall comic Max Linder, who had worked as writer, director and performer for Pathé since 1905. In a series of films from 1910, Max recovers from escapades often linked to over-commitment, whether to affairs practical or romantic. Although arguably not as inventive, he is to my eyes more endearing and funny than the man who soon eclipsed him, Charlie Chaplin. Chaplin was hired in the United States by Mack Sennett's Keystone outfit in 1913 and made his screen debut in the alias of the little tramp in *Kid Auto Races at Venice* in 1914. In a continuing joke about walking in front of a camera while a photographer attempts to capture the racing drivers at speed, Chaplin gave the first outing to a persona – dignified in indignities, apparently modest yet audacious – that he would set for good in *The Tramp* and *The Bank* the following year. That stylised quality of the underdog, of the immigrant in a land of incomprehensible rules which he slyly flouts, proved 'translatable' into many languages and cultures.

Asta Nielsen never managed that translation. The year after *Afgrunden*'s release, she decided to accompany Urban Gad to Germany to make films. The salary was high – the highest so far paid to any screen performer – but, despite a brief visit to New York, she would not achieve the fame or recognition of another, younger, Scandinavian. In 1925, Nielsen starred in a German film, *The Joyless Street*, directed by G.W. Pabst. It was set in Vienna in the immediate aftermath of the First World War with the street as a microcosm of corruption and degradation, including prostitution and murder. Forty-three-year-old Asta Nielsen and a nineteen-year-old Swede, Greta Garbo, played characters of similar age – the latter virtuous, the former, Nielsen, well and truly fallen. Not surprisingly the film was cut by the censors: Nielsen was left uncredited while Garbo travelled to America and became a legend.

Garbo later paid tribute to Nielsen for teaching her much, praising the older woman's versatility which she acknowledged she could never approach. Even to modern eyes, Nielsen's first performance in *Afgrunden* seems naturalistic: by her own account, this freedom from theatrical gestures was born of a certain abandon. She wrote in her autobiography, 'I realised that one had to detach oneself completely from one's surroundings in order to be able to perform an important scene in a dramatic film. The opportunity to develop character and mood gradually, something denied the film actor, can only be replaced by a kind of auto-suggestion.' The audience, in turn, can fill that vacuum with their own experience and fantasies. In the case of *Afgrunden*, Magda's behaviour may finally attract the punishment that contemporary morality demanded but women in particular would have appreciated that time spent with the flawed but sensual Rudolf might have had its compensations – at least in comparison to the prospect of marriage to the virtuous Knud.

G.W. Pabst, who had directed Nielsen and Garbo together and would go on to work with such forces of screen nature as Louise Brooks and Leni Riefenstahl, observed of Nielsen: 'One has long spoken of Greta Garbo as the "divine" – for me Asta Nielsen has always been and will always remain the "human being" *par excellence.*' Audiences clearly responded to that humanity but American studios were plotting a trajectory for their future stars – from girl next door to goddess – that would be all too obvious within the next few years.

THE BIRTH OF A NATION (1915)

USA

Director: D.W. Griffith

Cast: Lilian Gish, Mae Marsh, Henry B. Walthall

Black and white, silent

Two comfortably off families, the Stonemans in the north and the Camerons in the south, have young and attractive children. Relations between the two households are cordial, the young people visit each other and are variously attracted but friendship and romance are soon disrupted by war between the Union and the Confederacy. The battlefield claims sons from both families and reduces the Camerons to poverty before peace is finally restored, although the broker of that peace, Abraham Lincoln, is promptly assassinated. So ends the first half of this three-hour onslaught.

In the second part, the Stoneman patriarch, an abolitionist senator, works closely with black or mixed-race characters (white actors in black-face), including a conniving housekeeper and a protégé with an eye for his daughter Elsie (Lilian Gish). Once they have access to political power the blacks in the South are caricatured as corrupt, drunken and lazy. The heroic young Cameron, 'Little Colonel' Ben, forms a Clan (otherwise recognisable as the Ku Klux Klan) on behalf of the now intimidated and disenfranchised whites. A black renegade pursues Cameron's highly strung younger sister, Flora, in the woods with some kind of sexual intent; rather than face dishonour she throws herself off a cliff. The heavily costumed Clan then ride to the aid of the white folks, the cream of the Cameron and Stoneman

23

youth are joined in marriage and two final histrionic tableaux herald an end to war and a lasting, Christian, peace.

The Birth of a Nation is an epic film of extraordinary style and ambition with loathsome politics. If it were not so compelling, it would be unwatchable. It was adapted from a 1906 play, *The Clansman*, by a North Carolina Baptist minister, Revd Thomas Dixon Jr, and an early intertitle sets the tone of its argument about the causes of war between the states: 'The bringing of the African to America planted the first seed of disunion.'

The film had an unprecedented budget of $100,000, but brought in $10 million in box office receipts in its first years of successive rereleases. It would prove the highest grossing film of the silent era, confirming cinema's potential as a lucrative industry.

By the time he directed *The Birth of a Nation*, the Kentucky-born David Lewelyn Wark Griffith had already made some four hundred and fifty short films for the Biograph Company, including a dozen about the civil war. This epic, though, was of a different order; launched with its own score, played by a forty-piece orchestra, it brought together many of the best of the nascent techniques of cinema from around the world. With the crucial skills of cinematographer Billy Bitzer working with relatively simple equipment, Griffith incorporated location filming, including ambitious crowd scenes, in the street or on the battlefield (the latter set up on a San Fernando plain), varieties of camera angles, moving shots like a track or pan, panoramas and long shots, keeping the camera close to faces for moments of intensity, lighting Lilian Gish in particular, so that her face is a dazzling oval in the frame, or narrowing down the audience's focus to a specific detail with the use of lighting or a masking device known as an 'iris'.

Alongside the epic comes the domestic detail of the Stoneman and Cameron families with the carefully constructed interiors of their homes and their garden plots. For the Camerons, the ravages of war deplete their possessions markedly as the narrative advances, culminating in Flora trimming her threadbare dress with puffs of raw cotton instead of fur or feathers – an anticipation of Scarlett O'Hara's sartorial resourcefulness in *Gone With the Wind*, one of many echoes between Griffith's film and Margaret Mitchell's book and its subsequent screen adaptation.

Cross-cutting, the alternation of two narrative strands to increase tension or pathos, had been used for a decade since Edwin S. Porter's *The Great Train Robbery* (1903). Griffith cited the weaving of storylines in the work of Charles Dickens as an inspiration for his use of the technique. The pursuit of Flora to the cliff top, for example, is made more poignant by simultaneously showing her anxious brother searching for her on the lower slopes. Towards the film's end, the Clan gallop variously to save a family besieged in a cabin, to rescue Elsie from the threat of abduction, and to quell fighting in the streets. By intercutting these strands, Griffith's great achievement was to tell a complex story that was not only sustained but cumulative; it made sense (up to a point) yet it also roused powerful emotions.

Griffith denied any suggestion that the film was racist but so blatant was the demonisation of black characters that the National Association for the Advancement of Colored People, established in 1909, condemned it even before its release as 'a flagrant incitement to racial antagonism'. Protestors attempted to prevent screenings. On the other hand, the representation of the Clan gave new vigour to its old supporters. Identified as a terrorist organisation by a Federal Grand Jury in 1870, it had all but died out. In November 1915, the Ku Klux Klan was formally relaunched; shops began to sell Ku Klux Klan hats and aprons, in New York there were Ku Klux Klan parties and the organisation used the film in its recruitment drive, an initiative that was boosted by rereleases of the film over the next few years. Within a decade, from a few thousand members the Klan's supporters had grown to a peak of some five million. *The Birth of a Nation* was by no means the only factor but it clearly provided a focus for the cause.

The film's popular appeal was buttressed by its claims to historical accuracy. Set-piece sequences like the surrender of General Robert E. Lee or the assassination of President Lincoln in Ford's Theatre are described as 'historical facsimile' with specific visual sources – paintings or photographs – cited. These sections are like animated photographs, specific in detail. Griffith even had a replica of Ford's Theatre built. Half a century after the film's release, however, historian John Hope Franklin, writing in *Birth of a Nation: Propaganda as History*, destroyed many of its historical pretensions. While the documentary accuracy of the 'facsimile' tableaux was undoubted, he found no evidence for the depiction of intimidatory rule in the South by blacks and regretted the mix of fact and fancy: 'As an eloquent statement of the position of most white Southerners, using a new and increasingly influential medium of communication, and as an instrument that deliberately and successfully undertook to use propaganda as history, the influence of *The Birth of a Nation* on the current view of Reconstruction has been greater than any other single force.' More than that, the myth of the Clansman perpetrated throughout the film used 'a powerful and wonderful new instrument of communication to perpetuate a cruel hoax on the American people that has come distressingly close to being permanent'.

The Birth of a Nation was released on the fiftieth anniversary of the end of the civil war; despite Reconstruction, loss and division were still enduring themes and the need for a myth of unification was powerful. If Griffith cited Dickens and Tolstoy as his models for narrative technique, he might also have summoned up the spirit of Sir Walter Scott in the early nineteenth century. In cinematic terms, Griffith was attempting the American equivalent of Scott's literary evocation of a legendary history for Scotland and England.

Even more apparent, though, was the recent influence of the classical epics of Italian cinema. Italian filmmakers employed subjects from the country's ancient past, as in biopics of Nero, Julius Caesar and the destruction of Pompeii, to bolster the idea of enduring Roman/Italian values. The largest company in Rome, Cines, produced *Quo Vadis?* (1913) and with its sights on the American market signed an agreement with Chicago-based George Klein distribution company. In the year it was filmed, according to historian Gian Piero Brunetta, 420 films were shot in Rome, 120 in Milan and 569 in Turin. In 1914 a Turin production, *Cabiria*, directed by Giovanni Pastrone, opened in April and was shown in New York a month later. Set during the Second Punic War around the turn of the second century BC, it concerns a young girl who is sold into slavery in Carthage before a principled Roman nobleman rescues her.

Cabiria does not have the economy or consistency of narrative of Griffith's film but its visual ambition is impressive. Griffith would even duplicate a specific shot with a crane for the Babylon section of *Intolerance* (1916), a film he was already planning when he made *The Birth of a Nation*. Pastrone had filmed in Sicily, North Africa and the Italian Alps with sequences that employed not just thousands of extras but erupting volcanoes, tumbling temples, real elephants tramping across mountain ranges and a much-imitated scene in the temple of Moloch in which a great automaton of the deity devoured children, their little legs kicking, as they were poured by the devotees into its fiery maw. (Fritz Lang would refer to this in his depiction of the voracious industrial machine in *Metropolis* (1927)). Like *The Birth of a Nation*, *Cabiria* is a patchwork of styles and techniques, from the naturalistic to the exotic. One of my favourite sequences has a noblewoman relaxing at home, chatting in her garden while an untethered cheetah wanders in and out of shot, apparently at random.

Both Italy and the United States, with their recent unification and tension between urbanised north and agricultural south, sought to define themselves in cinema terms by the proven method of identifying the nation in contrast to a less attractive threat. Thus, we are what you are not. In *Cabiria* the civilised Romans stand out in contrast to the bloodthirsty Carthaginians. *Cabiria*'s look may have been inspired by fine painting but its florid intertitles are credited to Gabriele D'Annunzio, the poet, dramatist and martial and political adventurer who saw himself as a national leader. The film had a topical resonance: the site of Carthage was known to be in Tunisia, which in 1914 was a French colony. In the Italo-Turkish war of 1911–12, Italy had just gained territory in neighbouring Libya. So close was the parallel that it was not hard to find historical justification in *Cabiria* for Italy's expansionist ambitions. In the same way, *The Birth of a Nation*, for all its pious epilogue on the evils of war, is clearly a call to union for white Americans and the force that binds them is simply what they are not, the threat of 'the African'.

Epics on a historical theme recur over the decades, revising history as they go, playing with ideas of national identity through proxy situations. The hugely expensive 1925 *Ben-Hur*, an American production, was filmed in both Italy and California with a cast rumoured to number tens of thousands. Film historian Kevin Brownlow describes in compelling detail the epic struggles and disasters during production, including hostility between pro- and anti-Fascist Italian extras. The ingenious mixture of live action and miniatures worked to great effect in the thrilling chariot race but this depiction of the establishment of Christianity did not attract universal approval. Mussolini banned screenings when he saw the Roman, Messala, was defeated and China condemned *Ben-Hur* as 'Christian propaganda decoying the people to superstition.' The chariot race was closely reproduced in the 1959 colour version and the 1950s in particular favoured stories of individuals rising up against the tyranny of a decadent Roman Empire. Into that you might read a Cold War polemic, the rejection of totalitarian rule. Yet the tyrants were often played by British actors – Peter Ustinov as Nero in *Quo Vadis?* (1951), for example, Ernest Thesiger as Tiberius in *The Robe* (1953) and George Relph as the same character in *Ben-Hur* (1959). In his essay 'Imperial Projections', Martin M. Winkler suggests that this casting signifies more than actors with stage authority and clear diction; their presence reinforces the idea of Rome as a power against which the (American) individual struggles to emancipate himself. Memories of British domination became a shorthand for the oppressor. These linger long beyond any political reality with echoes as far as George Sanders as a patronising critic in *All About Eve* (1950) or the evil tiger Sher Khan in *The Jungle Book* (1967) or indeed Jeremy Irons's voicing of the villainous Scar in the Disney animation *The Lion King* (1994).

Widescreen epics of antiquity for post-Second World War audiences also called to mind images of rallies during the Third Reich, closing a historical circle, since the styling for Imperial Rome had been the model for Italian fascists and, after them, the Nazis. Nero's straight-arm salute and the salutation 'Hail, Caesar' were further reminders. Commenting on the 1959 *Ben-Hur*, the story of a Jewish nobleman struggling against Roman oppression, Bosley Crowther of the *New York Times* commented: 'in the hero's conversations with Messala, one can hear echoes of the horrible clash of interests in Nazi Germany. In the burgeoning of hatred in *Ben-Hur*, one can sense the fierce passion of revenge that must have moved countless people in Poland and Hungary.'

Historical films cannot help but be the creations of the time when they are made. Filmmakers often show us what we want to see. Historical accuracy, the weakness of *The Birth of a Nation*, has rarely been the director's or screenwriter's priority, from classical epics like *Cleopatra* (1961) right up to Mel Gibson's tale of thirteenth-century Scottish patriot William Wallace battling effeminate Englishmen in *Braveheart* (1995) or Baz Luhrmann's *Australia* (2008), which depicts Aboriginal peoples as working alongside the heroic white drover and his gentlewoman consort in the cattle-driving epic of Australian survival. Together they face the threat of a Japanese invasion in 1942. The Australian critic and academic Germaine Greer identified several factual errors (not least the exaggeration of Japanese incursions into Australian waters) and was outraged at what she saw as political expediency – 'this fraudulent and misleading fantasy is designed to promote the government's policy of reconciliation [towards Aboriginal peoples]' – pointing out that an Australian tourism body had contributed to the film's funding.

Australia was not a success, either critically or at the box office. *The Birth of a Nation*, however, did more than fill theatres for years; it sold an idea of American unity that persisted beyond the specific political interests of 1915. Its model of storytelling led towards a particular conclusion: after terrible, spectacular events and mighty conflict, the heroes and heroines – young, healthy and beautiful – come together for the pursuit of happiness in brightly lit prosperity. In the suggestion that they will work to rebuild their homes to their ante-bellum splendour, *The Birth of a Nation* gallops to a particular union of story and emotional force the Hollywood way.

THE CABINET OF DR CALIGARI (1920)

Germany
Director: Robert Wiene
Cast: Conrad Veidt, Werner Krauss, Frederic Feher, Lili Dagover
Black and white, silent

A well-dressed young man, Francis, is the storyteller. He relates how he visited a fair in a small town with his fiancée, Jane, and his closest friend, Alan. There they encountered a panda-eyed clairvoyant somnambulist, Cesare, who, when not dozing in a coffin-shaped box, sloped about in a tight black outfit like a narcoleptic Hamlet. Cesare's appearances were strictly managed by the sinister magician Dr Caligari. When Francis and Alan consulted Cesare on what the future might hold, he promptly predicted Alan's imminent death. Alan was duly found murdered the next morning and Cesare became the chief suspect. Then Jane was violently abducted. Who could be behind this series of strange events? Was Cesare a psychopath or Dr Caligari the real evil genius? Then again, there might be another explanation altogether that would subvert these suppositions . . .

Shot in the Weissensee studio in Berlin in November 1919, *The Cabinet of Dr Caligari* is a mystery story that is also among the original examples of horror film; it is a romance, yet also a confidence trick for it contains the best-known early instance of a twist ending, the cinematic equivalent of literature's unreliable narrator.

If *The Birth of a Nation* is about convergence and reinforcement, then *The Cabinet of Dr Caligari* is designed to disturb, disjoint and discombobulate. It begins with the distinctive expressionist sets of gawky, cartoonish houses and streets, all angles and vertiginous perspective squeezed into frame with no attempt at realism. Sections of the film were originally tinted in eerie green, brown and blue. The acting styles vary from exaggerated mime to naturalistic. Yet in the midst of this apparent theatricality, the film has a conventional narrative beginning: a man wants to tell us a story. Francis's account, via action and intertitles, pulls us through this nightmarish landscape to a conclusion that, unluckily for us, is no consolation at all. For Francis, moderate and plausible as he first appears, turns out to be an inmate in a lunatic asylum. All the other characters he has summoned up in his story are recognisable as fellow patients and the histrionically evil doctor proves to be a psychiatrist, the magisterial director of the establishment.

Writers Jans Janowitz and Carl Mayer first conceived the idea for Dr Caligari in 1918. During the war, Mayer had reportedly clashed with a military psychiatrist possibly as he tried to elude service with the classic artist's defence – a claim of mental fragility. Caligari's appearance is strongly reminiscent – in a caricatured way – of portraits of Jean-Marie Charcot, a nineteenth-century neurologist who made a particular study of hysteria and hypnosis and had taught Freud. Charcot's reputation had dwindled over the years and his public exposition of patients, sometimes in a semi-conscious state, in open lectures that verged on the theatrical, was condemned.

Volumes have been written about the depiction of pathology in *The Cabinet of Dr Caligari* and the relationship of psychosis to Germany's post-war trauma. Expressionism – the artistic presentation of the world through a subjective prism – had been established for some years in literature, drama and the visual arts. It now reached film with sinister and oppressive settings, skewed camera angles, characters dogged by dread and fear and dramatic chiaroscuro lighting (although lighting is less important than scenery in *Caligari*).

Friedrich Gundolf, the German-Jewish literary scholar who at one time numbered Josef Goebbels among his pupils, wrote in 1920 that expressionism '. . . belongs very essentially to the war and is not its consequence but the spiritual symptom of the same crisis whose worldly symptom is the war'. Although war makes no explicit appearance in *Dr Caligari*, the young men are nervous and volatile and Cesare, the somnambulist, seems all at once traumatised, stunned, demonic and haunted while having much the same effect on those around him. The idea of insanity and the nightmare of incarceration (as a fairground attraction, Cesare is Dr Caligari's prisoner, after all) seeps into the various characters' encounters in the narrow and jagged streets. Modernism was seen as an expression of national malaise. It is as if the architecture itself has been either blown apart by explosions or deranged by design.

Writing about German cinema after the Great War in *Shell-Shock Nation*, Anton Kaes cites a passage in Wilhelm Lamszus's 1919 book *The Insane Asylum: Visions of War*: 'We were drawn into this war as into an insane asylum, and we were mentally ill, even before the first bullet was fired . . . Even as I outwardly displayed composure before the horrible events, it felt to me as though the world had become an insane asylum.'

So it is with *The Cabinet of Dr Caligari*, which takes the audience into a world where there are eccentric parameters of plot and design and, just when we have accepted them in the interests of following the story, they are overturned. It is as if we have run down one of the foreshortened, wonky alleyways in the little town only to bang up against the back of the set. Dr Caligari is a cheap showman. Cinema was still barely an art, often considered a rabble-pleasing show. Psychiatry was an increasingly powerful yet distrusted profession.

In his influential 1947 study of German inter-war cinema, *From Caligari to Hitler*, Siegfried Kracauer found signs of the future in the film itself. He believed these indications to be as horribly accurate as Cesare's fairground premonitions. Like the citizens of the town, according to Kracauer, Germans were disturbed and chaotic; they sought order, even if it came in the form of totalitarian dictatorship. 'Self-appointed Caligaris hypnotised unnumerable Cesares into murder.' Certainly, the final view of Caligari himself in the film is as an authority figure. Wild hair now slicked back, he gazes straight into the camera, both steely and unknowable – more frightening than before. Whether this makes him a proto-Hitler is harder to establish, just as it is hard to be precise about the significance of the framing device that turns Caligari from sinister showman to man of science and reason, and Francis from reliable hero to deluded patient. (It also tidies up the strange appearance of the town in Francis's account – before he begins his story, and later when he is seen as a patient in the asylum, the style of the setting is relatively naturalistic.) This framing was apparently added later to make the film somehow less disturbing. If that was the intention, it failed.

In a clever piece of teasing advance publicity, posters appeared in Berlin weeks before the film's release, declaring *'Du must Caligari warden!'* – 'You must become Caligari!' without any further explanation. It is in fact a reference to another of the film's stylistic innovations, the floating of that phrase in text over the action in one sequence – a modernist mix of graphic and photography.

The film was received well in certain countries. Japanese audiences found similarities in its stark design and expression to traditional theatre forms. They also enjoyed another film from the same year, set in the Prague ghetto, *The Golem*, as well as *From Morn to Midnight,* a film with even more exaggerated sets, and F. W. Murnau's vampire tale *Nosferatu* (both 1922).

The Cabinet of Dr Caligari was first shown in New York in April 1921, where some audiences were bemused and even angry, demanding their money back. The writer and critic Carl Sandburg wryly summarised the differing audience reactions – it might be a combination of intrigue and puzzlement, or scepticism or lofty enthusiasm for a film that was primarily by and for artists. He also made the droll suggestion that if it had been made in Hollywood rather than Berlin it would probably have been titled *Who's Loony Now?* All the same, writing in the *Chicago Daily News*, Sandburg thought it a timely arrival to raise the game and open other possibilities to American filmmakers. Even though *The Birth of a Nation* was only six years old, not all practitioners aspired to Griffith's production standards. Alfred Kuttner in the March 1921 edition of *Exceptional Photoplays* was blunt: 'In *The Cabinet of Dr Caligari* the motion picture has proved its kinship with the other arts . . . it comes to us at a critical period in our motion picture industry when the public is jaded by many inferior domestic pictures and our producers themselves are still at a loss as to how to get out of their rut.'

By the end of the second decade of the twentieth century, German cinema was the nearest, although not close, competitor to the United States in terms of the number of films produced. The USA, however, had many more theatres. International exchange rates and their technical and artistic style ensured that German films made their way across the Atlantic and the filmmakers would start to follow too. Conrad Veidt, the young Cesare, for example, would work in the United States in the 1920s before emigrating to Britain in 1933. One of his last roles was as the Nazi Major Strasser in *Casablanca* (1942).

Like the crazy convergence of lines and angles in the set of *Dr Caligari*, the film itself represents a crucial meeting of several elements that would point the way forward for film. There was psychology; there was art; there was entertainment in the form of sensation and mystery. The critical reception for it in New York in 1921 represents a shift in the status of film from popular attraction to art. For the first time, aesthetes began to talk about the new form seriously: it was worthy of dedicated criticism and had the potential to develop more experimental styles, perhaps centred on smaller theatres or universities.

Virginia Woolf, who had been dismissive of films made from literary works, noting that a fur hat and jewels are not enough to create Anna Karenina onscreen, conceded a limited role for cinema so long as it realised its limitations. Filmmakers should do best to avoid all that is accessible to words.

However, the rerelease of *The Cabinet of Dr Caligari* in 1926 appeared to trigger a revelation, albeit somewhat grudgingly expressed in an article on 'The Movies and Reality' that she wrote for *New Republic* in August of that year.

At a performance of *Dr Caligari* the other day, a shadow shaped like a tadpole suddenly appeared at one corner of the screen. It swelled to an immense size, quivered, bulged, and sank back again into nonentity. For a moment it seemed to embody some monstrous, diseased imagination of the lunatic's brain. For a moment it seemed as if thought could be conveyed by shape more effectively than by words. The monstrous, quivering tadpole seemed to be fear itself, and not the statement, 'I am afraid.' In fact, the shadow was accidental, and the effect unintentional. But if a shadow at a certain moment can suggest so much more than the actual gestures and words of men and women in a state of fear, it seems plain that the cinema has within its grasp innumerable symbols for emotions that have so far failed to find expression. Terror has, besides its ordinary forms, the shape of a tadpole; it burgeons, bulges, quivers, disappears. Anger is not merely rant and rhetoric, red faces and clenched fists. It is perhaps a black line wriggling upon a white sheet.

Woolf made an assumption about the accidental effect of the shadow. It seems odd that she did not also notice that Cesare throughout is like a tadpole himself and that *The Cabinet of Dr Caligari* seethes with the visual equivalent of wriggly black lines on white sheets. There is a moment, some forty minutes into the film, when the somnambulist is heading towards the bedroom of the sleeping innocent, Jane. He is both inexorably drawn and reluctantly dragging his feet. One arm raised to make him almost two-dimensional, he slides along a wall and around a slice of scenery, becoming almost part of it. It is both inhuman and touching, repulsive and rather beautiful – difficult to put into words, perhaps even for Mrs Woolf – and that is the sheer power of it. It is not painting or music or literature: it can only be cinema.

1920s

GAZING UP AT THE STARS

n June 1920, Mary Pickford and Douglas Fairbanks arrived in Europe on honeymoon, having spent the first few weeks of married life at their showcase home, Pickfair in Beverly Hills, California. Exuberant crowds greeted Mr and Mrs Fairbanks in the various European capitals as they met the exiled Kaiser Wilhelm II in the Netherlands and dined in Paris with two hundred eminent French actors. According to the *New York Times*: 'Arriving in London, the pair were "mobbed" to such an extent that they had to spend one weekend at Lord Northcliffe's place in the Isle of Thanet and another at one of the country seats of the Duke of Sutherland.'

In just ten years, actors in moving pictures had gone from anonymous ciphers to personalities so recognised and respected that they might mingle in the notoriously exclusive enclosures of European aristocracy and the artistic elite. They were models of social mobility. The previous year, 1919, the couple had toured the United States with Charlie Chaplin, promoting

Liberty Bonds. Fairbanks, a stage actor, had been making films for just four years, Chaplin for five, while Pickford, the screen veteran, had first appeared in a short in 1909, yet here was the US government needing their help to support its debt management. On that Liberty Bond caravan, the trio decided to start the first 'star' studio, United Artists. Not satisfied with being recognisable faces and then familiar names, they wanted control and the freedom to write and produce.

The era of mass entertainment had begun with two media – radio and cinema. While audiences were growing for sporting events with the construction of large stadia, they were tiny compared to the hundreds of thousands, even millions, who might hear the commentary by radio, like the first American sports broadcast of a boxing match in Pittsburgh in 1921. Variety and comedy acts soon found their way into living rooms in the Western world. Sales of radios quadrupled over the decade, making it the primary form of entertainment in the home. In Britain the British Broadcasting Company (BBC) began in 1922 as a consortium of telecommunications interests intent on developing the medium but by 1927 it was incorporated by Royal Charter as a public institution with the motto 'Nation shall speak peace unto nation'. The National Broadcasting Company (NBC) in the United States was founded in 1926 .

By the 1920s, radio and cinema had a symbiotic existence. The Russians, for example, used cinema at home to promote the ideals of the Revolution but radio to spread the message abroad. Despite fears that Bolshevism might spread and a series of minor revolts break out in European countries, the overwhelming evidence was that people outside the Soviet Union were more interested in emulating those richer and grander than themselves, than in overthrowing them. It was also true that politicians were demonstrating rather less interest in the people than they had originally promised. With the constant excuse that they were guarding against the threat of revolt or chaos, leaders in many European countries moved to the right; democracy was limited.

F. Scott Fitzgerald remarked of the Jazz Age that it had no interest in politics; put another way, after the privations of global war, people in countries with access to any degree of luxury might seek glamour, sex appeal and sophistication if politics apparently offered little comfort or promise of improvement. The simplest and cheapest route to a glimpse of a better life was perhaps once or twice a week to visit a newly built picture palace, and watch stars like Greta Garbo and John Gilbert lure them into another world in *Flesh and the Devil*. In 1920, fifty million people a week in the United States went to the cinema; by 1929 the number was approaching eighty million. Women were considered the most active filmgoers. The evidence is hard to pin down although it was clearly the perception at the time. Pioneering film critic Iris Barry's *Let's Go the Pictures*, a chirpy 1926 bestseller, had a sub-chapter, 'The Cinema Exists to Please Women', which noted that an estimated three out of four cinema seats were occupied by females. Women were certainly generally active, having gained suffrage in 1920 in the United States and, with various restrictions of age and marital status, across Europe during the decade. As economies recovered from the Great War in the second half of the nineteen-twenties, it was now possible, though still rarely affordable, to have domestic appliances like the electric refrigerator at home, and the look, if not quite the texture, of the rich was increasingly available to those on more modest incomes. Developments in man-man fibres brought the cellulose-based textile Rayon, sometimes known as 'mother-in-law silk', to the market in 1924. There was now a practical aim to seeing how the rich dressed and lived in the opulent costume and interior designs of romantic comedies: it could be copied, more or less, at home.

At the beginning of the decade, Cecil B. DeMille comedies such as *Don't Change Your Husband* and *Why Change Your Wife?* were made specifically to capture the new female market. Jesse Lasky, vice-president of Famous Players, advised DeMille to make something 'that would portray a girl in the sort of role that the feminists in the country are now interested in . . .

who jumps in and does a man's work'. The films even equate female independence with conspicuous consumption, granting their audience entry into the homes of the rich and famous, and inviting them to gaze in awe at the art deco parlours, the master bedrooms with their fine linen, and above all the sumptuous bathrooms. DeMille was famous for his bathrooms, with their stained-glass windows, silk shower curtains, sunken baths and ornate fixtures. Made in an era when any bathroom at all would have been a luxury for most of his audience, the pleasures of a DeMille romcom were mostly vicarious, like window shopping in a gleaming department store.

Other luxuries were within reach. Max Factor Sr, who in 1914 had developed a thinned down 'invisible' greasepaint for film actors, launched his own branded company. In 1927 he began to sell to the public a range of what had previously always been known as cosmetics, using the new term coined on film stages – 'make-up'.

Newsreels such as British Pathé and, later, Movietone provided vivid glimpses of foreign countries and political events outside the picture houses – it might be a celebration of Armistice Day in Shanghai or a comparative study of African clothing to European fashion, or the demonstration of an invention, such as the 'novel folding umbrella', which, from the evidence of one Pathé featurette, was as tricky to open then as today. Technology brought clanking automobiles – the Baby Austin took to British streets in 1922, the Ford Model A appeared in the United States in 1927 – Charles Lindbergh's flight across the Atlantic, experimental rockets pointing spacewards and the culinary time travel of frozen food. All these developments were a source of wonder but also, inevitably, of frustration and comedy. The complex relationship between humanity and machine drove the surreal escapades of many onscreen adventurers, among them silent film comic Buster Keaton, whose seminal picture, *The General*, retells a true story of a stolen train, placing the magnificent steam engine itself at the centre of the narrative.

Colonial and imperial powers were unravelling, leaving countries to rename themselves and to realign. A struggle for control of oil reserves eventually resulted in American and European drilling and extraction in the Middle East and East Indies, launching an era of industrial growth fuelled by imported oil. KLM and Qantas, two of the first airlines, began commercial flights in 1920. The world, for the affluent, was shrinking. Touring holidays became more popular. Indulging their curiosity about foreign lands was no longer the exclusive preserve of the wealthy and cultured. Watching a documentary like the phenomenally successful *Nanook of the North* (1922) satisfied that interest but also, in subtle ways, gave the audience a sense of appropriation. The 'Eskimo' took on an identity in part created by another culture.

Film made its way into the streets and daily lives, too, and not just in Russia where film projection was established in mobile units. Bermondsey, in London's East End, became the first British municipality to produce films with a Public Health film department that drove around projecting in a specially converted van: a typical title might be *School in the Sun*, about children with TB visiting Swiss sanatoria.

Early in the decade, American filmmakers grew concerned about competition from the impressive quality and numbers of imported German films. UFA, the leading studio founded to make propaganda during the First World War, had later merged with other studios to become the dominant producer of all kinds from musicals to documentaries. *Dr Mabuse* (1922) and *Metropolis* (1927), directed by Fritz Lang, were just two of its distinguished products. The rise of Hitler would prompt Lang to emigrate to America in 1933; the director of the vampire film *Nosferatu*, F.W. Murnau, was among those who had left earlier; his 1927 American film *Sunrise* brought high-production stylised expressionism – with elaborate metaphorical sets – to a tale of marital love tested and reasserted.

For the Americans the riposte to all this art onscreen was to become bolder and more spectacular. Fairbanks flashed his eyes and his sword in

The Mark of Zorro (1920) and bounded back on to screens in *Robin Hood* (1922), and *The Thief of Baghdad* (1924). Rudolph Valentino promised sex in the Arabian desert in *The Sheik* (1921) while the Gish sisters – Dorothy and Lilian – struggled through the French Revolution in *Orphans of the Storm* (1922).

For all this, cinema takings took a dive in 1925. This lapse was blamed partly on the success of radio and John Logie Baird soon provided a glimpse of a new threat with the first long-distance television signal. Hollywood responded, as it would over the decades, by piling on the action with the First World War drama *Wings* (1927) and Cecil B. DeMille's biblical epics. Ambitious innovations made impressive, if short, excursions: Abel Gance's *Napoleon* (1927) used Polyvision, a novel triptych screening process, and the first 3-D movie, *The Power of Love* (now lost), where viewers wore goggles with one red and one green lens, was shown in Los Angeles in 1922.

At the beginning of the decade, as Pickford and Fairbanks conquered Europe, newspapers and magazines like *Photoplay* ran hagiographic pieces on this new aristocracy, their lovely homes, romantic adventures and charitable deeds. In 1921, however, the controlled dissemination of saccharine snippets was disrupted by a murder trial in which the accused was Fatty Arbuckle, an oversized comedian who at one time rivalled Chaplin for popularity. During the course of three hearings into the death of actress Virginia Rappe at a party, it was revealed that Hollywood actors drank heavily (this during Prohibition) and were promiscuous. There were even suggestions in the press that Rappe had been sexually abused with a champagne or even (a greater blow to America's image) a Coca-Cola bottle. Arbuckle was acquitted of manslaughter but, as an editorial in the *New World* newspaper put it, 'The publicity has put an unbearable burden of infamy on the motion picture. Every individual within the industry will in some degree feel the stigma of it.'

At another level, the Arbuckle trial ushered in a certain exoticism and raciness to Hollywood's depiction of itself. As the years passed and further scandals emerged, audiences forgave their stars a few peccadillos that enriched the gossip sheets but major transgressions clearly hit box office takings. In the wake of the Arbuckle trial, Universal demanded that its actors sign a morality clause, with any breach resulting in dismissal. The definition of morality appeared to be anything that undermined their screen persona, although for vamps like Theda Bara or Clara Bow who, with her distinctive Max Factor lipstick, embraced the role of 'It' flappergirl in 1927, the reverse held. Bow was offered a half-million-dollar bonus if she avoided scandal. She never collected. The shivers of conservatism within the industry began with the establishment of a trade organisation, the Motion Picture Producers and Distributors of America under the chairmanship of Postmaster General William Harrison Hays Sr. This organisation, which would instigate the idea of 'ratings' to guide consumers as to what they might expect to see, was in effect the beginning of cinema's official self-censorship.

In 1924, Julien Luchaire, director of the International Institute of Intellectual Cooperation at the League of Nations claimed, 'Only the Bible and the Koran have an indisputably larger circulation than that of the latest film from Los Angeles'. Yet Hollywood did not necessarily lead in everything. For all that Europe and the United States worried about the spread of revolution, Russia came to occupy the same vanguard position as cultural innovator that France had held in previous decades ever since socialist theorist Henri de St Simon had declared in 1825 the social importance of the arts as 'avant-garde' for progress.

In Russia the New Economic Policy of the 1920s encouraged experimentation in the arts and training in new skills, including film. With three films over five years – *Strike* (1924), *Battleship Potemkin* (1925) and *October* (1929) – Sergei Eisenstein demonstrated a radical use of the technique of montage. The most celebrated of the three, *Potemkin*, commemorated the twentieth anniversary of the failed 1905 revolution, but its aim was not purely narrative and its approach went far beyond socialist realism. With its juxtaposition of images, and using the technique of montage, it drilled into the viewer's senses rather than their intellect for cumulative dramatic effect. The splicing of one image and set of associations with another was skilfully intended to manipulate the audience to produce a visceral response. It might be disgust (squirming maggots on meat) or danger (a pram wheel teetering on steps) or fear and pity (shattered glasses and a bloodied eye). At the cinema the viewer was assaulted at greater speeds – with less time to process each new stimulus than, say, in the contemplation of a painting or a sentence – just as modern life gave brief contrapuntal flashes of the world from trains, automobiles and escalators.

Montage and juxtaposition were echoed in literature, particularly in prose that emulated the 'stream of consciousness'. John Dos Passos's novel *Manhattan Transfer* (1925) appears to reflect Eisenstein's technique in words, as does cinema enthusiast James Joyce's *Ulysses*. Eisenstein was a great admirer of Joyce's work (but thought Dos Passos a poor imitator of cinema) and met the writer in 1929 in Paris in the first of a series of encounters, intrigued by the possibilities of including interior monologues in film. Freudian ideas of the subconscious had already influenced the arts. With the growth of expressionism in cinema and its claim to reach the deepest recesses of the soul, previously touched only by art, literature or music, it was inevitable that Freud would be approached to collaborate, as he was by both the German studio UFA and the American producer Samuel Goldwyn. He refused both but his psychoanalytic associates Hanns Sachs and Karl Abraham advised on the making of the silent film *Secrets of a Soul* (1926), directed by G.W. Pabst, who would go on to make that famous study of female libido, *Pandora's Box*. Plot synopsis of *Secrets of a Soul* is all but futile – but at its simplest, a chemist (Werner Krauss, who, six years before, had appeared as the crazed Dr Caligari) is obsessed with knives and possibly with murdering his wife; he has fantastical and surreal dreams which sometimes involve flying; he visits a certain Dr Orth who retraces childhood memories with him and 'finds' the cause of his anxieties. Much of the time, the audience may be confused: why do those people nod at one another? Why is the room full of puppies? Contemporary psycho-analysts have no problem spotting the themes of resolution and detection that run through the film although Sachs and Abraham's involvement at the time caused criticism within the movement.

As a kind of lucid dreaming, the film anticipates Luis Buñuel's *Un Chien Andalou* three years later. From his student days in Madrid, Buñuel had been close to the poet Federico García Lorca and the painter Salvador Dalí. On his journey from studying natural sciences to philosophy to film, Buñuel worked as an assistant to director Jean Epstein in France. He claimed that seeing *Battleship Potemkin* made him want to tear up paving stones in the street when he left the cinema. His own first film (a collaboration with Dalí), the sixteen-minute short *Un Chien Andalou* (1929), was more likely to leave audiences holding their heads in confusion. An unforgettable collaboration of film and visual art, its images continue to be recycled by filmmakers nearly a century later – from David Cronenberg to Terry Gilliam to David Lynch.

Ironically, for all its shock value, the longevity of *Un Chien Andalou* may derive partly from its dependence on conventional narrative techniques to keep the audience engaged. Having hooked them with what may be a love story, but is at the very least a set of attractive characters in an appar-ently ordinary setting, the film literally turns the knife, as a man suddenly slices the eyeball of a woman who may be his lover. Buñuel and Dalí claimed it all arose from a conversation one day about dreams. Bunuel's vision was of a moon, like an eyeball, sliced by a sliver of cloud; Dalí topped that with a severed hand crawling with ants. In its obviously artistic way, however, *Un Chien Andalou* was simply pushing the parameters of what regular cinema was doing with its increasingly elaborate historical epics – Fred Niblo's *Ben-Hur* or Murnau's poetic dream stories. The picture onscreen had to be convincing even if it was bizarre – a fantastic world the audience had not yet visited, at least not consciously.

Up to this point, silent cinema had never really been mute; few performances were unaccompanied by music or even occasional effects (sounds to suggest thunder or a cockcrow, for example) provided in the theatre. Onscreen, noise was implicit: silent films often feature musicians or dancers or an explosion or a scream – all of which demand the audience to supply an interior soundtrack, which Jean-Paul Sartre recalled doing with gusto. In his study of Sergei Eisenstein's counterpoint of sound and vision, Robert Robertson describes the Russian filmmaker's preoccupation with fugue and advanced ideas of the sound film. As early as *The Strike* or *October*, he was teasing the audience's reflexes with tinkling chandeliers, machine-gun fire or factory whistles, using images and cutting to suggest the acute pitch of these noises – perhaps even more urgently than the actual sounds themselves would have done. Eisenstein knew that if sound was already implied in silent cinema and his system of visual montage could 'colour' a sequence by its juxtaposition with the images that preceded and succeeded it, then aural prompts and teases could enrich the mix still further.

In the event, when sound was eventually possible, the technical challenges of early recordings often hobbled directors' options. Microphones had to be placed precisely, limiting the frame of the shot, and whirring cameras were confined inside soundproofed boxes, ostracised from the action. This cumbersome business was famously satirised much later in *Singin' in the Rain* (1952) which also gets laughs from the fact that the new sounds did not always please the audience.

Vitaphone invented a synchronised sound and picture system with a geared turntable in 1925 and the following year Bell produced a variation for a Warner Brothers music track. On 6 October 1927, Warner Brothers released the first sound picture with sections of both music and dialogue, *The Jazz Singer*. Leading man Al Jolson (born Asa Yoelsen in Lithuania) was already as popular a recording star as Caruso. Onscreen he came to utter his prophetic catchphrase 'you ain't heard nothin' yet'. Six months later came the first complete talkie, *The Lights of New York*, a gangster picture that would set the pace for the films of the following decade.

Silent film purists would continue to argue that dialogue and music were little more than a distraction from the visual artistry. Mary Pickford, for example, famously derided the addition as 'lipstick on the Venus de Milo'. The American Academy of Motion Picture Arts and Sciences was formed in 1927 and Douglas Fairbanks hosted the industry's first self-congratulatory Oscars ceremony in 1929. The 'talkies' were not eligible, although the *The Jazz Singer* did get a special one-off award. That same year a prototype Hollywood musical was released – *Broadway Melody* (1929), with sections in two-strip Technicolor. The last silent pictures were made in 1931.

By the end of the decade, following the 1929 stock market crash, corporations were shaking down and sometimes out all over the world. In Hollywood, a series of mergers and takeovers left five major studios – Fox, Loew's/MGM, Paramount, RKO and, thanks to the success of their sound pictures, Warner Brothers. They had beaten off the challenges from Europe but were constantly seeking new ways of bringing in the audiences. The Pickfords and Bows were adored, for a while, but at heart was the paradox that Pabst identified – they were recognisably human. They might have lived on your street – that is, if your neighbours had access to the finest lighting and make-up. Adorable was fine but it did not guarantee an enduring relationship between those on screen and those below in the auditorium. The studios started to devise a way not just to make stars, but to create enduring legends – as Pabst suggested of Greta Garbo's unattainable beauty and aloofness – with something close to divinity about them.

The key to this was the genius of cinema – the ability to create a timeless yearning, a communal longing where each person in the audience is convinced that their relationship to the star is unique and special, like waking in the clutches of a dream so sweet and disarming that already the dreamer loses the power to describe it. They have been to a place of such complete oneness with their ideal – whether a person, a place or simply a state – that they are helpless and hurt by its withdrawal. More than visual art or literature, cinema established a circle of desire without hope of fulfilment. Yet in the dark anonymity of the movie house, perfection can seem so close . . .

FLESH AND THE DEVIL (1926)

USA
Director: Clarence Brown
Cast: Greta Garbo, John Gilbert, Lars Hanson
Black and white, silent

Childhood friends Leo and Ulrich, played by John Gilbert and Lars Hanson, return from service in the Austrian army. The real challenge, however, lies ahead of them: they will become entangled with the inappropriately named Felicitas whose guiding impulse appears to be to cause agony all round with no great reward for herself, either, except an impressive wardrobe. Defining this elusive European, close up but untouchable, is Greta Garbo in one of her earliest American films. The protégée of the all-too-human Asta Nielsen was about to attain screen divinity.

The first encounter of all three onscreen sets up the tension – eroticism, narcissism and yearning. On leave from their regiment, Leo and Ulrich have just emerged from a train. Meeting them on the platform are a stout matron (Leo's mother) and a ringletted girl (Ulrich's little sister). Familiar greetings are exchanged – the relations are fulsome, ordinary and just a little embarrassing. Then, behind them, a woman steps down from the carriage and Leo is instantly transfixed. In a dark, fur-trimmed coat, carrying flowers, hat low over her eyes, Garbo as Felicitas is more a presence than a personality. Her face is barely visible, although her form is elegant. As she gets into a cab, the bouquet falls to the ground. Leo picks it up and returns it to the mysterious woman, asking with his eyes (rather more heavily lined than hers, as it happens) if he can take a gardenia for remembrance. She acquiesces, both amused and languid (this sort of thing clearly happens all the time), and slips into the cab, distanced from Leo, as from us, by a pane of glass.

Flesh and the Devil is a gorgeous film to watch, an evocation of lost Austrian elegance, of snow and open fires and huge vaulted drawing rooms where the sun pours in through the tall windows. Its brilliance lies in its structure, however, an isosceles triangle of thwarted desire with Felicitas at its apex. In the early scenes it is soon clear that old friend Ulrich only really has eyes for Leo; his infatuation with Felicitas comes later. Poor Ulrich – his default position throughout is pure longing tinged with the premonition of disappointment. In emotional terms, this is Ulrich's film, the audience shares his agony. A series of triangles is set: Ulrich loves Leo, Leo loves Felicitas, Felicitas has a husband. In time, the husband having been despatched in a duel, Ulrich will fall in love with – and eventually marry – Felicitas. But then she will resume her affair with Leo. All these complications are ahead. At this early stage, however, it is the audience that must fall for this fatal creature. In our second glimpse of Felicitas after her initial railway station appearance, she is obscured by less glamorous women. Then, like the sun, she emerges into view. Framed by a neckline of pearlescent tulle, she positively gleams.

So how did the director Clarence Brown achieve this radiance for Garbo? Cinematographer William H. Daniels diffused the light on Garbo's face with special lenses (75 or 100 mm) as well as gauzes to focus on her best features – the cheekbones, the eyes (and the lashes in particular) and the eternally dissatisfied mouth. The light usually lost the shadow on her nose, for example, but on occasion, by using half-tone lights from the side, Daniels could also create a chiaroscuro effect which further added to her allure. He would continue to find Garbo's most intriguing and desirable aspects in *The Mysterious Lady* and as a double agent in *A Woman of Affairs* (both 1928). However, Daniels always maintained he lit to serve the purpose of the character and scene; he did not devise a specific 'look' for Garbo. So if the scene called for dramatic action as when, for example, Leo (not unreasonably) tries to strangle Felicitas, then the foreground and the faces would be cast in shadow to bring the struggling couple into a stylised silhouette. Over the next four decades, Daniels would contribute subtle details to enhance the beauty of leading ladies – in 1958, he made a modern goddess of Elizabeth Taylor in *Cat on a Hot Tin Roof*, the light reflecting from her classical white gown up to subtle shading on her face that frames the famous violet eyes.

However, the testimony of another cinematographer suggests there was indeed a characteristic consistency in the way Daniels lit Garbo that set a pattern for her image. In 1925, an American-raised Austrian, Josef von Sternberg, directed his first feature, *The Salvation Hunters*, a tale of a young couple's struggle out of poverty. Its female lead, played by Georgia Hale, was an implacable but minor-league enchantress exercising an almost super-natural power over the men in her way. Von Sternberg would develop the emotional intensity of this central female character in subsequent films. By the end of the decade he had travelled to Germany to film *The Blue Angel* (1930), making along the way the disconcerting discovery of Marlene Dietrich. Von Sternberg encouraged Dietrich to accept a contract with Paramount and, once she was in the United States, he worked with cinema-tographer Lee Garmes to create a system of lighting specifically for her. Garmes tried illuminating from the side, so that one half of Dietrich's face was in shadow; he soon realised that he was replicating Daniels's approach and that Dietrich had begun to look like Garbo. He changed the direction of light so that it poured down from above, striking Dietrich's cheekbones and 'losing' the awkwardness of her nose. (Plastic surgery would soon help matters there.) She was perpetually bathed in a halo of light and therefore somewhat immobile, an effect she maintained through lighting and costume up to her final cabaret performances in the 1970s.

The particular lighting treatment of stars (and female stars in particular), as if they travelled with a gilded microclimate, was and remains essential to the Hollywood look. The triangular lighting setup of a 'key' light to the front or top, a more flattering 'fill' light to the side to bring out the best features, and a backlight to pick out details and highlight the hair is what makes a star look special and not like the rest of us caught on CCTV. The lighting directs your attention, the equivalent of the quasi-divine shaft of Renaissance painting. With women, lighting is often softened or diffused to flatter. That preferential treatment may be so extreme that it sometimes risks unbalancing the whole mixture of setting and storytelling, the *mise-en-scène*. In *Masters of Light*, a series of conversations with contemporary cinematographers published in the 1980s, Lázló Kovács, the Hungarian Director of Photography for Scorsese's *New York, New York* (which is itself a tribute to Vincente Minnelli musicals of the 1940s), talks of the challenge of edging into a soft lighting system for the star, Liza Minnelli, by using diffusion on other shots in the scene leading up to her close-ups. He cites, as an example of how not to do it, close-ups from old Doris Day pictures which 'stick out like a sore thumb', misty and fuzzy where the other shots are clear and bright.

These 1920s lighting schemes for Garbo and later, from 1930, for Dietrich demonstrated a fundamental truth. Desire in the cinema does not necessarily require two people onscreen gazing at one another. In fact, the most important relationship is more often between the star and the audience, with the rest of the cast there to support or echo that relationship. Josef von Sternberg may not have been the first to establish the galvanic link between audience and star but he was the one to define its quality – the need to fill the 'dead space' between the two, the gap between the eye of the camera and the subject, with diffusing light which would draw the audience in. This creation of a magic zone between Them and Us is clearest in a quartet of films he made with Dietrich and cinematographer Lee Garmes.

Their first collaboration, and Dietrich's American debut, was *Morocco* (1930) where she is initially glimpsed leaning on the ship's rail, wearing a hat with a spotted veil. In an interview with Charles Higham in the 1960s, Garmes recalled the layers of interest – latticework, fans, dust – that the director placed between subject and camera. Von Sternberg would take this technique to extremes in the luscious, excessive *The Devil Is a Woman* (1935) in which Dietrich fascinates by appearing through undulating streamers at a ball or between the branches of a frosted forest – a cinematic dance of the seven veils. In the same year Garbo appeared famously on a station platform in *Anna Karenina* (1935) alluringly obscured by steam. The technique passes on down the decades through Bette Davis's hats, Ava Gardner's scarves or Marilyn Monroe's sunglasses. Even those fingers in front of her eyes in Uma Thurman's *Pulp Fiction* dance make jokey reference to the erotic power of the veil.

Barriers between the audience and the star may not always be veils or curtains, however. In *Flesh and the Devil*, Garbo and Gilbert fall into a vigorous clinch yet frustrated love is what the audience feels for Garbo. At the time, she was involved offscreen with Gilbert in a romance reportedly even more passionate than the one the audience glimpsed onscreen, a lightning strike that Garbo claimed shook her out of her professional distance. Garbo and Gilbert let it be known that they had fallen in love while filming a romantic scene (director Clarence Brown later claimed that he soon realised what was happening, and motioned the crew over to another part of the set to 'let them finish what they were doing'). Their subsequent relationship certainly seemed to have been scripted like a romantic comedy. *Photoplay* even dedicated a ditty to them:

Off again, on again, Greta and John again
How they have stirred up the news for a while
Making the critics first sigh with them, die with them
Making the cynical smile.

Appropriately, it was Gilbert who was the one doing the more obvious yearning, allegedly proposing to Garbo on a regular basis and, from time to time, being accepted. She was even reported to have set a date, 8 September 1926, only to leave him waiting at the altar. ('Yackie' eventually forgave her and their affair staggered on for a few more years.) If this were true, they were planning to get married before *Flesh and the Devil* was even in cinemas. What a happy coincidence for the publicity department!

By the time of the premiere, the public were frantic to see the couple onscreen. Audiences hoped to see the real thing, the compact between fantasy and fact that gives that addictive sense of ownership over the romance, as if they were there when the thunderbolt struck. Carl Sandburg must have spoken for many filmgoers when he proclaimed, 'if there was ever, in screendom, as earnest an exchange of kisses as that between John Gilbert and Greta Garbo let him who knows of it speak now or forever hold his peace'. *Variety* claimed that the love scenes 'will make anyone fidget in their seat and their hair rise on end'. Unsurprisingly, *Flesh and the Devil* broke house records in a number of American cinemas.

Gilbert did not last in Garbo's affections, nor did his style of acting survive the fast-talking 1930s, yet his place in her arms was pivotal to a generation who took lessons in love from the movies. 'I place the blame not on my inability to imitate what I have seen on the screen, but someone else's inability to imitate Greta Garbo's receptive qualities,' concluded an impressionable youth, one of many correspondents in a controversial survey on movies and conduct by Herbert Blumer in the early 1930s. The aim of the study was to detect whether or not cinema was destabilising children and young adults. In some ways, this was simply an updating of the moral concerns that attended any romantic art, from novels to dancing. Yet there was something different about sitting in a film theatre. Since romantic films appeared more enveloping and sensual they might well 'induce strong yearnings for amorous experience'. Blumer even adopted the term 'emotional possession' to describe the spell. 'The observer may be so absorbed in the glamour of the scene as to be swept by the passion portrayed therein. In such circumstances one detects again the surging upward of impulse, the relaxing of ordinary inhibitions, the readiness to yield to importunities for love experience – and so a readiness to participate in conduct before which one might otherwise hesitate.'

Blumer calculated that one third of teenagers imitated the love scenes, or the 'art of necking', they had just witnessed in their local fleapit. Garbo and Gilbert became role models, both fantasy figures and physical instructors in real or imagined love lives: one male college student admitted that 'almost all of my knowledge of sex came from the movies . . . the first time I ever kissed a girl was after I saw Greta Garbo and John Gilbert'. A girl confessed: 'I can picture John Gilbert and Greta Garbo rehearsing a love scene right now, but in my mind it isn't Greta Garbo, it's me!' Another pictured herself 'the recipient of Gilbert's kisses. Folded into his arms I could forget all my school worries.' According to Blumer's correspondents, the movies were a liberal education in the art of loving: girls learned how to flirt or play the vamp, boys embraced cinematic techniques of hand-holding, seducing and smooching. And where better than in the dark? As one twenty-one-year-old college student put it, 'a highly charged sex movie puts many girls in an emotional state that weakens, let us say, resistance'. The cumulative effect of witnessing all these 'sex movies' worried Blumer, who argued that it might encourage a regular filmgoer to 'live a kind of life different from his prior career', and that 'the kaleidoscopic change that is involved in mood and receptivity of the spectator is so great that emotionally it may put demands on him which make him callous, or leave him indifferent to the ordinary requirements of emotional response made upon him in his workaday world'. His argument built to a solemn conclusion, 'the emotional possession induced by passionate love pictures represents an attack on the mores of our contemporary life'.

Garbo and Gilbert are still the most famous of screen couples who carried the act into their domestic life with celebrated effect. Others followed, among them Bogart and Bacall, Burton and Taylor, Cruise and Kidman. As they gaze at each other, knowing they can see themselves in close-up later, their gaze excludes, rouses and fascinates us, the third party in that trio. Yet the convention of film often has love scenes played over the shoulder of one or both of the participants. So, but for a few degrees, we are in the eye-line of the beloved, that third side of the triangle.

The format of the trio will be repeated time and time again, initially with Garbo and Gilbert and then down the years through Celia Johnson's virtual betrayal with Trevor Howard of dear husband Fred in *Brief Encounter* (1946) to Jeanne Moreau's fatal vacillation between *Jules et Jim* (1962) and the desert storm of *The English Patient* (1996).

Yearning is among the sweetest and most powerful of cinema's weapons. This is not simply a matter of sex, however, or of gender. Some element of the unattainable or forbidden is always alluring to an audience. Even such an obvious object of desire as the narcissistic young biker in Kenneth Anger's experimental film *Scorpio Rising* (1964) is out of reach. The director may fetishise his male body in the way that Scorpio buffs up his motorbike yet he is not there for the taking; Anger literally puts the shadow of death right behind him. We can gaze but never possess.

Films work best at manipulating our emotions when we can share the onscreen experience, whatever the genre. In *The Way We Were* (1972) gorgeous, shallow goyish writer Hubbell (Robert Redford) finally ends up in the apartment of clever Jewish political activist Katie (Barbra Streisand) who has yearned for him since their college days. Drunk, he passes out in her bed but recovers sufficient consciousness to roll over and have sex. Afterwards, she is blissful and yet melancholy: 'Hubbell, it's Katie,' she whispers, 'You do know it was Katie?' For a moment, she's as anonymous as anyone in the stalls.

Lured by the cinematography, setting and plotting the audience gazes on the unobtainable star. When Leo returns from exile midway through *Flesh and the Devil*, having served time for killing Felicitas's husband in a duel, he arrives once again at a railway station. His beloved friend Ulrich meets him, a little more tremulous than usual. In an echo of the first encounter, there is another vehicle waiting outside the station; all that can be seen of its occupant is a shapely ankle. When Garbo is finally revealed, her eyes are downcast, her face guarded, her hat pulled down. She briefly extends a gloved hand and greets Leo formally. Ulrich, the innocent, then blithely delivers the terrible news: she is now his wife. Leo gazes at her, rapt but destroyed – whatever he does from now on is wrong: either he deceives his friend or himself. When he meets her again secretly, as he must, the island where they meet is shrouded in alluring mist.

By the artificial means of their mists and veils, their gauzes and shadows, filmmakers of the 1920s instilled in the audience a lovely and lasting yearning for what lay beyond. If that absorption sometimes makes us 'indifferent to the ordinary requirement' of life outside the cinema then we are bound, like Garbo, to remain eternally dissatisfied. To be miserable like Garbo was an aspiration indeed.

. . . .

NANOOK OF THE NORTH (1922)

USA
Director: Robert J. Flaherty
Cast: Allakariallak, Nyla
Black and white, silent

If cinema can demand your adoration, so it can also fling open the shutters on to a panorama. From the birth of cinema, people learned about the world in their local picture house. Almost as soon as the movie camera was invented, it became part of the explorer's kit. Photography from expeditions was hugely popular. The travelogue was one of the most successful genres in the early days of cinema, introducing audiences at cavernous lecture theatres to new races and species, glimpsing environments and societies they could barely dream of – Aborigines, nomadic tribes and Native Americans. These films, though, were shorts, illustrations of a lecture, and it was not until 1922 that audiences were shown the first ethnographic film and the beginning of the modern documentary.

From 1911 Gaumont had released a series of short films from the early stages of Captain Scott's British Antarctic Expedition by the official photographer, Herbert Ponting. After the death of Scott and his colleagues, Ponting travelled lecturing with the footage and, then, in 1924, he released a feature, *The Great White Silence*, complete with illustrations, intertitles and reconstructions, which told the story of the ill-fated expedition.

In the interim, however, the man who brought glimpses of the frozen wastes (although from the environs of the North Pole rather than the South) into the local picture house was Robert J. Flaherty. Since 1913 he had taken a camera with him on prospecting trips into the Hudson Bay on behalf of Sir William Mackenzie, the Canadian railway magnate and entrepreneur. Several weeks upriver in the inhospitable Arctic he observed people, customs and landscape that persuaded him that there was a story to be constructed of Eskimo life, one that people would pay to see.

Story is the key word. *Nanook of the North* may have been a window on the world for its wide-eyed audiences but you could still pitch it today to the money men: warm-hearted people battle fierce beasts and savage elements to survive! An introductory text to the film sets the tone: here in the endless frozen whiteness of 'short bitter days – the brass ball of sun a mockery in the sky' we will see the struggles of the sealskin-clad heroes befriended by Flaherty.

Against this hostile backdrop Nanook glides in, guiding his canoe through the ice floes. Our first glimpse is tantalising. The light is so bright, the contrast so extreme, that his features are barely visible as he pulls up alongside the camera, unloads a cute fur-wrapped child from the prow and hauls himself with some difficulty from the canoe's central opening (those bear-pelt trousers make him twice as wide around the hips as the shoulders). Then, like a magician, he proceeds to pull from the hull not rabbits but a wife, Nyla, a baby, an older child, Alleghoo, and finally a husky puppy – an Arctic family variety act! How strange their habits, but how endearing!

And heroic. With his troupe on the verge of starvation, Nanook picks his way fleetly across the ice floes and, great hunter that he is, spears in the icy waters a great fat fish which he kills with a bite behind the gills. The family sights a walrus. Everyone runs to the edge of the ice; the small child claps his hands in excitement. After much to-do, Nanook spears the great beast through a hole in the ice, lassoes it and wrestles with the rope (will he be pulled in?) until together the family heaves the walrus out. Then they're off to trap an adorable Arctic fox (probably not for a pet, judging by the wall of pale pelts back in the trading post), build an igloo in less than an hour and settle down to sleep naked under furs. The narrative doesn't entirely make sense but almost a century later the energy and ingenuity of the individuals shine through.

Interviewed in the 1950s, Robert Flaherty's widow Frances Hubbard Flaherty, described *Nanook* as a new use for the motion picture, a portrait of the spirit of a people. As well she might: the original conceit of the film was hers. She attributed its eventual appeal to what she called 'one-ness', observing that 'when Nanook and Nyla and little Alleghoo smile out at us from the screen we are completely disarmed. They are themselves; we become ourselves in turn; all that might separate us from these people falls away; a feeling that is profoundly liberating that we are one with all people and one with all things.' But she warned that 'one false gesture, one hint of artificiality' would destroy that unity.

Yet *Nanook of the North* is laced with artifice. As Flaherty's widow confirmed, the intention was never to make an ethnographic document but a commercial feature for audiences who expected narrative. What emerged was a hybrid – the first successful documentary feature, authentic in its way but not entirely natural. Igloo building was a thing of the past; walrus hunting was staged for the camera and Nanook's family wasn't even his own. His name was really Allakariallak. Feature film techniques made the staged looked 'natural'. How else would we have seen the family at rest in their igloo, light pouring down on them through a 'window' like a glacial nativity scene? The igloo was an Arctic filmset, a half-moon section built for the benefit of the camera. That walrus was dead long before Nanook hauled it out from below the ice; in fact, he and friends had pushed it down there in the first place. The tussle with the rope was his friend on the other end. No wonder they seem to be laughing so much. The whole sequence is cut for comic timing.

This artifice plays both ways. The play-acting revealed something of reality, too. Critics claimed they were seeing something never seen before, natural man in his habitat. Courtesy of a narrative film, cinema audiences knew about Eskimos. Even if Flaherty's reconstructions weren't entirely accurate and offered an outdated view of Inuit life, a new frontier was opened to Western audiences. It began with the Inuit, who gleefully bought this version of themselves and their life. In the preface to *Nanook*, Flaherty describes what effect his footage had on its subjects: 'As soon as I showed them some of the first results, Nanook and his crowd were completely won over.'

So it was with audiences around the world. Frances Taylor Patterson in *New Republic* was proud of this American production: 'We are excessively weary of adaptations from the other arts . . . Here at last begins our native screen language, as original in concept as *The Cabinet of Dr Caligari*, yet as natural as that is fantastic.'

The 'nature' boy had an ice-cream pie named after him in Germany, the Nanuk, a drink in America, a line of furs, an icebox and so on. His death from starvation on an unsuccessful deer hunting trip a year later made international news, neatly reinforcing the melodrama of the feature film. The words Eskimo and igloo became part of common parlance, a song was written about the star of the movie:

> Polar bears are prowling
> Wintry winds are howling
> Where the snow is falling
> There my heart is calling:
> Nanook! Nanook!

This apparently spontaneous reaction to the Frozen First Family was actually the product of a sophisticated machine, an early example of marketing. As the decades pass, this commercial element will prove the incidental music of film's history, tying real and reel worlds together. Back in 1922 the campaign book that accompanied the movie suggested ways of selling Nanook to small-town America: local shops could display igloos in their windows or employ people to dress as Eskimos and stroll around the streets with a sled.

After his hero's death, Flaherty consoled himself with the notion that the film 'has gone into most of the odd corners of the world, and more men than there are stones around the shore of Nanook's home have looked upon Nanook, the kindly, brave, simple Eskimo'. The Inuit people were now established in international popular consciousness. Eight decades later, in 2001, the Inuit finally made their own film based on an ancient legend, *Atanarjuat: The Fast Runner* – story, production, finance and sixty cast, crew and support staff were all Igoolik Inuit. They won prizes at international festivals from Toronto to Edinburgh to Cannes. Some critics considered the story a little weak but at least it was their own.

Like Flaherty's *Nanook of the North*, Ermanno Olmi's 1978 portrait of a group of tenant farmers in Italy at the beginning of the twentieth century, *The Tree of Wooden Clogs*, is both a constructed story (events laid early in the narrative have later repercussions) and a mesmerising evocation of a way of life. The majority of the actors were actually small-scale farmers from a part of Lombardy where many of the same methods were still in use; Olmi himself was born in the region. The film is not simply documentary. At one point, a newly-wed couple journey away from the hamlet, gliding downstream on a barge. After two hours immersed in the struggles of the little community, the audience is transported by the wonder of the young couple's adventure. It arouses a particular understanding of what it was like to be alive at that moment, and for those who took part – and the director himself – there is a desire to communicate that hidden way of life to a wider audience.

Since *Nanook*, film has regularly served as diplomacy by other means. In 1950 *Rashomon* pulled back the rice-paper screen on Japan with an unreliable tale of something mysterious in the woods. Ingredients included a beautiful maiden, treachery, farce, theft, magic and sword fighting. Barely five years after the end of the Second World War, *Rashomon*'s fairy-tale structure, its depiction of violence, desire and above all its sexy nature-boy lead (Toshiro Mifune) provided an insight into the culture that was enlightening for Western audiences. As a *Times* review put it in 1952: 'Whether or not a country truly expresses itself through the medium of the films does not admit any decided answer. No American, for instance, would agree that Hollywood reflects the real America, but something, some hints of a country's habit of thinking, some perhaps unconscious reflection of its prejudices and preferences, filters through the lens of the camera to perplex or amuse the foreigner.' The *Baltimore Sun*'s reviewer was less equivocal: 'If anyone still regards the Japanese as a phlegmatic, undemonstrative race, then he should take a look at *Rashomon*.' *Rashomon*'s appearance at the Venice Film Festival (where it won the Golden Lion) was the result of a broader marketing campaign for a whole nation. As part of Japan's post-war reinvention, a decision was made to transform it into a leading cultural country and, according to Donald Richie in *The Japanese Film*, 'cinema was to be Japan's cultural emissary', with international film festivals the equivalent of ambassadors' receptions.

Yet when it came to deciding which films to submit, it was difficult to choose for best effect. Which images were the most attractive exports? Maybe not the people sitting on tatami mats; to Western eyes they might look uncivilised. Perhaps studious but pleasing travelogues might deliver a better image. In the end, despite the agonising, *Rashomon* was selected for Venice almost by default. When, against expectations, it was lauded, even with an Academy Honorary Award in 1952, *Rashomon* restored Japan to the international cultural map.

British director Stephen Frears observed in a BBC interview that his generation learned about Paris from the movies, particularly the battered monochrome streets of the French *nouvelle vague* of the 1960s. These films were an antidote to the garish US fantasy Paris of 1950s musicals like *An American in Paris* (1951) and *Gigi* (1958), a distinct run of features that gave unofficial support to the Marshall Plan's attempts to boost American tourism in war-torn Europe. So obvious was this strategic blend of art and politics that a correspondent for the *New York Times* remarked in 1956 that 'Paris had never looked more like a Hollywood backlot than it does these days'. For Woody Allen that artistic version of the Marshall Plan was effective. He told the LA Weekly Blog, 'before I ever went to Paris, I was in love with the city because Hollywood was in love with the city. Whenever you saw Paris it was the city of romance, music, wine, beautiful hotels, *Gigi*.'

Mainstream blockbusters have taken audiences *Around the World in 80 Days* (1956), on a *Roman Holiday* (1953), and in pursuit of *The Thief of Baghdad* (1940). The David Lean epics, like *Lawrence of Arabia* or *Dr Zhivago*, gave us a cinema Kingdom of Saud or a Russia that informed international perception of the country for decades, even though the romantic ice-palace of Pasternak's novel was actually constructed from frozen beeswax in Spain. Fellini satirised but also peddled picture-postcard Rome with statuesque Anita Ekberg splashing about before the Baroque sculpture of the Trevi Fountain. Areas of New York – Manhattan, the Bronx or Queens – have a cinema persona thanks to Woody Allen or Martin Scorsese or Spike Lee.

Each decade, film opens new borders. In the 1970s, Fassbinder and Wenders revealed small-town industrial Germany while daily life in Poland opened up to international audiences in the eighties, with Iran in the nineties and South Korea in the 2000s. Many directors have wanted to follow in Flaherty's footsteps and bring wilderness into the picture house. Sergei Bodrov took his cameras to areas of the Caucasus never before photographed in *Prisoner of the Mountains* (1996) and for his troubles was held hostage by his own bodyguards who were demanding a pay rise. Werner Herzog mixed feature and myth in the drama *Where the Green Ants Dream* (1984), about the conflict between a mining company and indigenous Australians; arguably, he adopted Flaherty's more dubious practices by dreaming up his own green ant Aboriginal myths. The more exotic the location, the more the audience must take on trust – unless they want to travel to see it for themselves.

Lecturer Burton Holmes, who introduced those first travelogues to cinema audiences in 1897, was credited with providing greater incentives 'to start people travelling than anyone except Henry Ford'. The influence of films on tourism over the years can be measured in the huge marketing sums spent on promotional tie-ins such as *Star Wars* tours in Tunisia, *Sound of Music* tours in Salzburg and *Lord of the Rings* tours in New Zealand. The New Zealand government went to extraordinary lengths to promote the country on the back of Peter Jackson's trilogy. A multimillion-dollar advertising campaign reminded potential travellers that the spectacular scenery was not computer-generated but home-grown; on conventional road maps of the two islands, imaginary places like Helmsdeep were marked next to the real spots where they were filmed. The rural town of Matamata now has dual identity as Bilbo Baggins's home of Hobbiton, one name in green ink, the other in red. After the campaign, there was a reported 22 per cent rise in tourism to New Zealand, a mini-boom still referred to as 'the Frodo economy', the Kiwi equivalent of Australia's 1980s 'Crocodile Dundee effect' when the outback comedy appeared to double the number of US visitors to Australia.

Over time, locations can take on the perspective of films made there. Is Texas more western because of the cowboy genre? London more London because of Universal horror films? A visit can bring disappointment. Not all of London's landmarks are conveniently around the corner from each other as in the live-action remake of *101 Dalmatians* (1996), for example.

A nameplate has already established that canine leads Pongo and Perdita and their human pets inhabit a deceptively spacious mews house in SW7 – South Kensington, north of the Thames and west of Hyde Park. One evening, a pensive Pongo wanders out to the roof terrace to gaze across the Thames . . . as if from the *south* bank towards the Houses of Parliament and Big Ben. Blow me down, as Dick van Dyke might observe, if he isn't slap bang opposite the best known landmark in London. Luvverly.

And so it is. This snowscape globe view of London owes much to the aesthetic of the original Disney cartoon from 1961. It presents a cute and cosy London with no landmark more than a short dogtrot away, an attractive notion that is played out in less obvious but just as seductive ways in films like *Four Weddings and a Funeral*, *Notting Hill* and *Wimbledon*. The screen geography is like one of those mid-century film posters where scenes from the action appear in cameo around the title. The film takes possession of the location and audiences, in turn, feel they own a little bit of Westminster or Montmartre or Arctic Canada, maybe even of Nanook himself.

THE GENERAL (1926)

USA

Directors: Clyde Bruckman, Buster Keaton

Cast: Buster Keaton, Marion Mack, Glen Cavander

Black and white, silent

If cinema made audiences yearn and wonder at marvels, it also had its imps, the apparently ordinary guys with extraordinary talent for doing what we might like to do but dare not. The catharsis of cinema is that they get away with it on our behalf – or if they don't get away with it, they bounce back from their punishment seemingly unscathed. Sometimes, the encounter is with authority – the heavy in the uniform – but more often, and more memorably, it is with an entire system and in the 1920s cinema universe that system is often manifest in technical ways – with innovations and machines.

After France's Max Linder, Charlie Chaplin had become cinema's chief imp of misrule; Chaplin's persona was that of a charmer with unparalleled skill at manipulating audience sympathies. Yet a more effective vessel of the great audience unconscious may be the beautiful, radical, dangerous comedian Buster Keaton who, in an extraordinary run of creativity throughout the 1920s, did something that is arguably more durable. He never asked for sympathy; he rarely showed any emotion. The audience was there to supply that. A classic case is *The General*, named for a magnificent steam engine, and set in the American Civil War. Keaton rated it his favourite film.

The General is based on a true story from 1862 when a bunch of Unionist spies in disguise stole a railroad engine in Georgia and drove her north, sabotaging lines, wires and bridges along the way. The train's rightful crew, patriotic Confederates all, chased after them and eventually recaptured their locomotive.

65

Keaton perceived the close match between the circumstances of this story and his screen strengths. There is a machine – a great clanking, steaming warhorse that, playing the character of the train's engineer, Johnnie, he learned to drive. There is another claim to his affections, the lovely Annabelle Lee (Marion Mack). There is a predicament (lost train and the threat of lost girl, since she believes erroneously that he is too cowardly to enlist to fight for the South). There is a great narrative in the civil war itself, made even greater by our hero's apparent obliviousness to the terrible events going on around him.

The film is distinguished by matching sequences – the journey north pursuing the train, the flight back ahead of the Unionist captors – but none more impressive than Keaton's breakneck progress through the actual battlefield, with soldiers played by four hundred members of the Oregon National Guard. First he travels north, facing away from the galloping horses, exploding cannon and charging infantry of a full-scale battle taking place behind him. And then, moments later, he goes back the other way unaware of another charge, this time of an army in darker uniforms – it's an economical yet dazzling and witty summation of the individual's role as bit player in the great events of history.

Keaton's films are technically sophisticated studies of humanity in a mechanical environment. Some even took the name of a contraption (here it is the train, two years earlier it was the ship *Navigator*). He was the outstanding example of the French philosopher Henri Bergson's 1901 essay on laughter. 'The laughable consists of a certain *mechanical inelasticity*,' wrote Bergson, 'just where one would expect to find the wide-awake adaptability and the living pliableness of a human being.' The first recorded example of film comedy (if you don't count that sneeze) is a Lumière fragment shown in 1895. *L'Arroseur Arrosé* (*The Sprinkler Sprinkled*) shows a man watering his garden with a hose. Suddenly, technology appears to turn on him and he is drenched. What follows is the pursuit of the prankster who had masterminded the jape, but the real impact of the comedy lies in the perception that the hose has acted not like a piece of rubber but a malign snake.

In one situation after another, from the two-reeler *One Week* (1920), where newly-wed Keaton has to erect a house from a kit in a remarkably precise prefiguring of the Ikea generation ('assemble according to numbers' etc), to the hapless photographer in *The Cameraman* (1928), the mechanised and manufactured world finds ways to bite Buster. He, of course, devises just as many ingenious ways to retaliate. In a sophisticated industrial age, Keaton was Man versus the Machine par excellence, although in fairness he was usually also in love with it and a willing agent of its chaotic power.

There is a scintillating moment in *The General* as Johnnie and his girl speed along in the steam train, alternately chasing or fleeing from enemy soldiers who are in another locomotive. Speed is essential: the furnace must be stoked. She helps – flinging in logs, prettily sorting and selecting the choicest. She rejects one because it has a knotty hole, flinging it to the ground in favour of a dainty branch which she lobs into the fire. Keaton watches, impassive as ever, but a beat longer than the supposed pace of the scene would dictate. As the train rockets along at breakneck speed, he leans down and picks up a splinter, courteously presenting it to her. Thrilled, she lobs it into the flames. Keaton lunges forward, the provocation is too much: his hands close around her throat and for a moment she is thrown backwards as he makes to choke her. Then the stranglehold is quickly relinquished in favour of an embrace, he plants a swift kiss on her lips and they get back to the serious business of evading the enemy.

Whether in a full-blown battle or on board a sinking ship or in the icy reaches of Alaska (Keaton's *The Frozen North* appeared not long after *Nanook*, as did Chaplin's Alaskan adventures in *The Gold Rush* (1925) – snowy landscapes and new frontiers were clearly suited to film's monochrome) Buster Keaton is untouched by the extremes, concentrating instead on the ordinary detail, such as the way his sword swishes, or his hat falls, the little things that the rest of us, bystanders to history, are probably watching, even as great events unfold behind our backs.

Yet at the same time the stunts Keaton performed were real – with real threat to organic material, his body . . . He did run down a mountain pursued by boulders, leap from buildings, stand steady while a house fell around him, and he had the fractures to prove it. He carried off one of the most spectacular effects even to this day – not to be repeated, no second chances, no substitutes – when a train in *The General* careers across a flaming bridge over a river and plunges into the waters below. More than Chaplin, whose sentimentality gave him a winsome distance, Keaton looks straight from the screen into our heads. His strangely beautiful visage is complicit with the audience – we are all in this together, there is no mitigation. (Keaton's expressionless style earned him the soubriquet 'The Great Stone Face' early on in his film career; he may even have been the first recipient of the description 'deadpan' in a 1928 *New York Times* article.) His surroundings were often a kind of atmospheric moonscape, too – a flat ocean or a wide plain – so nothing would distract from the gaze.

The Playhouse (1921) is an early Keaton short, less than twenty minutes in duration, that sharply points up key aspects of the relationship of cinema to audience. Overall, the short may not have the depth of invention of the later features but the first third of its twenty minutes is a brilliant showcase of the duality that makes a star. It is set in a vaudeville theatre where a succession of acts perform. Keaton was raised in the traditions of music hall; as an infant with his parents, he made up the family act the Three Keatons. So skilled is Keaton's playing here, and so seamless the technique, that it only gradually dawns that he is playing every role. With the help of impressive multiple-exposure filming, Keaton is the conductor, cellist, percussionist, trombonist and stagehand, among others. Then, onstage he plays a troupe of dancers and minstrels to the most amazing effect, startling even by the standards of modern computer-generated imagery, that is not so much an effect as a loop in time. The six Keatons you see hoofing onstage are actually six performances by the same man, step-perfect for cameraman Elgin Leslie who had devised an ingenious system. Leslie masked off sections of the film, shot Keaton's dance, rewound to the exact point, covered another section, captured Keaton again further along in frame and so on until there was a whole line-up for the delight of the audience. Keaton is the audience, too, naturally – that little boy with the sticky lollipop and the grand lady in the evening gown with the old soak consort (him, too) – but at the same time he's always essentially himself. And you. And me. On our behalf, in what is licensed chaos, he struggles with frustrations and carries out those fantasies of revenge that we can never dare to enact. So close is the identification that Keaton's 2004 biographer Edward McPherson admitted to the shock of hearing Keaton's recorded voice for the first time. It was 'deeper, huskier – not at all the voice I had heard in my head, which, I realized, was modelled (in a cheerfully narcissistic way) after my own internal monologue'.

Then, after six minutes of virtuosity, *The Playhouse* takes a truly weird turn. We see Keaton snoozing on a bed so it must all have been a dream. In fact it isn't – the walls slide away to reveal that he's actually on a stage and then the narrative edges into a semi-autobiographical chaos of yet another vaudeville show. This becomes so confusing that Keaton begins to doubt his own judgement and signs a pledge not to drink (a resolution he didn't necessarily keep offscreen). He's as dazzled and dizzy from the whole thing as the audience is.

Keaton's characters often fall into dreams. He gazes out at us and simultaneously points sideways. He is both in and out of the frame – the bridge that lets us in, his gaze as direct and arresting now as in 1921 or 1926. In part, he was using old stage techniques. His father had discovered that their hyperactive physical comedy routine picked up more laughs when the boy apparently failed to react when he was flung around the stage. Keaton's genius was to raise the stakes around him, making that impassivity his greatest appeal. In film after film, he played characters who ought to have been equipped to deal with situations but suddenly found themselves at a loss – an engineer on a runaway train, a millionaire cast adrift – but determined to carry on with what dignity was available. The critic James Agee, writing in *Life* in 1949, observed,

> . . . he used this great sad motionless face to suggest various related things: a one-track mind near the track's end of pure insanity; mulish imperturbability under the wildest of circumstances; how dead a human being can get and still be alive; an awe-inspiring sort of patience and power to endure, proper to granite but uncanny in flesh and blood.

So why did so many complex interpretations arise from something so apparently blank? In a cinema, there are two beams directed at the screen simultaneously – one from the projectionist's booth, the other from the eyes of those in the seats below. Each individual in the audience projects his or her own characteristics, ideals and prejudices on to actors. The stone faces, like Keaton or Garbo, whose wide-boned structure was often described as a mask, are the best receivers for these unconscious broadcasts.

Even today something of that effect lingers with inexpressive actors like Bill Murray in *Lost in Translation* (2003) or pretty much every Clint Eastwood performance. Terence Stamp in his autobiography credits Michael Caine with teaching him the technique of stillness, which allows a screen actor to be the conduit of our interpretation. By contrast, actors schooled in old theatrical traditions like Laurence Olivier can seem over-expressive or even hammy when their faces are fifty foot high. The old advice to actors – don't just do something, stand there – may be a joke, but it reveals a truth about screen acting: less is more. Stillness is a precious quality in cinema, a fact recognised as early as the teens and twenties when actors were encouraged to rein in their stage techniques.

'I did bigger business in Europe than I did in the United States. I was a box-office draw in the darndest country in the world. . . . Russia. I was a bigger box-office attraction than Chaplin in Russia,' Keaton admitted with some pride in an interview with Christopher Bishop in a 1958 edition of *Film Quarterly*. Russian filmmakers in particular would have recognised Keaton's technique. In the late 1910s, the Russian film theorist Lev Kuleshov had conducted experiments in film craft with his students, including Sergei Eisenstein. In his most famous trial, he filmed the expressionless face of actor Ivan Mozhukin looking at an unidentified object or person out of the frame. Kuleshov then edited the same image with a shot of a bowl of soup, a dead woman in a coffin and a child playing, and asked audiences to tell him what Mozhukin was feeling. When they saw the actor juxtaposed with the food, they thought he was hungry, next to the coffin he appeared sad, and so on. This experiment was primarily to reveal the power of montage in the creation of meaning in cinema, but it also illustrates the link between screen acting and the process of identification. The audience is not passive – our active imaginations get to work on these beautiful spaces left open for us. Hitchcock recognised that *Rear Window* (1954), a film all about voyeurism and looking for clues and motives, was an example of the Kuleshov effect. As he explained to the French director François Truffaut, in the shot of James Stewart gazing through his binoculars at a dog lowered in a basket, Stewart is seen with a kindly smile, 'but if in the place of the little dog you show a half-naked girl, exercising in front of her open window, and you go back to smiling Stewart again, this time he's a dirty old man!'

In 1926, the year *The General* was released, Buñuel presented *Un Chien Andalou* to cinemagoers, with its shocking opening. A solid, heroic looking man (played by Buñuel himself) sharpens a razor on a strop. He goes outside on to a balcony and gazes up at a full moon. The next shot is of a woman staring straight into the camera. The man, now standing behind her, brings the razor across the screen – right to left – towards her eye. Cut to the moon where a sliver of cloud cuts – right to left – across its face. Then a close-up shot of what we take to be the blade slicing the woman's eyeball. Totally unprepared, the audience is horrified and disoriented. Yet they are not in fact unprepared: the action is more easily comprehensible because it has been prefigured in the previous shot of the moon. What the audience lacks is the plot or psychological reasoning.

Still, viewers are not free to project a meaning of their own on to puzzling images or the blankest of screen faces. Many factors shape the audience's response: the editing, the narrative, the character type, the roles actors have played in other films and what we know about them offscreen, or, rather, what we *think* we know about them. Keaton's blank style, for instance, was imaginatively attributed by one journalist to some unspecified 'secret sorrow'. The sad clown label stuck to Keaton, an early film example of the confusion between the real person and their assumed identity that stage actors had long exploited.

When we watch a film we are by no means passive, we might even have specific ambitions for the action – something film plots have recognised over the years. Our eagerness to put ourselves in the picture, that crossover between reel and reality, regularly appears as a dramatic device. In *Sherlock Jnr* (1924) Keaton plays a projectionist who dreams of starring in the detective movie he is screening. Before long he is up there taking part in a series of scenarios, a lifetime before actors had to cavort in front of a featureless 'green screen' so that a computer-realised background could be added in later in post-production. As the audience sees it, Keaton climbs up from the auditorium, struggling to adapt to the changes in location that are happening behind him – a garden, a street, a house. Keaton was pulling apart the conventions of an industry that was barely twenty years old. Many other filmmakers would copy him in years to come.

In Woody Allen's *The Purple Rose of Cairo* (1985), Mia Farrow gazes up at Jeff Daniels as the leading man, Tom. Moments later, they are together; his character has stepped out of the screen and into the real world, with chaotic consequences, As Farrow's character, Cecilia says, 'I just met a wonderful new man. He's fictional but you can't have everything.' Later he squares up to the fact that's it's recession-hit America and jobs are hard to come by. As Cecilia puts it, right now the whole country's out of work. Tom's response is suitably romantic heroic – Well, then, we'll live on love. We'll have to make some concessions, but so what? We'll have each other. Cecilia, though, has tired of his square-jawed optimism. That's movie talk, she sighs. But for a while, there was a compact between Tom and Cecilia, screen idol and audience, and that compact stretches across the decades.

1930s
. . . .

STRUGGLING THROUGH

I
n barely a quarter of a century film had moved from fairground attraction to a sophisticated industry with regular consumers. Now that
cinema-going had become a regular habit, that industry had to contend
with what might prove its first serious reverse – an international economic
crisis that seemed to threaten all the progress of the previous decade. Yet,
despite the financial stringencies that followed the Great Crash of 1929,
audiences flocked to the Odeons, Pantheons, Alhambras and Colisseums
in ever increasing numbers. In 1930 eighty million cinema tickets a week
were sold to an American population of 123 million, still an all-time record.
By the end of the decade in the United Kingdom, 23 million were sold to
a population of 48 million. Hollywood had entered its golden era, which
would run until the end of the 1940s. Cinema was providing by turns a
prop, an instruction manual and a warning.

Not only had the stars grown luminous, the locations exotic and the exploits extraordinary, film suddenly had a voice. Some filmmakers agonised over the introduction of sound. Looking back from 1970, the French director René Clair, who made his first film in 1924, recalled: 'Media of expression develop gradually in the course of centuries; for example, music did not pass suddenly from Gregorian Chant to the symphony orchestra. But we were being asked to change our tools and our language in a few months.'

Artists often fear the incursion of variety and novelties that might pollute the form, suspicious of the commercial forces that drive them. Filmmakers who considered themselves artists were particularly anxious that the intrusive reality of human voices and other everyday sounds would undermine the fantasy, the spell of cinema. In a neat reversal of Virginia Woolf's grudging concession that cinema might have some limited artistic potential, Clair wondered: 'Can the talking picture be poetic? There is reason to fear that the precision of the verbal expression will drive poetry off the screen just as it drives off the atmosphere of daydream.' He observed that people emerging from sound films did not have that 'comfortable numbness that a trip to the land of pure images used to bestow upon us'.

Clair, who could have been speaking of Buster Keaton when he noted that silent film heroes 'spoke to the imagination with the complicity of silence', nevertheless went on to make a remarkable trio of sound films, including the first French musical *Sous les Toits de Paris* (1930), which embraced song, musical dialogue and dazzling studio sets. The musical, hitherto impossible, would prove a financial blessing to the American studios like Warner Brothers who, in time, would make additional profits from the sale of sheet and recorded music.

At first sound itself and dialogue in particular did not always please the audience. They might dislike the accent or the nasal whine of their favourite silent stars; many films (like Josef von Sternberg's first collaboration with Marlene Dietrich, *Der Blaue Engel/The Blue Angel* from 1930) were made in parallel versions with the dialogue in different languages.

Post-synchronisation – dubbing – brought the possibility not only of putting another language into the mouths of the actors but of increasing the dramatic impact by adding sounds you might not expect to hear, or taking away those you might.

The limited auditory range of microphones restricted the action. At one end of the spectrum were the worthy, static, stage-to-screen adaptations of successful plays where the actors simply intoned their lines without moving too far from their allotted marks. At the other were experimentalists who pushed at these constraints, understanding that sound montage, just as much as picture montage, could contribute to the atmosphere, tension and general manipulation of an audience's reactions.

Alfred Hitchcock delivered a striking example in his first talking film, *Blackmail*, in 1929, as a young woman with a guilty secret sits around a table with her family. For her the word 'knife' repeatedly stands out from the mundane exchanges. The language itself becomes an assault, a staccato reminder of a recent horrific experience. In Fritz Lang's *M* (1931), a film about a child murderer, a woman is disturbed by children chanting play-ground songs beneath her apartment, but her neighbour reassures her: at least if you can hear them you know that they have come to no harm. Then, in cruel parallel, music is also used to denote threat: the killer whistles Edvard Grieg's 'In the Hall of the Mountain King'; and soon, the sound alone is enough to suggest his presence. If you can hear him, the children are not safe.

Sound could also enhance verisimilitude. In post-production, once filming had finished, the American director Lewis Milestone built up the noises of battle for *All Quiet on the Western Front* (1930). The following year, with a less arduous subject, he captured realistic sound by devising a way to free a camera and sound-recording equipment from cables and booths and follow the protagonists in the first screen version of the whipcrack dialogue stage play *The Front Page* (1931). Howard Hawks would make his own version at the end of the decade with Cary Grant and Rosalind Russell, as *His Girl Friday* – a film that still holds the screen record for words per minute, as if challenging the new recording equipment. Women appeared onscreen who could talk back and – like their audience – went out to work, got divorced and wore trousers. Garbo and Dietrich might never convince as working girls but Russell, Katharine Hepburn, Carole Lombard, Olivia de Havilland, Joan Fontaine, Ginger Rogers and Claudette Colbert, not forgetting Hollywood's baby sisters, Judy Garland, Deanna Durbin and Shirley Temple, could as easily be stenographers as society princesses; best of all for the times, they could speak up for themselves. Joan Blondell's turn as the hard-up wannabe star in *The Gold Diggers of 1933* proved that anything was possible for those who were not afraid of hard graft.

President Franklin D. Roosevelt's New Deal of restorative economic measures began in 1933. In June that year the first drive-in cinema opened in New Jersey. The movie houses on both sides of the Atlantic were temples for the celebration of the opportunity and bounty that advanced societies could promise, even if the audiences were themselves short of cash.

The studios were not immune, riding financial upheavals, labour problems, insolvencies and eventually an anti-trust suit from the government. After various shake-outs and mergers, five big studios dominated. MGM, purveyor of shiny, popular fare had stars of the wattage of Clark Gable, Jean Harlow, Jeanette MacDonald and Nelson Eddy. Paramount was home to European émigré artists from von Sternberg to the Marx Brothers. Fox, which merged with Twentieth Century in 1935, turned out general entertainment with likeable stars such as Shirley Temple and Betty Grable. There was eclectic RKO, with a mixture of talent, from Astaire and Rogers to Katharine Hepburn to the tyro Orson Welles, while Warner Brothers specialised in social comment and gangsters blasting machine guns from the rooftops, but displayed a special loyalty to the New Deal.

If thrift and uncertainty sat on the chests of cinemagoers like a great grey incubus, for a couple of hours they might wrestle free into a frenetic

Marx Brothers caper or a lavish costume picture or the ultimate poor guy and rich girl romance – Clark Gable and Claudette Colbert in *It Happened One Night*. The surprise hit of 1934, directed by Frank Capra, it was the first of the 'screwball' comedies that defined a new egalitarian romance and helped to bring Columbia Pictures out of the minor studio league. The film opened inauspiciously with mixed reviews but tickets soon built on word of mouth. Audiences admired Gable, who was lithe and funny as the newspaperman down on his luck; they adored Colbert as the spoilt heiress escaping from her father to marry a society aviator. The backchat when these two hook up on the road, the contrast of riches and hardship, the suppressed raciness (the couple share a room, but proprieties are maintained by a ludicrous barrier of a blanket strung up between the beds) and the competitive spark between them (hailed as modern but clearly owing much to Shakespeare's sparring couples) made this the first film to win all five major Academy Awards.

Frank Capra knew how to mix the cocktail of stimulant and entertainment. For all its laughs *It Happened One Night* neatly skewers the follies of the rich and extols instead the virtues of careful husbandry – Gable wins Colbert's respect when he turns down a $10,000 reward in favour of settling a debt of $39.60. The couple travel through America on a bus, glimpsing hunger and deprivation along the way. Each day brings a negotiation of limited resources (being a runaway, she has no access to her millions) as they scratch an existence, sleep rough and scavenge carrots. When they hole up at an Auto-Camp, a continuous tracking shot follows Colbert bundled up in Gable's old bathrobe as she picks her way past their fellow mobile-home residents – kids play in the dirt, men fix cars and weary figures take what rest they can – until she joins a queue for the showers with a group of bare-faced, straggle-haired women. Colbert's character, Ellie, demonstrates her worthiness to be the hero's mate by the ease with which she chats to them. By contrast, her wealthy beau turns up for their wedding in a ridiculous helicopter; he is clearly not the man for her.

Capra's manifesto for common sense in difficult times would develop in *Mr Deeds Goes to Town* (1936), *You Can't Take it With You* (1938) and, in 1939, with *Mr Smith Goes to Washington*. In this last film James Stewart plays Jefferson Smith (the name combines both American President and political thinker with Everyman) who is head of the youth group, the Boy Rangers. Smith is adopted as a political candidate by a group of cynical Washington manipulators who see him as the man to get some questionable legislation through. Despite attempts to exploit him, Jefferson is armour-plated by naiveté and an unwavering idealism. He finds support from a Washington aide, the realistic and hardworking Clarissa (Jean Arthur as a paragon of humorous but professional career girl). When it comes, Smith's heroic moment is also ludicrous: he stands for hours on end in a filibuster in the Senate demonstrating both the power of democracy and the effectiveness of political persistence.

By contrast, European films of the time expressed dark foreboding. As Hitler and Mussolini tightened their controls over the populations of Germany and Italy, and sought to acquire new territories, Stalin instigated purges in Russia, civil war broke out in Spain and France's Popular Front briefly succeeded then collapsed. The French director Jean Renoir, who was associated with the Popular Front, made *La Grande Illusion* (1937), a drama about the First World War, and the first foreign-language film to be nominated for an Academy Award; it was banned in Germany, being condemned by Goebbels for its depiction of the futility of war. *La Bête Humaine*, the film Renoir made in 1938, combined a profound darkness with a fatalism that owed much to Freudian notions. Its brooding premonition is more powerful for being set not amongst soldiers or statesmen, but working people in the naturalistic surroundings of a railway yard.

British apprehension about events unfolding in continental Europe produced a memorable science-fiction film around the pessimistic theme of politicians' inability to avert disaster. *Things to Come* (1936) was based on H.G. Wells's 1933 novel in which war breaks out in 1940, devastates the planet and sends much of its population back to the Dark Ages. Decades later, as these people are stricken by a ferocious plague, a band of sleek technophiles arrive to build a new civilisation in Basra, Iraq. Progress wrestles with primitive nationalism, set to a score by Arthur Bliss.

In the United States, threats came in more immediate form, recognisable from newspaper headlines. Prohibition had provided the ideal conditions for one particular industry – organised crime – and its executive, the gangster. The St Valentine's Day Massacre of 1929, in which one Chicago gang rubbed out rival members of another, brought Al Capone to the forefront of the Most Wanted, in more than one sense. Out in small-town America, outlaws like John Dillinger, Clyde Barrow and Bonnie Parker held up banks with shotguns and outwitted the law. At the cinema rapid-fire dialogue and bullets mixed with social grit in *Little Caesar* (1930) and *The Public Enemy* (1931) and – most notorious of all – *Scarface* (1932).

America's Catholic bishops denounced Hollywood for producing films that glorified gangster life and instigated a pledge by concerned members of the Church to reject their corrupting influence. Measures to restrain the content of films were obvious from 1930, when the Motion Picture Production Code (originally the Hays Code) was adopted by several studios, but its effect was really evident from 1934 through the administration of the Breen Office, so-called after the Catholic censor, Joseph Breen, who headed the operation. Its tenets were to ensure that no film would 'lower the moral standards of those who see it'. This precluded any screen ridicule of the law or of religion, any naked or suggestive dancing, depictions of venereal disease or childbirth, specific methods of crime or murder that might be imitated, excessive and lustful kissing or mixed-race relationships. Overall, the Code was in favour of marriage, the United States and good taste. Breen was even initially wary that *Mr Smith Goes to Washington* might bring the political system into disrepute with its portrait of corruption and graft but eventually conceded that it fully buttressed the ideal 'of the people, by the people and for the people'.

Polling and survey pioneer George Gallup's success in predicting Roosevelt's presidential victory helped make legitimate the practice of opinion polling, which could then be applied to all forms of social study. Academics such as Dr John T. Tigert, president of the University of Florida, weighed in with pronouncements on the successful new mass entertainment: 'For the purpose of making and influencing public thought, the motion picture in its present stage is the most powerful influence now known.' Across the Atlantic, the MP and novelist John Buchan in a debate in the House of Commons described cinema as 'the most powerful engine of propaganda and advertisement on the globe today'. He had reason to appreciate its force: Alfred Hitchcock adapted his thriller *The 39 Steps* in 1935.

The global reach of film was also the concern of H.J. Forman, whose 1935 volume *Our Movie-Made Children* was the first large-scale study of the influence of cinema. His work was based on a series of experiments commissioned by the Payne Fund, a group largely composed of social scientists from the University of Chicago who described themselves as an 'organisation interested in the radio, motion pictures and reading in relation to children and youth'.

Their methods employed the latest technology, such as the psycho-galvanometer: children watched excerpts from films with their fingertips on electrodes in liquid. The scientists concluded that the children underwent 'a powerful emotional experience that affects their young brains and nerves with almost the force of an electric charge'. One experiment suggested such effects might last for up to seventy hours. The symptoms were likened to 'emotional possession', 'impulses that are ordinarily restrained are strongly stimulated'. Women might become aggressively amorous and youngsters turn to crime – fears laid out in chapters such as 'The Path to Delinquency' or 'Movie-Made Criminals'.

Britain had a similar band of anxious academics, magistrates and doctors under the collective title the Birmingham Cinema Enquiry. They tackled the problem as social malaise rather than physiological disorder, seeking to discover 'how far unhappy homes, divorce, illegitimacy and disease were due to the pictures'. Cinema was presumed guilty. The Enquiry's national conference in 1932 brought together representatives from twenty-two educational institutions, forty-two social bodies, nineteen religious groups and four medical organisations. Dr W.A. Potts of the National Council of Mental Hygiene blamed a 90 per cent rise in indecent assaults on boys and a 62 per cent increase in assaults on young children generally on the 'sex content' of films. Maybe Fritz Lang's 'M' could be heard whistling outside.

Worse condemnation was to come. Journalists R.G. Burnett and E.D. Martell declared in their book *The Devil's Camera* that the motion picture industry was the greatest threat yet to Western civilisation. Britain and the United States were in peril from the glamorous depiction of crime and violence onscreen. What was more, the 'persistent portrayal of immorality among white people cannot fail to produce the worst possible effects among the so-called backward races'. In Britain a Labour MP complained that films were 'creating erroneous impressions of Western civilisation and probably doing incalculable harm in Asia and the East generally'. These and other fevered responses are described in greater detail by Professor Jeffrey Richards in *The Age of the Dream Palace*.

Yet film also had its champions within the Establishment. In his own published study, *Are We Movie-Made?*, legal expert Raymond Moley found fault with the methodology of the Payne Fund's experiments and disparaged linking criminal activity to cinema-going as 'dangerous as well as humorous'. In Britain, Sir Herbert Samuel, the Home Secretary, agreed with police officers who noted that cinema kept the young off the streets and out of pubs. 'On the whole, the cinema conduces more to the prevention of crime than to its commission.'

It could even educate – the Middlesex Experiment of 1932 found it particularly effective at drumming in facts about hitherto unfamiliar foreign countries, what you might identify as the *Nanook* factor. Overall, concluded the report, *The Film in National Life,* also published that year, 'the film is a stimulant, not a sedative. It is much more likely to wake up the dull or lazy boy than send him to sleep.'

The studios were working on another stimulant – colour. To the old two-strip process – red and green – blue was now added. Short films of decorative events displayed the new vibrant hues, with the stars in their finery. *La Fiesta de Santa Barbara* (1935) showed Hollywood celebrities enjoying the festival Old Mexico-style in western costumes, chatting not so casually together at tables outdoors. A trio of dark-haired sisters, the Garlands, sang 'La Cucaracha' in bright dresses, with the smallest one looking and sounding many years older than thirteen. It was Judy's first Hollywood appearance.

That same year RKO produced the first three-strip Technicolor feature, *Becky Sharp,* directed by Reuben Mamoulian with Miriam Hopkins as Thackeray's bold heroine. Its effects were strongest in the ball and battle scenes where the bright red coats of the English soldiers caught the eye. As the trailer put it, 'the screen becomes the palette for life's great canvas'.

The producer of *Becky Sharp,* David O. Selznick, was aware that colour had to be balanced carefully. At one level it was a question of logistics. Studio floors were now complicated by sound equipment and engineers, and to this would be added the extra staff to supervise the colour both in front of and inside the camera. All this business might dilute the director's ownership of his picture. In a similar way to René Clair's reservations about sound, some felt that monochrome and the subtleties of its lighting created more of a dream-like environment, whereas colour would drag in realism and dilute that spirit. Maybe colour should be kept for musicals or costume pictures, with serious drama left to the more severe scheme of black and white. Yet there were already enthusiastic mannerists who appreciated that colour in both setting and lighting could accentuate mood or character – without aping reality. In fact, colour could be a fantasy or a character in itself. Selznick was reluctant to hold back – he was heading towards *Gone With the Wind* (1939) with its silhouettes against fiery sunsets. Close on its heels would come *Snow White and the Seven Dwarfs* (1937), *The Wizard of Oz* (1939) and in the next decade in Britain the films of Michael Powell and Emeric Pressburger.

When the thirties began, however, the luxuriance of colour was still a way off. Black and white was the tone of realism and horror, and in particular of the spinning newspapers that lifted stories off the streets and into movie plots.

· ·

SCARFACE (1932)

Director: Howard Hawks
Cast: Paul Muni, Ann Dvorak, George Raft
Black and white, sound

> *This picture is an indictment of gang rule in America and of the callous indifference of the government to the constantly increasing menace to our safety and liberty. Every incident in this picture is the reproduction of an actual occurrence, and the purpose of this picture is to demand of the government: 'What are you going to do about it?'*

The third of the great gangster films of the decade begins with a prologue in which director Howard Hawks skilfully ices a cake while eating it. With a screenplay by Ben Hecht adapted from Armitage Trail's novel, *Scarface* had the immediacy of newsreel: the audience knew that mobster Al Capone owed his nickname to three slashes on his left cheek from a knife fight; 'every incident' promised action which Hawks delivered with the steady rat-a-tat-tat of a machine gun and yet, to save everyone's face – and to get the picture past the authorities – crime must not be portrayed as glamorous. Or at least the glamour should gradually be eroded and then finally dispelled in a shower of bullets.

Handsome, ambitious young Italian-American Tony Camonte (Paul Muni) is the lieutenant of a crime boss in the bootlegging business up against a rival Irish gang. Camonte has ambitions first towards the boss's girl and then his empire. He starts to act unilaterally, clearing out the opposition's market in a series of spectacular drive-by raids on bars and restaurants. As he becomes more powerful, a vulnerability becomes apparent – an intense, almost incestuous, affection for his sexually adventurous sister, Ceska (Ann Dvorak). When she secretly marries his sidekick, Ceska unwittingly provides the key to her brother's downfall.

Though released in 1932, *Scarface* was actually shot in 1930, just a year after the St Valentine's Day Massacre. Al Capone had left his Chicago base to visit Hollywood in 1927 with an eye to some business (a gangster could take his pick of drink, drugs, prostitution, union management and general protection rackets in such an environment) but was distracted by other concerns, including the taxman. When he heard of the *Scarface* plans, Capone not unnaturally took an interest in a film that would take his own nickname for its title. Ben Hecht, closeted in a hotel room on a deadline to finish the script, claimed a couple of 'advisers' arrived with a draft, seeking reassurance that the film would not caricature their boss. Hecht insisted it was a generic portrait and, rather easily it seems, they were satisfied. Hawks later said he had invited Capone to view footage but he claimed to be otherwise engaged. It is likely that the gangster may not have registered that Hawks had chosen to elide 1930s mobster rule with the machinations of the fifteenth-century Borgias, with Tony as Cesare and Ceska as Lucrezia – down to the murderous jealousy towards the sister's lovers. Then again, he may have found the comparison flattering.

Films of the early thirties were dotted with simulacra of the gangster: *Scarface* shares elements and motifs with many of them. Edward G. Robinson in *Little Caesar* or James Cagney in *The Public Enemy* may be more fully realised psychopathologies but *Scarface* remains the exemplar. With photography by Lee Garmes, who was about to create the Dietrich 'look', it remains the most elegant, exciting, witty and viscerally shocking of the bunch.

Scarface was not finally released until two years later after a prolonged tussle with the Hays Office, which was concerned about the violence, sexual references and general moral ambiguity. The controversy, as ever, proved a great advertisement. The eventual compromises included giving the film a subtitle, *The Shame of the Nation*, and adding a sanctimonious statement that prefaces the action and extra scenes, not directed by Hawks, including a long 'editorial' speech by a newspaper publisher on the evils of gangsters and how they must be cleared from the streets. It simultaneously justifies media coverage of their exploits, and calls for punitive legislation. There was also a new ending where Scarface, rather than expiring operatically among the remnants of his lost dreams, is brought before a judge who sums up his villainy to camera (so that a chastened audience may atone for their previous enjoyment) before he is taken to the gallows. The hangman's noose is dropped over the camera, just in case any viewer were still in doubt as to the wages of sin. Luckily the film is almost always shown with its original ending intact.

None of these changes reduced the charisma of the figures at the centre. The police may denounce Scarface as a 'yellow rat' when he pleads for his life at the end, but the enduring memory is of Muni's open, good-looking face and the puppyish energy that can turn homicidal on the flick of a coin. Sensual Ceska makes an impressive appearance at a party; when she dances boldly for sidekick Guino (George Raft), all the jeopardy of the situation sparkles in her wide eyes. She is a kid, as Guino points out, but the eighteen-year-old knows what she wants. Her lethal, controlling brother may be just a few yards away but her will to break free is even more powerful, a force poignantly echoed in the siblings' final scene together. Raft himself is the poised mystery at the centre of the picture. A professional dancer, he had met and admired Capone and other mobsters, and he claimed to have incorporated his observations into *Scarface*. His role is like a piece of idealised choreography – he says little but moves with a watchful grace, flicking his trademark coin. Like a silent actor among the talking, he absorbs and reflects the frenzied emotions of those around him. His performance was admired by the very criminals who had inspired him and his mob connections continued over the years.

Gangsters were impressed and fascinated by cinema and films repaid the compliment, even making reference to them by name in the script. Michael Mann's John Dillinger feature *Public Enemies* (2009) not only recalls in its title the 1931 film but also the symbiosis – the movies made gangsters glamorous; the gangsters made movies thrilling and urgent. Paul Muni's spats were taken up as criminal footwear. John Dillinger was alleged to have made a habit of leaping over the counters of banks he robbed after he saw an actor do just that onscreen. He was eventually gunned down by the FBI in 1934 as he left the Chicago Biograph Theater performance of the newly released *Manhattan Melodrama* (produced by David O. Selznick) where we can assume he had enjoyed Clark Gable's repartee as the charming gambling-boss-turned-mobster.

The introduction of sound changed the public's appreciation of film-stars in another respect. They were no longer stateless, abstract paragons who might speak in the preferred voice of the viewer's imagination. George Raft was born in Hell's Kitchen, New York, to German parents, as was Clark Gable, but in Ohio; others were more recent immigrants and it could be discerned from their accents. Paul Muni had arrived in New York from Lwów in Poland in 1902 and Edward G. Robinson from Bucharest the following year. James Cagney was of Irish descent, with a touch of Norwegian. While this certainly added to their screen appeal, conservative audiences who defined their nation as Protestant and Anglo-Saxon might also find a subtle threat of The Other. The hectoring newspaper publisher in *Scarface* includes in his call to action, 'Put teeth in the deportation act!

These gangsters don't belong in this country!', while an apologetic spokesman for the Italian community wrings his hands, deploring the shame these delinquents have brought on his people. Scarface seeks to be included, even taking elocution lessons, until he loses control. Assimilation, the American credo, was the antidote to conflict.

That sense of needing to be recognised and to belong drives most gangster plots. It is brilliantly expressed nearly sixty years later in Martin Scorsese's *Goodfellas* (1990), which was closely based on the life of Henry Hill (played by Ray Liotta), a former associate of organised crime who turned FBI informant. With minor name changes, many of the characters are portraits of real people yet the film is also expressionistic as much as documentary. As with *Scarface*, the mood can shift rapidly, playful one moment, deadly the next. On top of this lies a deep irony; events are always unfolding that Henry does not entirely perceive or control. His first line in the film, delivered just after the gruesome despatch of an individual bundled into the boot of a car, concerns his sincere childhood ambition to be a gangster, as a big band leads Tony Bennett into the song 'Rags To Riches'. When Henry becomes a part of the organisation, he is able to impress Karen, the girl who will become his wife. In the film's most famous and dazzling sequence Henry takes his future wife into the Copacabana nightclub through the kitchens in one long unbroken travelling shot in which he greets doormen, waiters and guests – *his* people, he's showing her – dispensing jokes and tips along the way, until he and Karen are ushered to the best table in the house, right at the front of the stage, where they are hailed by the hoods seated nearby. Stunned and slightly unsettled by this virtuoso display of belonging and allegiance, Karen asks Harry, 'What do you do?' 'I'm in construction'. She looks doubtful, if excited: 'It don't feel like construction'. There, in one sequence, is the gangster's fantasy. As Henry says, on another occasion, mobsters were treated like 'movie stars with muscle'.

In *Scarface*, the dinner jackets and the jewels show that the criminal classes are not necessarily low. More than fifty characters die onscreen in the film, not all of them obviously thugs or hoodlums. The onslaught of the film, as scintillating as the shards of glass and as percussive as the explosions in the restaurant-hit sequence, accelerated the application of the Code. Another critical moment – although it seems ludicrous by comparison – was James Cagney's use of half a grapefruit as a weapon, pushed angrily into Mae Clarke's face in *The Public Enemy*. This unexpected domestic violence over the breakfast table reminded audiences that low life was not confined to bars and brothels.

When Will Hays decreed a moratorium on the gangster genre in 1935, Cagney had to serve his penance in *G-Men* (1935), as an FBI hero on the right side of the law and his career from then on included more dancing and fewer machine-guns. The following year, Edward G. Robinson went undercover as a police detective in *Ballots or Bullets*.

Filmmakers love *Scarface*. Brian de Palma remade the film in 1983 with Al Pacino as a Cuban mobster in Florida. Modern gangsters or would-be gangsters appear to feast on its flashy excess. Roberto Saviano's 2006 book *Gomorrah*, about the organised crime syndicate in the Naples area, Camorra, was itself made into a film in 2008. In the book Saviano details the gangsters' predilection for a Hollywood crime aesthetic. A Camorra boss, Walter Schiavone, apparently commissioned an architect to build an exact replica of Tony Montana's imposing Miami mansion with its marble colonnades, sweeping staircase, pink Doric columns and gold fountain, regardless of the fact that in the film the house is intended to appear ludicrous and vainglorious; much of it is destroyed in the endless bloody finale that will finish Al Pacino's character. (The film was also a key work for gangsta-rap. Sean Combs, aka P. Diddy, claimed to have seen the film more than fifty times; another artist has taken the name Scarface.)

When Saviano writes 'It's not the movie world that scans the criminal world for the most interesting behaviour. The exact opposite is true', he could be talking about the 1930s. He cites Francis Ford Coppola's *Godfather* films, inevitably, and Marlon Brando's appearances as Don Corleone as introducing the term *padrino* to the crime hierarchy. One senior member of the Camorra, Luciano Liggi, was described as jutting his chin out, Corleone-style, for photographs. Younger hopefuls are more likely to emulate characters from Quentin Tarantino's *Reservoir Dogs* or *Pulp Fiction*, memorising lines of dialogue and even holding guns at fashionably cool angles, which may help their image but not their accuracy. The Naples Forensic Division, according to Saviano, reports that gunmen now often appear to take more shots to finish off their victims. The consequence of not holding the barrel straight is that the first shot is to the stomach, groin or legs, rather than a more lethal body wound.

Maybe 1930s gangsters occasionally shot themselves in the foot if they swaggered, simultaneously laughing and firing a machine gun, as Paul Muni does when Scarface makes his last stand. The strictures of the Production Code might temporarily shut down the gangster film but much of its energy – the articulate and wilful women, the dangers of material excess – would have lingered with an audience still awaiting results from the New Deal. Scarface wants the American Dream and he wants it right now. As he dies, the camera pans up to the twinkling Cook's Tours sign, The World Is Yours.

GOLD DIGGERS OF 1933 (1933)

Director: Mervyn LeRoy
Cast: Warren William, Joan Blondell, Aline MacMahon
Black and white, sound

The advent of sound made possible a fresh genre – musicals – bringing together the exotic spectacle of musical theatre and the apparent realism of film. The series of Warner Brothers/Busby Berkeley musicals that began in 1933 with *42nd Street* and ran through the *Gold Diggers* films are lavish entertainments with an inescapably tough centre, complex legends of the Depression.

Four determined young women with theatrical ambitions sustain the plot of *Gold Diggers of 1933*, directed by Mervyn LeRoy. Times are hard – they sleep three to a bed and steal milk from the neighbours; they need to earn a living and a precarious Broadway production promises employment; love, when it appears, is compromised by money, usually the lack of it. There may be fairy-tale elements – the prince in the form of the rich young man who is working incognito as a songwriter; the ogres of a sclerotic old social order impeding the new egalitarian vigour of show business and, always, the shiny, dazzling transformation as the hard-pressed chorus girls become glittering fairies and princesses onstage. Time after time the Busby Berkeley numbers travel from the quotidian to the Olympian: one moment a couple are wandering through a local park, the next the stage and screen are transformed with beautifully clad figures in an Elysian landscape, the same faces in idealised surroundings. Across the spectrum of film, sophisticated idols were being replaced by attractive more ordinary types who could polish up well.

The production of a Broadway show was a handy model for 1930s economic challenges. The plots hang on simple finances (loans and returns/ backers and audiences); solid hard work finds reward; the neglected underdogs get recognition while those in positions of privilege have to 'earn' their riches through some moral awakening. The so-called 'gold diggers', the workers, are never as cynical or venial as the wealthy folks: working people struggle with two jobs, while a rich widow grudgingly gives paltry tips. Yet in the persistent fantasy that love stumbles unknowingly upon riches, the perky medical student may yet get to marry the heiress. Certainly, the formula was effective for the Warner Brothers studio: the first musical in the cycle, *42nd Street*, was a box office success that alleviated its $15 million debt.

Busby Berkeley observed of his musicals' popularity with audiences, 'it took their minds off the troubles and worries of the day'. So was it purely escapist, then, to sit in the cinema for two hours, watching spangled girls chirrup 'We're In The Money' in the midst of the Great Depression? Was cinema already an opiate? Box offices appear to defy recession: *Variety* magazine remarked of the downturn that began in 2008, 'cinema gets bump from slump', noting that, in five of the last seven recessions, box office revenues increased, a trend industry analysts attribute to a combination of relatively low cost entertainment and the temporary sanctuary from economic reality.

George Orwell certainly perceived filmgoing as an evasion. In *The Road to Wigan Pier* in 1937 he wrote, 'cinema is one of many cheap luxuries that provided an escape into fantasy'. He might not have been as dismissive as the poet Bryher, friend of Joyce and Hemingway, who condemned the medium's drug-like effect in an article she wrote in 1928 for the magazine *Close-Up*: 'To watch hypnotically something which has become a habit and which is not recorded as it happens by the brain, differs little from the drugtaker's point of view and it is destructive because it is used as a cover to prevent real consideration of problems, artistic or sociological.'

Did either Orwell or Bryher ever consider Joan Blondell, in *Gold Diggers of 1933*, as she stops in a mean street to offer a cigarette to a down-and-out, before dropping a shoulder and intoning a bluesy lament for the unemployed?

> Remember my forgotten man,
> You put a rifle in his hand.
> You sent him far away,
> You shouted hip-hooray,
> But look at him today . . .

The camera then moves to a series of illuminated windows in which figures – a black woman, a downtrodden white mother with a baby and an old lady – languish, regretting their lost or damaged menfolk. Then the screen darkens and suddenly, from the theatricality of a Broadway tableau, we seem to have travelled to the midst of a battlefield.

Shortly before, in May 1932, the same year FDR laid out his New Deal, Busby Berkeley had been moved by a war veterans' march in Washington that ended in violence, with troops firing on former soldiers. Roosevelt himself had made mention in a speech of the 'forgotten men' who returned from the First World War and were unable to find work. Within a year, Berkeley had recreated the mood and scale of the march in this hugely ambitious expressionistic musical number. Soldiers tramp across rain-sodden stages; the sequence dissolves to lines at soup kitchens and welfare centres; infantrymen march in silhouette in giant arcs like an animated memorial, while women below reach up, powerless to help or touch them. That is the note, with Blondell centre stage beseeching us to remember, on which the film ends, not with the sweetness of a romantic clinch or the fizz of a final joke, but with a cry of pain. When they saw the thematic strength of the images and music, producers Jack Warner and Daryl F. Zanuck made the extraordinary decision to make this their finale.

'Remember My Forgotten Man' is a powerful riposte to the argument that social commentary in American cinema lags behind events, only appearing at the end of the 1930s with John Ford's film of John Steinbeck's *The Grapes of Wrath*. The film parable of the Broadway musical with its celebration of individual talents and collective action – the cumulative impact of scores of dancers in one great choreographed symbol – is in itself a graphic and memorable social comment. The plots always suggest there was some extra energy to be taken from everyone working together that could yield dividends both material and metaphorical. In a famous essay in the 1970s, 'Some Warner Brothers Musicals and the Spirit of the New Deal', Mark Roth saw them as being 'essentially political', a blueprint of how Americans could pull together to get through bad times.

Looking at it now, it is hard to ignore the bitterness of a number such as 'We're In The Money' or the ominous Lullaby of Broadway section from the follow-up *Gold Diggers of 1935* with its carefully drilled phalanxes of tap dancers in militaristic leather-look uniforms. Such images were familiar to those who watched newsreels of political developments in Germany and Italy as Susan Sontag argued in her 1970s essay, 'Fascinating Fascism'.

As the 1930s advanced the restraints of the Production Code forbade passionate clinches between screen lovers: they had to make do instead – as, much later, Bollywood stars would – with elaborate dance duets. This sublimation of the earthy and base into the aesthetic took films away from tenements and Broadway theatre stages into the abstract pearly art deco opulence of the cruise liner and luxury hotels. If you can't be sexy, be glamorous. Yet even in Fred Astaire and Ginger Rogers musicals like *Gay Divorcee* (1934) and *Top Hat* (1935), there may still be a social connection. In his book *Popular Filmgoing in 1930s Britain*, John Sedgwick observes that Rogers' and Astaire's characters typically 'do not represent superior people but rather, ordinary people who happen to operate in these luxurious places'. For escapism to work, it needs a realist entrée or an avatar, a Cinderella figure who provides the point of connection to the dream.

One of the first colour features which made that entry to a more luxurious world an explicit journey was a David O. Selznick production, *A Star Is Born* (1937), a movie fable so enduring they remade it twice – in 1954 with Judy Garland and again in 1976 with Barbra Streisand. Country mouse Esther Blodgett (a sweet but firm-jawed Janet Gaynor) will transform herself into Vicki Lester, Hollywood star. The film begins with her mother deriding her escapist dreams of being a star like Garbo, 'You and your movies, it's all you think about . . . The other day, I caught her talking to a horse with a Swedish accent!'

Her tough old grandmother, a former pioneer, is all in favour of 'going out and making something of yourself'. After all, didn't her generation forge a new country, burning in the fields in summer, freezing in winter, conquering the wilderness? Maybe, she concludes, stretching the metaphor a little, Hollywood is your wilderness. Don't just dream, do. Vicki does, working from obscurity to 'the girl who won the heart of the world' as the announcer describes her when she arrives not long after her husband's suicide for a Hollywood gala in her honour. As she emerges into the flashbulb glare, Vicki Lester shows barely a second's hesitation before she visibly swells in the public gaze. Vicki's celebrity comes at a cost to Esther's happiness, but it would have been a crime to throw away her chance to fix her own identity as self-made woman and star. What's more, she has her approving grandmother by her side, who lent her the money to go to Hollywood in the first place and who would never let her give up on the dream. As the most discreet of tears coordinates with the diamonds at her throat and in her hair, Vicki is sad but resolved – she has overcome unemployment and the one-in-a-thousand odds to make it. Does anyone in the audience doubt she made the right choice?

That kind of grit was also personified, in very different packaging, in the musicals of Gracie Fields, Britain's biggest filmstar of the period. Since the Cinematograph Act of 1927, British studios had been encouraged to battle the dominance of Hollywood pictures. Cinemas were required to screen a quota of British films, initially 7.5 per cent but rising to 20 per cent in 1935. At home films were expected to bolster British values which, with luck, they might even export.

In *Sing As We Go* (1934), Gracie plays a champion of workers' rights who is fighting the closure of the mill where she works: comic relief is provided by her dippy room-mate who falls asleep clutching a copy of *Film Weekly* to her chest, with an array of celebrity photographs forming a halo on her pillow. Gracie herself was no pin-up, the antithesis of a Hollywood starlet, both plain-looking and plain talking, or, in the words of a *Film Pictorial* profile, 'if she doesn't like a thing, she says so, and that's that'.

Numerous letters to film magazines testified to her appeal to her working-class audience – 'she doesn't pretend to be what she ain't!' Despite

95

her fame, Fields was happy to preserve traces of the former millworker who had been born above a Rochdale chip shop. In an article written in 1936 for *World Film News*, Joanna Macfadyen identified the core of Gracie's phenomenal appeal: 'Gracie's act puts the men in a hearty family mood (no vicarious love affairs with her), the women adore her (they share her dress sense, there are no envious wish-fulfilments nor are wrecked marriages the basis of her entertainment) and children enjoy the general racket.'

Scripted by J.B. Priestley, *Sing As We Go* may poke fun at Hollywood glamour but it has its own choreographed massed ranks – millworkers or holidaymakers in the bracing pleasure gardens and lidos of Blackpool. With her determination and optimism, Gracie appears single-handedly to be pulling Britain through the recession, carrying the workers' woes on her broad shoulders. When she is sacked along with the rest of the mill employees, she makes the stoical yet sunny claim, 'If we can't spin, we can still sing.' She does indeed keep warbling through adversity, batting away the fears of unemployment and literally getting on her bike to find any job that will bring in the money – whether maid, clairvoyant or even human spider in a travelling show. *Film Pictorial* observed at the time, 'even in the hardest times, Gracie Fields still keeps us Looking on the Bright Side'. Like Frank Capra's folk heroes, Fields is a sympathetic role model and unlikely leader. In the 1930s, cinema protagonists, like cinema audiences, no longer simply gaze in wonderment; they get up and do something.

Graham Greene, however, despised Fields's films for their provision of simplistic solutions to profound problems. 'Unemployment', he observed, 'can almost be wiped out by a sentimental song, industrial unrest is calmed by a Victorian ballad and dividends are made safe for democracy.' Film for him was in danger of becoming another kind of drug, neither narcotic nor opiate but panacea. Ealing Studios chief Michael Balcon, reviewing his own considerable output three decades later, regretted that none of his films 'in any way reflected the despair of the times in which we were living . . . one cannot escape the conclusion that we could have been more profitably engaged'.

Social engagement emerged more obviously in the fledgling documentary movement. In 1934 a correspondent to *Film Pictorial* regretted: 'We have no Dickens in this generation but we have an even greater power in the screen. A film dealing with life in the slums, if ably produced, could do more than anything else to alleviate this terrible situation.' The following year the information film *Housing Problems* (1935) gave viewers evidence, often in forensic close-up, of the rat-infested slums that many residents of Stepney, in London's East End, called home. For the first time, members of the working class directly addressed the camera and spoke about their experiences.

Yet the concerned correspondent to *Film Pictorial* had provoked a riposte from another reader: 'when will some people realise that the screen is to provide *entertainment* and not to act as a medium of certain forms of propaganda? . . . Confine beauty and art to the cinema and avoid sordid reality.' Another film fan, a secretary from Weston-super-Mare, made an even stronger claim for escapism in *Picturegoer* in July 1932: 'Would you please inform the critics that I do *not* want to see myself on the screen? . . . It does not follow that because I am a typist I want to see films about typists. On the contrary, I like my heroine to be a duchess or a chorus girl or one of the thousand things I am not. Greta Garbo is nothing like me and her roles are quite unlike the ones I play for thirty-five bob a week. Yet when watching Greta, I am Greta. Typists are blessed with more imagination than the film critics.' The magazine's editor appended a line to her letter – 'this looks like our friend Realism vs Romance again'.

And so on over the decades. Filmmakers often bemoan audience reluctance to watch the dramatisation of challenging current affairs. *Body of Lies*, Ridley Scott's fast-paced, big-budget thriller about CIA practices in the Middle East, for example, failed to outperform the comedy *Beverly Hills Chihuahua* in 2008. Oscar-winning director and screenwriter Paul Haggis, whose film about traumatised US servicemen returning from Iraq, *In the Valley of Elah*, pleased critics but failed at the box office, concluded that the public was unwilling to confront difficult events in real time.

Yet it may be that audiences simply prefer parables; perhaps they feel something false even in the most skilfully realised representation of contemporary events. If they can perceive the framing of a genre – gangster film or idealised biopic or musical – then the resonances are not compromised by constant comparison to fact. Some 1930s musicals worked as parables on a number of levels, as superhero action films did in the first decade of the twenty-first century. Christopher Nolan's *The Dark Knight* shows Batman reacting to fanatical terrorism with questionable force; however exciting the action sequences and dazzling the effects, this is a sombre film. *Iron Man*'s director Jon Favreau, on the other hand, believes the strength of the comic superhero is precisely what Graham Greene hated, simple solutions to complex problems, 'a fantasy and escape so that we could see a solution, no matter how fantastical, that we could all cheer for'. Alongside Iron Man, or Gracie Fields, you could rank the Greek island matriarch played by Meryl Streep in the record-breakingly successful *Mamma Mia!* as she pulls an unconventional dream family out of the chaotic web of modern relationships. The *New York Times* noted, 'relatable nonthinking comedies . . . are the perfect balm for the recession'.

So what is 'nonthinking'? Successful entertainment is rarely that simple. *Gold Diggers of 1933* is a wry, often ridiculous, portrait of a grim time. On the one hand, it features a saucy extravaganza that was originally planned to close the film – 'Petting In The Park' (a hilariously kinky number laced with erotic references, some silhouetted nudity, a bizarre form of metallic bondage and a disturbingly lascivious baby) which was the last salacious giggle of the Warner musicals before the Code clamped down in 1934 and drove sex onscreen into innuendo and sly metaphor. On the other hand, the number that actually closes the show is 'Forgotten Man' and most of the female characters are more than types (even if some of them do raise their heads from the pillow first thing fully made up with false eyelashes) who talk about lovers and money with remarkable frankness. In the big 'get-up-and-go' speech the world-weary comedienne Trixie (Aline MacMahon) admonishes reluctant Gordon (William Powell) who is shy of appearing on stage, to come to the aid of the production that will provide jobs for the chorus girls. If not, 'God knows what will happen to those kids. They'll have to do things I wouldn't want on my conscience and it'll be on yours. Now you can go out and sing, Gordon – and put this show over.'

The director of *Gold Diggers of 1933* was Mervyn LeRoy, the man who had directed two of the most impressive portraits of men on the wrong side of the law – Edward G. Robinson in *Little Caesar* and Paul Muni in *I Am a Fugitive from a Chaingang.* LeRoy would go on to be head of production at MGM, commissioning, producing and directing parts of *The Wizard of Oz* (1939). When I watch *Gold Diggers,* I like to think of him as Barney Hopkins, the producer struggling to put on the Broadway show, as he fishes around for a winning idea. He considers the plight of his cast (everyone's broke), hears a snatch of melody, catches half a remark and jumps to his feet: 'This is what this show's about – the Depression! . . . The Big Parade of Tears!'

LA BÊTE HUMAINE (1938)

Director: Jean Renoir
Cast: Jean Gabin, Simone Simon, Fernand Ledoux
Black and white, sound

Jacques Lantier (Jean Gabin) is a railwayman on the line between Paris and Le Havre. The film opens with a four-minute ride through the northern French countryside, immediate and exciting as documentary, as the train hurtles along the tracks. Sometimes the spectator's perspective is that of the driver on the footplate but, later, the point of view shifts to the front of the train itself as it bends around curving bridges, through tunnels and pulls into the station, the urgency of the engine blending into a big orchestral score that both celebrates the magnificence of the machine and promises fatal drama. In those first minutes, viewer and train have been briefly united. Lantier himself is bound not only by professional pride but by a strange, almost sexual, bond to his locomotive, *La Lison*. He is a model employee – dependable, strong and diligent. Occasionally, he has uncontrollable episodes when he yearns to kill.

The film begins with a quotation from the 1890 novel by Emile Zola on which the film is based. *La Bête Humaine* was published towards the end of his twenty-novel cycle about the Rougon-Macquart family, members of which have a deadly flaw which leads them to destroy others and ultimately themselves through addiction and violence. The prologue sets up Lantier's plight: 'At times he was very conscious of his hereditary failing. He began to think he was paying for the others, his forebears who had drunk, generations of drunkards whose bad blood he had inherited. His mind exploded from the pressure. He suffered the agony of a man driven to act against his will for reasons he did not understand.'

This troubled psyche is further agitated by proximity to Séverine, the young wife of the deputy stationmaster at Le Havre. Travelling as a passenger on the train, Lantier inadvertently glimpses the couple just after they have committed a murder. When the body is discovered, the investigating officer asks Lantier whether he saw anyone in the corridor. Séverine's huge eyes are fixed on him. When he explains that soot in his eye prevented him from seeing clearly, he is already complicit. Lantier – like so many *film noir* leading men to follow – is in deep trouble.

Even though he was born into a vaudeville family, Jean Gabin brought a working man's integrity to his roles; thickset and energetic, he anchors the melodrama as a man adept at his work but often lost in the 'thick smoke that fills my head and distorts everything'. As Séverine, Simone Simon is literally kittenish – the first glimpse is of her fondling a baby cat; later she sits stroking a luxuriant fur stole on her lap – a child-woman with wide-set eyes, eyelashes as defined as whiskers, sophisticated but animalistic. The story, like the train, moves fast; the locations are realistic (the rail company SNCF helped with filming although the plot was hardly an advertisement for its employees); Lantier's transformations from stolid railwayman to murderous beast are as mysterious to us as to him. The first of these episodes, the most shocking, takes place in broad daylight, as Lantier and a girlfriend move from a sunlit meadow beside the train track. There is no warning, nothing sinister in the setting: the crisis arrives as suddenly as a passing train – he puts his hands around her throat and squeezes. Afterwards, the violent spasm passed, Lantier discusses his 'sickness' with the girl, in a matter-of-fact way. That is how it is.

Fatalism underscores this thriller. There is yet a chance that Lantier may escape his genetically determined hell, if he could only avoid that dangerous woman, Séverine. Don't do what she tells you; don't go in that room; keep away. Don't be caught in the trap between events outside and the beast within.

The sense of dread and helplessness *La Bête Humaine* engenders in an audience would have been familiar in late 1930s Europe. Jean Renoir later explicitly connected the film to his pessimism following the collapse in 1937 of the Popular Front in France, the governing alliance of left-wing movements under Léon Blum. Renoir described the Front as 'a magnificent exposition of human brotherhood'. Their rallying cry of '*Tout est possible!*', made just a year earlier, had given way to infighting, cynicism and despair. With such disorganisation in government and Hitler's actions in Austria and Czechoslovakia, the country was set on a track to another major conflict in Europe, just as Lantier and *La Lison* are locked to the rails hurtling between Paris and Le Havre. When Lantier kills, it is in desperation.

Renoir maintained that the study of humanity, in all its imperfection, was the artist's best defence against fascism's inhuman drive to perfection. For all Lantier's tendencies, Jean Gabin's charisma and naturalism ensures that he is a figure to be understood, even loved. Freudian ideas had permeated the vocabulary of popular cinema by the end of the 1930s: there was a vague understanding that the subconscious could work away and lead, like the Rougon-Macquart bad blood, into pre-determined alleyways. Actions might be affected as much by prior events as an active morality. Familiarity with the process of psychoanalysis and its influence on film would become more apparent in the next decade.

La Bête Humaine was by no means simply an isolated riposte to fascism. The alchemy is always mysterious or, as director and writer Paul Schrader later observed, 'a case of artistic and social forces magically interacting and coalescing'. France's first internationally successful sound film, *Sous Les Toits de Paris* (1930), directed by René Clair, had opened with a shot of chimneys and travels along the roofline and through the smoke down into a city street, expressive by its narrow architecture of the melodrama of ordinary folk that is to follow. French critics at the time questioned its depiction of criminals and other degenerate individuals but, by the end of the decade, murderers and deserters were regularly protagonists. In 1932, Jean Renoir had directed the first adaptation of a police procedural thriller – an early Maigret novel by Georges Simenon. In 1938, the same year as *La Bête Humaine,* Jean Gabin also played the lead in *Le Quai des Brumes,* directed by Marcel Carné, a relentlessly lugubrious tale of an army deserter caught in an ugly standoff between a beautiful woman and her 'protectors', also set in Le Havre.

Shot in black and white, *La Bête Humaine* is a testament, if not to the technological innovations of colour photography, then to the subtleties of lighting and sound. The noises of the railway are immersive; steam pistons and levers click and release into a percussive track; at moments of intensity – a decision taken, a glance exchanged – a hugely impressive and ominous orchestral score sweeps everything aside. The focus may be 'deep', bringing to light the complexity of a scene, allowing us to look beyond the foreground action to revealing details far in the background that we may not even be aware we are taking in. Sometimes, in discreet ways, this acts as a visual distillation of social context. The lighting varies from bright sunlight to romantic diffusion in the love scenes, to chiaroscuro dappling in moments of anguish or indecision to expressionist shadows and the reflection from puddles for the ugliest deeds – a mixture of realism and nightmare.

In 1940, after the German invasion of France, Jean Renoir left for America and Gabin joined him. The sanitisation of the Production Code had prompted American audiences to look abroad for darker material. Filmmakers around the world reacted to economic and political hardship in different ways but the Europeans were more obviously agitated about the clash of ideological and martial forces around them. What had emerged in France was a distinctive style that both respected the narrative sophistication of the Americans and the irresistible (and not always attractive) pull of animal instinct. It was the beginnings of *film noir*, which would not actually get that name until the mid-1940s and was then applied to earlier films retrospectively. *Film noir* has proved one of the most powerful and enduring moods in cinema.

A complicated chain of influence brings about the genre. In the silent era, in 1915 and 1928, there had been two film adaptations of Zola's 1867 novel of adultery and murder, *Thérèse Raquin*, a thematic precursor to *La Bête Humaine*. In 1934, the American writer James M. Cain published a short novel, *The Postman Always Rings Twice*, which drew on the facts of a 1928 trial in which an adulterous couple murdered the husband, but there were clear echoes of *Thérèse Raquin*, too. In France in 1939, Pierre Chenal directed a version of Cain's story, *Le Dernier Tournant*, but it was Renoir's film of *La Bête Humaine* that more clearly influenced subsequent remakes such as *Ossessione*, directed in Italy by Luchino Visconti in 1942, and, most famously, the Hollywood version using the original title, *The Postman Always Rings Twice*, in 1946 with Lana Turner and John Garfield – one of the most celebrated examples of *film noir*.

The beast of the unconscious made less subtle appearances, too. Before the Code cracked down in the United States, *Dracula* (1931) and *The Black Cat* (1931) had been box office successes. *The Black Cat* is a real shocker of hidden terrors with houses built on war graves, a sophisticated architect who happens to be a murderous Satanist and a final, gruesome flaying. In 1931 Fredric March's Oscar-winning slide from romantic kiss-curled Dr Jekyll to simian Mr Hyde was both louche and violent. He greets his hairy apparition as Hyde in the mirror with a triumphant yelp of 'Free at last!' In *Blonde Venus* (1932) Marlene Dietrich in a big gorilla suit lopes along a nightclub stage after a shapely chorus of girls (un)dressed as tribal Africans. Dietrich peels off the head to reveal luminous pale skin and a halo of fair hair to intone 'Voodoo Magic' ('. . . that beat gives me a wicked sensaaaa-tion, my conscience wants to take a vacaaaation'). The beast was inside the woman inside the beast.

The Hays Code would put those rampant creatures safely behind bars. By 1938, when *Dr Jekyll and Mr Hyde* was rereleased, it had been heavily censored, particularly for scenes depicting sexual sadism. Filmmakers at the end of the decade had learned to suggest rather than show. Director Jacques Tourneur and producer Val Lewton's *Cat People* (1942) concerns Irena, a girl of Serbian descent who is afraid of what may happen when her sensuality breaks out of its cage, constantly mindful of an ancient legend in which aroused women turn into panthers. This slinky mix of psycho-analysis, sex and horror (*film/chat noir*, as it were) was summarised in *Variety*'s review: 'a weird drama of thrill-chill caliber, with developments of surprises confined to psychology and mental reactions, rather than transformation to grotesque and marauding characters'.

Like Lon Chaney Jr's chagrined *The Wolfman* (1941) or Jean Marais's elegant Beast in Jean Cocteau's *La Belle et la Bête* (1946), Irena (Simone Simon) is saddened by her nature. Only four years have passed since Simon played feline Séverine, the minx who bewitches the train driver in *La Bête Humaine*, but the cat has grown less curious and more cautious, lurking in the shadows.

1940s
·············

EMERGING FROM THE DARK

A global war that left more than fifty million military and civilian dead, with European and Asian countries devastated, infrastructure collapsed and economies crippled, might have been expected to halt the progress of an entertainment medium. Yet the 1940s produced films – sometimes under the harshest, least promising conditions – that contain some of the most distinctive images and scenarios in film history. It would have been hard to predict that the combination of four decades of technical advancement in filmmaking would intersect with a terrible urgency of expression to such brilliant effect.

The Second World War finally marked the end of European domination of world events and the United States emerged most notably as the economic victor. By the end of the 1940s, half of the manufactured goods in the world were produced in American factories. In March 1941, Congress had passed the Lend-Lease Act which gave aid in particular to Britain and the Commonwealth countries in return for support for US forces stationed abroad.

During the depressed thirties and into the war, much American cinema had been designed to keep spirits high; the Hays Production Code had been devised to purge film of negativity or decadence. Throughout the war itself, themes of morale raising and loss run through cinema in more or less overt ways. The positive and colourful sides of Hollywood were on show to the American domestic market: patriotic musicals continued to be lucrative for the studios, even if the grin seemed a little fixed occasionally. Screen gangster James Cagney now appeared reformed as Broadway star George M. Cohan in *Yankee Doodle Dandy* (1942). Bob Hope and Bing Crosby's five-film *Road to . . .* series began in 1940 in Singapore and carried on through Morocco in 1942, around the time that US troops landed there. A strong vein of nostalgia ran through *State Fair* (1945) and *Meet Me in St Louis* (1944) where the fragility of domestic happiness is always threatened, as you can hear in Judy Garland's wistful rendition of 'Have Yourself A Merry Little Christmas', sung to her little sister in the film as they face the prospect of having to give up the family home. Vincente Minnelli's musical is the first in which song, story and camera all blend together; there is no separation of dialogue and dance number, as there was in earlier musicals like *Gold Diggers of 1933*, and the film is set in an ordinary household with neither the glamour of the wealthy nor the glitz of Broadway. Zing, zing, zing went the heartstrings all the same.

Feature films found oblique – and not so subtle – ways of lobbing missiles at Hitler or Mussolini. Fictionalised dictators appeared onscreen – lampooned by Chaplin in *The Great Dictator* (1940) or vanquished by swashbuckling heroes in historical adventures like *The Sea Hawk* (1940), where Errol Flynn sees off invasion by the Armada. Offscreen, Hollywood figures like Clark Gable and director Frank Capra served in the forces and stars like Bette Davis, Hedy Lamarr and Marlene Dietrich cooked or waited on table in the Hollywood Canteen, the celebrity servery for servicemen set up on Cahuenga Boulevard in Los Angeles.

Censored newsreels showed to the people at home in the United States and Britain footage from the front, shaped to keep resolve strong, sometimes filmed on new cameras like the Arriflex 35, which for the first time allowed the operator to see through the viewfinder exactly what might be exhibited on screen. The White House instigated a 'Visual Presentation' unit so that the President could be provided with the latest information in the most accessible format. Representatives of the film industry contributed, including Walt Disney, whose Donald Duck followed a Hollywood tradition when he was pressed into service to sell war bonds.

Ironically, the film that is now recognised as a masterpiece of American cinema – if not the greatest film ever produced by the nation – Orson Welles's *Citizen Kane* (1941), with its virtuoso deployment of techniques from expressionism to newsreel, is an account of American achievement as grandiose failure.

Certain governments – German and Italian, notably – actively encouraged feature film production during the conflict. In France, the exigencies of occupation forced the industry into Hollywood-style genre – glamorous comedies, in particular, to make the French forget what they were missing from America. In Britain, although the cheap and cheerful 'quota quickie' initiative was over by 1938, it had provided a basis for an industry that would turn out drama that might apparently ignore the conflict (as with the preposterous Gainsborough costume melodramas made between 1943 and 1947, although themes of danger and separation do creep in there, too) or move towards a quasi-documentary style, reflecting with a new realism how people actually lived. Then there was *In Which We Serve* (1942), an unashamedly stirring effort, directed by David Lean with Noël Coward who also starred and wrote both words and music. A hymn to loyalty, fortitude and social cohesion, for audiences and critics it seemed to transcend its own purpose as propaganda.

Countries had suffered in very different ways, the full details of which might not emerge for decades. One in six of the population of Poland are now known to have died, one in seven of the population of the USSR, one in twenty-five in Japan, one in a hundred in the United Kingdom, one in three hundred in the United States. The circumstances of deaths whether civilian or military, close or far from home varied hugely – the willingness or ability to express loss was coloured by cultural difference. The threat of oppression or bereavement found forms as different as the historical parable of persecution and death in Denmark, Carl Theodor Dreyer's *Days of Wrath* (1943) or the sylvan struggles of the world's most famous motherless fawn *Bambi* (1942).

As the USA oversaw the establishment of an international monetary system with the Bretton Woods agreement in 1944 and extended support to keep Communism at bay with the Marshall Plan in 1948, so countries reacted culturally in various ways to this shuffle of global influence. Films made in the immediate period of reconstruction might be read as metaphor – such as the delicate domestic stories of Yasujiro Ozu in Japan, whether of a child left homeless by the war or an old man's loneliness. It might be an epic of political upheaval in post-Partition India or a celebration of Mao in China – or simply a sober account of what was happening outside the window. In Europe, where import and export bans had disrupted the regular distribution of American films, new styles and subjects emerged that diverged distinctively from the American model of storytelling.

By 1945, only one in seven cinemas remained open in Germany, showing mainly German-language melodramas and musicals made years earlier, mostly by UFA, the leading studio during the Weimar Republic. So powerful had the medium proved in the service of the Third Reich that the Allies were initially reluctant to allow any filmmaking at all. The Americans in particular preferred to feed the German people a diet of American values on celluloid. In the autumn of 1946, however, the first German post-war feature, *The Murderers Are Among Us*, had its premiere in East Berlin. The director, Wolfgang Staudte, had worked for UFA; after abortive attempts to get permission to film in the British and American sectors of Berlin, he eventually found support from the Soviet authorities in the eastern sector for an 'anti-fascist' film. Set in an apartment building, the plot concerns its residents, among them a traumatised doctor who has returned from the front and a young woman liberated from a concentration camp. Amid the shattered masonry and disorganisation of the city, they try to reconcile the horrors they have experienced with the stubborn persistence of commercial and domestic life. Some of their neighbours may even be perpetrators, prospering unpunished. *The Murderers Are Among Us* is the first of the so-called 'rubble films' (*Trümmerfilm*) among the ruins of the city, named for the women who cleared the detritus from the bomb sites, searching for anything of value.

In 1944 the grand Cinecittà studios in Rome, founded by Mussolini, became a refugee camp. Gian Piero Brunetta's *The History of Italian Cinema* cites a similar antagonism on the part of the Americans in Italy as in Berlin, quoting a senior officer in Psychological Warfare as claiming that Italian cinema was a purely fascist invention and must be suppressed. As it was, war had all but destroyed the industry: there was little equipment and an erratic power supply. Directors like Roberto Rossellini and Vittorio De Sica took their cameras outdoors and their inspiration and actors from the streets; the movement became known as neo-realism. *Rome, Open City* was filmed just months after the Germans had left the Italian capital; its subjects were resistance to the occupation and the suffering of ordinary people, like the woman played by Anna Magnani, shot down on her wedding day. It won Best Film at Cannes in 1946. In De Sica's *The Bicycle Thieves* (1948) a man and his son search Rome for the stolen bicycle that is essential to their livelihood. The backdrop is a devastated city; their job is to put up posters of Rita Hayworth, Hollywood goddess, in *Gilda* (1946). The tragic grandeur of the newly ruined city (adding another set of fallen masonry to this ancient capital) as the back drop, and the simple pathos of the action in the foreground was a striking new use of deep focus.

The Allies took up this approach in a more stylised form in dark entertainments such as Billy Wilder's cynical story of US post-war adventuring in Berlin, *A Foreign Affair* (1948), and the British thriller *The Third Man* (1949), directed in Vienna by Carol Reed – both stories of moral ambiguity (everyone is using someone else; few people tell the truth) and portraits of the shattered cities. Wilder made *A Foreign Affair* with US government assistance using the remaining studio facilities at UFA, but it is hardly propaganda for either Germany or the United States. The *New York Times* critic commented, 'Congress may not like this picture . . . the Department of the Army may find it a shade embarrassing.'

The effect of this new mood in cinema on moviegoers was now gauged in different terms. By the 1940s, social scientists no longer dipped fingers in electrolytic fluid; they now called on psychoanalytic methods. Sigmund Freud had died in London in September 1939 but his influence continued to develop alongside cinema. In the 1940s, the psychiatrist or psychoanalyst and their methods moved centre screen – most attractively in the form of Ingrid Bergman in Alfred Hitchcock's thriller *Spellbound*.

Psychoanalysts Martha Wolfenstein and Nathan Leites looked carefully at all the American, French and British films playing in New York cinemas for a year from 1945. The criteria for *Movies: A Psychological Study*, published in 1950, were relatively simple: 'where the productions gain the sympathetic response of a wide audience, it is likely that their producers have tapped within themselves the reservoir of common day-dreams'. So British films reflected a sense of lurking danger; the French a perception that human desires and wishes are thwarted by the nature of life itself; and Hollywood's output was mostly about the importance of winning.

Anthropologist Hortense Powdermaker, who had earlier studied South Sea islanders, turned similar techniques on the denizens of Hollywood – directors, producers, actors, technicians and audiences – whom she observed between 1946 and 1947. She found audiences more likely to believe onscreen events, however fantastic they might appear, if they were beyond their own experience. In fact, the entire medium was built for plausibility:

> Movies have a surface realism which tends to disguise fantasy and makes it seem true. This surface realism has steadily grown from the old days of the silent flickers to the modern technicolor talkies, with their increasing use of the documentary approach . . . It is this quality of realness which makes the escape into the world of movies so powerful, bringing with it conscious and unconscious absorption of the screen play's values and ideas . . .

By the 1940s, many analysts, analysands and other Freudian disciples had fled from Europe to work in British and American film. The conceits of guilt and shame, the patterns of repetitive and destructive behaviour that were familiar to European film audiences, now solidified in what came to be recognised as an American genre, retrospectively named *film noir* by a French critic Nino Frank. (Frenchman identifies American genre inspired by European films with French name – like much else in *film noir*, this plot is not always easy to follow.) Frank wrote in 1946 about the recent crime dramas imported to Europe from Hollywood, films like *Double Indemnity* (1945), *Murder, My Sweet* (1945) and *Laura* (1945). European émigré directors like Fritz Lang, Robert Siodmak, Curtis Bernhardt and Billy Wilder shaped the genre in the United States from German expressionism, French poetic realism, European neo-realism and a certain American post-war uncertainty to which was added a mysterious taste for the exotic. Their streets were rain-soaked and shadowy and their heroes lonely and heartbroken, vulnerable to predatory women in the guise of helpless victims. Stories unravelled in flashback with bitter hindsight; in these dramas, the mind is more important than the murder weapon.

In 1945, critic Lloyd Shearer, later editor of *Parade* magazine, asked in an article, 'Crime Certainly Pays on the Screen': 'Why at this time are so many pictures of this type being made?' Nearly thirty years later, Paul Schrader (who would go on to write *Taxi Driver*, a meditation on the disaffected post-Vietnam male) put the cause down to the hangover from the Second World War – 'the disillusionment many soldiers, small businessmen and housewife/factory employees felt on returning to a peacetime economy was directly mirrored in the sordidness of the urban crime film'. In *The Blue Dahlia* (1946), for example, Alan Ladd returns with a couple of traumatised comrades from the war to discover that his wife has been cheating on him. When she is murdered, Ladd becomes the prime suspect and then an outlaw in the very country for which he risked his life.

Readjustment to civilian life could indeed be traumatic. All those drifters and neurotics in *film noir* are easily interpreted as returning soldiers while the *femmes fatales* are in fact the women who had replaced them in the factories and found other men to share their beds. Rosie the Riveter, the poster girl of wartime female emancipation, had turned nasty. As the 1940s progressed into the 1950s, these metaphors of anxiety and paranoia became more complex, embracing both fears of the atomic age and McCarthyism.

From 1938 onwards, those called as witnesses to the House UnAmerican Activities Committee (HUAC) had had to answer under oath if they were now, or ever had been, a member of the Communist Party. In 1947, HUAC's investigations turned specifically to writers, directors and actors in Hollywood. If a witness refused to answer or to name known Party members they might well be blacklisted or – in the case of the so-called Hollywood Ten in 1950 – even imprisoned. Many of those who would not testify were practitioners of the new *film noir* genre – among them Edward Dmytryk (although he did later change his mind and talk) and Abraham Polonsky, whose thriller *Force of Evil* (1948) is set in a corrupt and conspiratorial milieu with little difference between gangster and businessman. Actor John Garfield's fatal heart attack at the age of thirty-nine was partly attributed to the stress of the witch-hunt.

*　　*　　*

In 1947, the British-American actor and producer John Houseman (who had worked extensively with Orson Welles) claimed in *Hollywood Quarterly* that 'every generation has its myth – its own particular dream in which are mirrored the preoccupations of its waking hours . . . a quick examination of our daily and weekly press proves quite conclusively that the "tough" movie, currently projected on the seventeen thousand screens of this country, presents a fairly accurate reflection of the neurotic personality of the United States of America in the year 1947'.

This type of discussion was a harbinger of the new intellectualism surrounding film. In France André Bazin, a young man who had secretly begun a society to show and discuss film during the Nazi occupation, was commissioned after the war to write on cinema by the editor of a philosophy journal, one Jean-Paul Sartre. Over the next decade, in *Cahiers du Cinéma*, the magazine he co-founded in 1951, Bazin would formulate an appreciation of cinema by specific directors, using the term 'auteur' for those whose imprint was distinctive not only in the visuals and settings but also in the handling of actors and even sometimes, the script – directors such as Jean Renoir, Alfred Hitchcock, Howard Hawks or Frank Capra and, most notably, Welles, who demanded from the studios greater control over their work. Bazin looked beyond Eisenstein's technique of montage, of splicing together picture and eventually sound for cumulative effect, and the expressionist style which nudged the audience into a reaction by means of sets and lighting, to reserve his highest praise for film as the closest representation of reality among the art forms. He was a huge admirer of *Citizen Kane*. For him, the composition and depth of focus apparently gave the viewer greater autonomy, a choice of where to look. Not so, in fact the gaze was guided, framing was always more art than accident and Welles's trademark placing of the camera low to the floor pushed the viewer into all kinds of judgements about character and perspective, arguably not so different from the way the Expressionists directed the viewer's gaze.

Then there was another emergent force, arguably as influential over the decades – one that could attempt all the effects and moods that cinema had ever achieved, switching between them with apparent abandon. Animation had become a popular form in the 1930s, enhanced later by colour but, more importantly, by sound. For the elements of fantasy or caricature in drawings to have real impact, they needed to be anchored by real voices, however weird they might sound. By the outbreak of war, Mickey Mouse, Bugs Bunny, Donald Duck, Popeye and a host of other characters had become recognisable stars. Within the decade, the first Japanese 'anime' film would be made and Ray Harryhausen would be pioneering 'stop-motion', where models were manipulated frame by frame to give the appearance of live action. Walt Disney's first feature-length animation using drawings on celluloid over a fixed background, the Technicolor *Snow White and the Seven Dwarfs* (1937), was a financial and artistic success, and awarded an Honorary Oscar for 'significant screen innovation'. It seemed a new form of cinematic image had been created – one that could sometimes express more with elaborate arrangements of hand-drawn lines than even the most realistic composition of live action. Animation provided a controlled universe within which some of the most acute threats could be described and confronted.

. . . .

BAMBI (1942)

Director: David Hand (Producer: Walt Disney)
Colour animation

On a soft bed in the wintry forest a doe curls around her fawn, breaking the perfect circle only to check that he still sleeps before she snuggles back down. When they emerge, they struggle to find food on the frozen ground. Imagine their relief when a patch of tender grass suggests spring has arrived and food will be plentiful. They feed happily until Bambi's mother catches the scent of the Hunter. As they race away across a wide field (and Bambi's mother has already warned him of the dangers of open ground) shots ring out. The little one runs on and on until, winded, he stops in the forest and looks behind him . . .

There are few more durable depictions of loss. The death of Bambi's mother, Steven Spielberg revealed in a *Newsweek* discussion in 2006, is the film event most likely to make him cry. As a child, simply recalling it would make him get up in the night to check that his parents were still alive. Her murderer, the Hunter, appears at No. 20 in the American Film Institute's record of worst villains. *Time* magazine listed *Bambi* among its top thirty horror titles. We never see the Hunter's face and Spielberg himself would employ an unseen threat for the early parts of *Jaws*, denoting the sinister presence by a series of low musical notes, just as the Disney film had done.

Generations of parents have had to explain to their distraught children what actually happened offscreen to Bambi's mother. As the years pass, they may find that the effect of the incident, while less shocking, is no less emotive since it may now relate to some particular experience. In a memo to a colleague in 1935, Walt Disney wrote of the appeal to the subconscious that gives animation its true vitality: 'The first duty of the cartoon is not to picture or duplicate real action or things as they actually happen but to give a caricature of life and action, to picture on the screen things that have run through the imagination of the audience, to bring to life dreams and fantasies that we have all thought of during our lives . . .'

Walt Disney had himself seen evidence of conflict first hand. In the First World War he had driven a Red Cross ambulance in France and Germany. In 1922, with his brother Roy and a small band of animators, he established a small studio. Disney was the first to use sound in animation in an early Mickey Mouse short, *Steamboat Willie*, in 1928, first to use three-strip Technicolor in one of the Silly Symphonies, the Academy Award-winning *Flowers and Trees* (1932). The feature-length *Snow White and the Seven Dwarfs* (1937) brought in sufficient funds to build a studio in Burbank, California. By then Disney was established as the dominant animation house, with an industrial-scale production and offices in London and Paris, a model of the corporate system he clearly endorsed.

Disney's skills and the aesthetics of animation were, by 1942, appreciated beyond the local picture house; the borders between high and low culture began to crumble. The opening sequence of *Bambi* is a slow pan across a forest glade with what is, even today, a remarkable depth of field, using the multiplane method in which layers of artwork move at different speeds away from a hugely complex camera. The effect is close to three-dimensional, although, unlike true 3-D, it does not require stereoscope. In *Bambi* we pass close to ferns and trees and beyond them see the undergrowth and trunks stretching back; in the background a tall, white waterfall cascades into a pool. Still the camera moves on towards a small clearing, an owl flies through shot and lands on the branch of a tree. The action is about to start. This opening may not have quite the gothic impact of the camera passing through the rusting fences, ornate gates and mist to glimpse *Citizen Kane*'s castle but it sets the mood with remarkable grace and economy. In the year of *Bambi*'s release, David Low wrote in the *New Republic* that Walt Disney was the most significant figure in graphic art since Leonardo da Vinci, while Harvard art historian Robert Feild eulogised his work as 'the most potent form of artistic expression ever devised'. Sergei Eisenstein marvelled at the juxtaposition of imagery and sound in *Fantasia* (1940) where comic characters and classical music waltzed together towards something altogether more abstract and ambitious. He particularly appreciated the musicality of Kandinsky-like shapes animated in apparent sympathy with the notes and rhythms. Eisenstein also made the claim – which Disney himself seemed to be moving towards in that 1935 memo – that the American animator had found a way to activate the 'purest most primal depths' and elicit a form of response in the audience that was 'pre-logical'.

The economy of line-drawing in animation does in fact recall expressive primitive images, a connection that emerges clearly in Werner Herzog's 2010 documentary, *Cave of Forgotten Dreams*, about the hundreds of paintings of animals on the walls of the Chauvet Cave in southern France. Apparently simple, these proto-cartoons suggest movement.

Bambi is most memorable when it suggests rather than tells, allowing us to provide our own imagined graphics. An early draft of the *Bambi* script, a version of an Austrian story by Felix Salten, had the fawn finding his mother dying in a pool of blood, but the scene was amended for less gore and more poignancy: if we cannot see the actual death, we are more likely to identify with the sense of loss, each supplying our own experience or fear of bereavement. Similarly, an early screening of the finished film still contained a sequence where, towards the end, the Hunter was glimpsed mortally wounded in the forest fire. Four hundred spectators apparently recoiled in disgust, shaken out of the film's spell by such realism. When death does actually strike onscreen in *Bambi* (a pair of pheasants lose their nerve, break cover and are shot, fluttering horribly into eternity), it is shocking but, in the tough I-told-you-so ethic of the nursery, they had been warned. And so had we – those foolish pheasants were not long for this animated world.

The film itself did not perform as well financially on its initial release in 1942 as when it reappeared in cinemas five years later; perhaps the reminder of death and separation was too acute for some audiences during wartime. Looking at what else was being made in American cinema at the time, however, it seems cinema provided many ways to rehearse not the unthinkable (for everyone contemplated with horror the possible early death of loved ones) but that which they most dreaded. For Disney this was something of a theme, building as he did on fairy-tale motifs: Snow White flirts with mortality in her death-like glass-case sleep and both

Pinocchio (1940) and *Dumbo* (1941) suffer excruciating separations from loved ones. Bambi, and other unlikely characters, led the audience to engage for a moment with the unbearable.

The afterlife is a popular location for 1940s cinema, so well visited in fact, that in the 1970s critic Peter L. Valenti coined the term *film blanc* for what he identified as a sub-genre. Qualifications for inclusion were fourfold: there should be a death (or a lapse into a dream so profound that it eclipsed everyday life), an encounter with a benign ambassador from another dimension probably called Heaven, the potential for romance and the subsequent 'transcendance of mortality to escape the spiritual world and return to the mortal world' – a rather cheery distortion of the Orpheus myth. Read that way, Bambi's apparently supernatural patriarch, the stag which briefly materialises to dispense guidance, would fit the benign ambassadorial role and the love of the young doe, Faline, and support from other cute animals fulfil the rest.

It's a *Wonderful Life* (1946) is an outstanding example of *film blanc* as James Stewart gets a second chance at the beautiful imperfection of existence. Other films presented the grim facts of war and bereavement in ways that managed both to confront and comfort their audiences. *A Guy Named Joe* (1943) is a neat example: by killing off its protagonist, bomber pilot Spencer Tracy, in an air raid, it appears to break the rules of popular, escapist cinema, presenting contemporary viewers with an unpleasant truth. This soon passes into soothing fantasy as Tracy turns guardian angel for another airman, even helping him to woo his bereaved girlfriend (grief transformed into hope has become a keynote). *Between Two Worlds* (1944) traces the stories of several people killed during the London Blitz who find themselves on a ship that has only two destinations: Heaven or Hell. In *film blanc* fashion it grants two of its characters the ultimate fantasy: a second chance at life. The greatest *film blanc*, of all, however, has to be Powell and Pressburger's masterpiece, *A Matter of Life and Death* (1946), in which a celestial slip-up means that David Niven's airman carries on living after he was scheduled to die. When Heaven's bureaucrats try to rectify their mistake, Niven fights for his right to life, on the legal grounds that he has fallen in love, and love, in cinema terms, is always the get-out-of-jail card.

In *A Matter of Life and Death*, airmen cheerily enter Heaven (boisterously in the case of an American crew) and carry on as if nothing has happened to them; there are no visible wounds, no messy grief. The only difference from the material world is that their celestial quarters are a tad colourless. As the summer edition of *Sight and Sound* put it in 1946: 'it is a fashion which springs possibly from the psychological needs of people who have known losses in war and who unconsciously may take comfort from the suggestion implicit in all these films that the other world is very close to the one they know, and that beings in it continue to interest themselves in the persons they have left'.

Sometimes the comedy was sharp, as in Ernst Lubitsch's *Heaven Can Wait* (1943); sometimes there was the bitter note of regret beneath the laughs. Who doesn't think in *Blithe Spirit*, David Lean's 1945 adaptation of Noël Coward's 1941 play, that Rex Harrison's charming but callous husband isn't better suited to his impossible, blowsy (and deceased) first wife, Elvira (Kay Hammond, vermilion lipstick setting off ash-grey ensemble from hair to chiffon hem), than to the living second – elegant, antiseptic Ruth? And how many 1940s couples did indeed get by, or not, with the shade of a first spouse hanging around?

Blithe Spirit is invigorated by Margaret Rutherford's bracing performance as the erratic medium Madame Arcati. Spiritualism and cinema had long been close bedfellows, the Victorian fascination having not diminished with two global conflicts. According to Jenny Hazelgrove in *Spiritualism and British Society Between the Wars*, readers of the newspaper *Sunday Despatch*, when asked to nominate favourite film endings at the beginning of the 1940s, favoured those where contented spirits could be seen in the afterlife – the outstanding example being the First World War drama *Three Comrades*

(1938) in which two German soldiers beckon their friend to join them. *How Green Was My Valley*, the Best Film at the Academy Awards in 1941, carries a powerful theme of the dead living on in memory and achievement ('Men like my father cannot die . . .' declares Huw Morgan, looking back on his childhood in the Welsh mining village. 'They are with me still, real in memory as they were in flesh, loving and beloved forever. How green was my valley then.').

The fawn, little Bambi, who is left to struggle in his own verdant vale with a band of comedy-animal comrades to nurture him to adulthood, looked, six decades later, like a straightforward metaphor to critic and screenwriter Peter Woollen: 'it is easy to interpret *Bambi* as a war film, with the hunters as Nazis, the forest fire as the Blitz, the father as missing, away at the front, and the mother as a casualty of war' (*Paris Hollywood*, 2002). Easy, perhaps and not without some truth, but reductive – and not an explanation of the endurance of the *Bambi* myth and imagery into the twenty-first century.

In 1942, the *Times'* review of 6 August had declared: 'It is at last possible to experience in the cinema the emotions proper to a work of art.' While *Fantasia* may have had artistic pretensions that were marred by self-consciousness, *Bambi* observed classical rules. It 'has qualities which belong to the older arts of poetry and painting and does nothing to disgrace them . . . Mr Disney challenges the old test of purging by pity and terror and survives it.'

Bambi survives to make a new generation of children tremulous because it is carefully and exactly rendered with delicate detail. It works also because its interpretation is not immediately transparent and because parables – fantasies of talking animals among them – liberate the imagination to tackle all kinds of subjects, some of them otherwise unbearable, others illuminating. One of the earliest successful animations, *Felix the Cat*, became a favourite of writer Aldous Huxley (who contributed to Hollywood screenplays for *Jane Eyre* and *Pride and Prejudice* in the 1940s). His 1925 essay 'Where are the Movies Moving?' cites a sequence where little black notes emanate from the cat's mouth to indicate singing, he catches them, fashions a scooter from them and rides off. It was simple, said Huxley, logical and natural . . . 'it shows how cinematography differs from literature and the spoken drama and how it may be developed into something entirely new. What the cinema can do better than literature is to be fantastic.'

After the war, Disney released a series of portfolio programmes for cinemas, collections of cartoon shorts. The features continued with *Peter Pan* but became somehow coarser and more formulaic, as if Bambi's huge eyes and curly lashes had been plastered with stage make-up. By the end of the decade, critics might grumble that Disney's work had become kitsch and commercialised. Its mysterious appeal had been harnessed by the government in short propaganda films to sell not only bonds but atomic power.

IN WHICH WE SERVE (1942)

Directors: Noël Coward, David Lean
Cast: Noël Coward, Celia Johnson, John Mills, Bernard Miles
Black and white

Captain Kinross (Noël Coward) commands the destroyer HMS *Torrin* which is attacked by air during the Battle of Crete. The ship sinks and as the crew hang on to the life raft, hoping for rescue, they think back to their last Christmas at home in a series of watery dissolves. Captain Kinross reflects on life with his clever children and lovely, understated wife, Alix (Celia Johnson), in the gracious home on the Sussex Downs; for Chief Petty Officer Hardy (Bernard Miles) the reverie is a terraced house in Bristol with practical spouse and mother-in-law, and Ordinary Seaman Shorty Blake (John Mills) thinks back to his larky East End family and his new wife.

The film is unashamed propaganda for the British war effort, its purpose to stir patriotism and stiffen resolve. The shipmates' names, Blake and Hardy, recall the achievements of notable British figures, the poet/artist and Nelson's heroic flag-captain. It ought to be risible and yet, decades later, there is still a frisson on hearing Coward's Royal Navy warship captain address his crew on deck about the benefits of 'a happy and an efficient ship'. It's time, he says, as they prepare to set sail, to send Mr Hitler a telegram: 'The *Torrin*'s ready: you can start your war.'

Coward was approached by producer Anthony Havelock-Allan to write the film just weeks after his play *Blithe Spirit* opened in London and a couple of months after the sinking of HMS *Kelly* in the Battle of Crete in May 1941. Kelly's commander, Louis Mountbatten, later Admiral of the Fleet and Viceroy of India, advised on the film's battle scenes and the character of Captain Kinross was clearly recognisable as a simulacrum; he even wore Mountbatten's own cap onscreen. Coward is credited as co-directing the film but the majority of the work fell to David Lean, who also did much of the editing.

The opening shipyard sequences, shot by Havelock-Allan and cinematographer Ronald Neame, have the immediacy and authenticity of documentary and a touch of the poetry of the British craftsman at work to be found in Humphrey Jennings's or Alberto Cavalcanti's records of the nation in the 1930s and 1940s. This opening slides into action footage of real battleships and aircraft and, before we know it, our fictional crew are launched into the Battle of Crete. Yet verisimilitude can suddenly give way to scenes of blatant theatricality, even camp. After an early skirmish with the foe, Kinross stands at the bridge sipping cocoa with his signals officer, known as 'Flags' (Michael Wilding). The lighting and set are clearly artificial and flattering; behind them is a back-projected mackerel sky, the morning light just coming up. It is the cinema equivalent of 'Make Do and Mend', the wartime dictum of getting by when resources were scarce.

Captain Kinross impeccably enunciates the dilemma:

'Here comes the dawn of a new day, Flags, and I shouldn't be surprised if it were a fairly uncomfortable one.'

'Very pretty sky, sir. Somebody sent me a calendar rather like that last Christmas.'

'Did it have a squadron of Dorniers [Luftwaffe fighters] in the upper right-hand corner? That's where art parts company with reality.'

The impossible elegance of Coward's commander (watch the expression of distaste as he swims through the oily waters of the studio tank) is also strangely moving. For all the film's clunking class discrimination (the honest seaman is more likely to perish than the posh officer), there is a sense of common purpose and sacrifice that American writer David Mamet identified as a contrast to American war films' 'inter-unit antagonisms' in which two guys struggle to win a girl or collect the most medals. Looking at *In Which We Serve*, Mamet singles out a speech by Celia Johnson at a dinner, given ostensibly as advice to a young woman about to marry a member of the Senior Service. The captain's wife talks about her supporting role and her feelings towards her main rival for her husband's devotion, his ship, the *Torrin* – emblematic of national sacrifice. Mamet praises the lack of sentimentality in Johnson's performance; it is instead 'filled with the truth of emotion withheld'.

Writing in *The Nation* in December 1942, on the film's American release, the critic James Agee judged it the most impressive new film that year, yet he also identified its particular British ambivalence, 'a hollow filled with persuasive shadows and echoes'. Coward's talent was also the shortcoming of the film, 'a peculiarly sentimental kind of sensitiveness which is common to many witty, sad, able and fastidious men'. This results, concluded Agee, in a kind of kitsch, a meticulous sense of form and detail and taste that take the place of profundity. The film is 'elegantly geared for almost too many "effects" . . . discriminating watchers . . . are liable to find it merely touching . . . whereas the undiscriminating watcher, taking this delicate imitation of power for power itself, is subtly hornswoggled'.

Hornswoggling of a patriotic nature is most persuasive when folded into entertainment, whether epic adventure or light musical, rather than in a blatant display of flag-waving. Within six months of Chamberlain's declaration of war, there were seventeen British films already on the propaganda production line, made in consultation with the Ministry of Information. Among their number were *Night Train To Munich* (1940), Carol Reed's espionage thriller set behind enemy lines, and *Let George Do It* (1940), in which comedian George Formby trounces a ring of Nazi spies. Raising the nation's morale were newsreels that explained why we were fighting and documentaries by the Crown Film Unit, the most exquisite being Humphrey Jennings's evocations of Blighty under siege, *London Can Take It* and *Listen to Britain*. Many of these techniques and moods find their way, in slivers and references, into *In Which We Serve*. As the British Ministry of Information concluded in another context, 'film, being a popular medium, must be good entertainment if it is to be good propaganda'.

In Russia, Bolshevik propaganda trains and Stalin's Tupolev propaganda flights may have incorporated galvanising film shows but they only reached tiny clusters of people at a time. Eisenstein's *Battleship Potemkin* ran for just four weeks on a single screen in Moscow on its release, hardly an exercise in mass persuasion; the director was disappointed his countrymen were not more appreciative. A dozen cinemas in the city at the time, however, were selling out screenings of *Robin Hood* with Douglas Fairbanks, which ran for eleven weeks while, among home-grown offerings, by far the most popular was *The Bear's Wedding*, a horrific tale of bestiality and carnage among the tsarists. For critics outside Russia, *Potemkin* appeared a propagandist triumph (after all, many believed after seeing it that there really had been a massacre on the Odessa Steps) but, by the Second World War, Eisenstein had shifted his method to historical parable. He began filming *Ivan the Terrible* in 1942, stressing the parallels between the sixteenth-century Tsar, with his repulsion of foreign threats and suppression of the Boyars, and Josef Stalin, who promptly endorsed such perspicacity by giving Eisenstein a state prize.

By 1939, the Japanese state had taken control of its film industry to turn out what were in effect militaristic advertisements. Action films in historical settings, the *jidai-geki*, were required to demonstrate the virtues of self-sacrifice and honour; the *gendai-geki*, which were concerned with quieter themes of domestic life and work, had to reinforce patriotic pride.

In Germany, Minister for Propaganda Josef Goebbels had already been guiding UFA studios for several years, proving time and time again that the most effective way to sway hearts was to produce crowd-pleasers – whether historical films about figures like Frederick the Great, Schiller or Bismarck who had shaped the nation's history, or musicals, crime thrillers and comedies that buttressed ideas of family, carrying the values of National Socialism in a bland emulsion. Goebbels wrote in a diary entry: 'even entertainment can be politically of special value, because the moment a person is conscious of propaganda, propaganda is ineffective'. In the early thirties, he had initially resisted the idea of Riefenstahl's documentary *Triumph of the Will*, thinking its hyperbolic heroic approach might be counterproductive, although he changed his mind later. Even *Jud Süss* (1940), the anti-Semitic melodrama recognised by historians like David Welch as a key tool in preparing German people for the idea of evacuation and eventual extermination of millions of Jews, is at one level a lavish costume drama designed to appeal to large audiences, far more powerful in effect than the strident, less artful *The Rothschilds* of the same year. Documentaries about attractive young athletes and outdoor pursuits, whether sport or mountaineering, came to represent an Aryan ideal. Leni Riefenstahl indirectly glorified the rise of the Nazis and Hitler in such marriages of aesthetic and ideology as *Olympia* and *Triumph of the Will*.

However abhorrent this use of cinema as propaganda may have seemed to Germany's enemies there was, paradoxically, no agreement about how effective a persuader film really was. A study by Paul Lazarsfeld and Robert Merton in 1943 concluded that film on its own could only reinforce existing values and ideas; it did not have the power to change minds. As Aldous Huxley had observed in 1936, 'The Propagandist is a man who canalises an already existing stream. In a land where there is no water, he digs in vain.'

Audiences had only so much appetite for hornswoggle. In 1940, a Mass Observation report cited a screening of *The Lion Has Wings* (1939), a would-be morale-raiser of British determination and intrepid airpower. Its opening line, 'This is Britain – where we believe in freedom', gives way to a litany of British achievements – from modern factories, homes, schools and so on going back eight hundred years. Not everyone was persuaded. Mass Observation noted that, when Merle Oberon inquires of pilot Ralph Richardson whether Britain is ready for war and he responds rousingly that the country has never been better prepared, repartee from the crowd included – 'Never been prepared, you mean' and 'Oh, God, what propaganda!'

A film guaranteed to irritate certain elements of the British audience was *Mrs Miniver* (1942), a confection Made in America from a British recipe – a series of columns about a Home Counties housewife which ran in *The Times* in the late 1930s. In the film, Mrs Miniver, key-lit for maximum glamour and played in full false eyelash and couture rig by Essex-born Hollywood actress Greer Garson, lives in an opulent house by the Thames. Her husband Clem (Walter Pidgeon) has a barely disguised Canadian accent and a job that involves boats. They variously deal with air raids and short-ages in their oversized refrigerator, Mrs Miniver captures a German pilot and Clem brings the boys back from Dunkirk in his river launch. The Luftwaffe blow the roof off the village church but the congregation carries on singing 'Onward, Christian Soldiers' and the vicar embodies church militancy: 'This is the People's War! It is our war! We are the fighters! Fight it then! Fight it with all that is in us! And may God defend the right.'

Director William Wyler admitted in his memoirs that in this context, at least, he was a warmonger: 'I was concerned about Americans being isolationists. *Mrs Miniver* was obviously a propaganda film.' Roosevelt used the vicar's speech in Voice of America leaflets. The film won six Academy Awards and did well financially but in Britain, although it topped the box office, the reception was at times ambivalent. Some loved the spectacle of familiar situations glamorised and pumped up into Hollywood melodrama; others would have agreed with a fifty-five-year old university lecturer from Aberystwyth who grumbled that it had 'interesting photography but the hidden propaganda is just a damned impertinence'. The American government's Office of War Information generally preferred a more subtle use of propaganda with crowd scenes featuring women in uniform or children doing their bit for the war effort. A united home front might be more impressive than any overt depiction of the enemy – an approach clearly taken by *In Which We Serve*.

There was, however, another kind of war film that concentrated solely on the enemy, a purposeful horror genre which sometimes mixed news footage of atrocities with elements of fiction, designed to galvanise by revulsion. James Agee saw an example, *Ravaged Earth*, in 1942, which claimed to show in grisly detail the brutality of the Japanese Imperial Army in Shanghai. His response in *The Nation* was to urge that the film be 'withdrawn until, if ever, careful enough minds, if any, shall have determined whether or not there is any morally responsible means of turning it loose on the public'.

In the 1940s commentators of the left, such as the Frankfurt School, saw a broader propagandist purpose in most commercial cinema, however – as a tool of capitalism. Theodor Adorno and Max Horkheimer had both left Germany after 1933 and settled eventually in the USA. Their 1944 *Dialectic of Enlightenment* contained a chapter, 'The Culture Industry: Enlightenment as Mass Deception', which accused the movie and other entertainment businesses of turning audiences into unquestioning, passive consumers. The celebration of individualism onscreen appeared to crush the individuality of those watching: as they put it, 'the film forces its victims to equate it directly with reality'. The 'relentless rush' of facts and sensations rendered the spectators helpless and incapable of critical thought. 'As soon as the film begins, it is quite clear how it will end and who will be rewarded, punished or forgotten.'

Disney has been accused by some critics over the years of pushing a particular set of American values – patriarchal, white, colonial and aggressively capitalist. During the Second World War, though, Disney creations were employed in the fight against facism. Apart from the Donald Duck war bonds initiative, popular cartoon characters went travelling. *Saludos Amigos* (*Hello, Friends*) (1942) was a quartet of animations in Spanish and Portuguese, tailored for consumption by Latin American countries – Brazil and Argentina in particular – known to have ties with Nazi Germany.

In Britain, all films, however good, had to meet with Ministry of Information approval. Without the support of Mountbatten, the King's cousin, there might have been more problems over the sinking of a British ship in *In Which We Serve*. The line between patriotism and realism or even satire was even finer in Powell and Pressburger's *The Life and Death of Colonel Blimp* (1943). Prime Minister Winston Churchill took against the idea of the film, believing it would perpetuate the image of a fusty old soldier, an image that sometimes seemed close to the PM himself. In fact, the film has a far more complicated ecology: it is at once celebration, elegy and lament while it lampoons the hypocrisy and eccentricity of the British Establishment and condemns the waste of war. The Ministry of Information seemed to appreciate this interplay and saw off Churchill's attempts to have the production shut down.

William Wyler's *The Best Years of Our Lives* (1946), about three returning American servicemen who must adjust to disability, unemployment and divorce, is more layered with regret and reflection than you might expect from the director of *Mrs Miniver*. Gregg Toland's deep-focus work here cleverly makes the contrast between the relative affluence of the fictional Midwestern town, Boone City, and the confusion of the veterans, unsure of what they have won or lost.

Back in 1942, on the gentle Sussex Downs, Celia Johnson gazes into a cloudless sky, the setting moments before of a dogfight between German and RAF planes, and remarks to her naval officer husband dozing on the grass beside her on his last day of leave, 'I can't believe it's so dreadfully wrong to forget the war, now and then, when one can, just a little . . .' When Noël Coward as Kinross silkily remarks on her ability to ignore the evidence of conflict over their heads, she responds, 'I made the most tremendous effort and pretended it wasn't real at all. They were just toys having a mock battle just to keep us amused.' Shameful, he teases her, that's sheer escapism. 'I don't care,' she responds and goes on to praise the sweet, green, peaceful countryside – everything around them they are fighting to protect.

SPELLBOUND (1945)

Director: Alfred Hitchcock
Cast: Ingrid Bergman, Gregory Peck
Black and white

'Our story deals with psychoanalysis, the method by which modern science treats the emotional problems of the sane.' Alfred Hitchcock's eighth American title opens with a frontispiece announcing *Spellbound*'s purpose in highlighting the virtues of Freud's therapy in driving 'the devils of unreason from the human soul'.

The action is set in a discreet Vermont mental hospital with the suburban title of Green Manors. It could easily be a country club. Psychiatrist Dr

Constance Petersen (Ingrid Bergman) takes her new patient, an amnesiac played by a queasily ambiguous Gregory Peck, back through his unconscious to the one key event that can unlock his present confusion and clear him of suspicion of killing a man. So psychoanalysis becomes a kind of murder mystery that can be 'solved' as Dr Petersen uses her professional skills to unblock Peck's memory, giving rise to the idea of 'flashback' as a moment of revelation.

Spellbound was released at a time when many Hollywood practitioners were themselves on the couch. It was the creative offspring of two beneficiaries of psychoanalysis – Hitchcock, and producer David O. Selznick who had been fired with evangelical enthusiasm by his own experience. Later filmmakers have had more ambivalent attitudes to the use of psychoanalysis in the creative process. Some, like David Lynch, adopt the why-should-I-give-them-the-good-stuff defence, believing analysis can only deplete creative resources. Others, like Bernardo Bertolucci, are convinced that psychoanalysis freed them to make more 'open' films. As he said in conversation with psychoanalyst Dr Andrea Sabbadini in 1997: 'Since I started psychoanalysis I found that I had in my camera an additional lens, which was – it's not Kodak, it's not Zeiss, it's Freud. It is a lens which really takes you very close to dreams. For me movies, even before knowing Freud, have always been the closest thing you can imagine to a dream. First of all, the movie theatre in this amniotic darkness for me has always been like a womb, so we are all dreamers, but dreamers in the womb.'

Spellbound, though, for all its inspiration is essentially a thriller, but a highly influential one. Hitchcock might later dismiss it as 'another manhunt story wrapped in pseudo-psychology' but its use of dream sequence sets a pattern for film psychology and plotting. As Dr Petersen tries to find the cause of Peck's amnesia he is asked to recall a dream. The sequence, one of the most famous in cinema, was designed by Salvador Dalí, who had collaborated with Luis Buñuel on *Un Chien Andalou*. Quoting Freud to her supervisor, Dr Petersen points out that 'a man cannot do anything in amnesia that his real character would not have done'. Peck is then told that dreams 'tell you what you are trying to hide'; he duly obliges by recalling a theatrical sequence of nightclubs and curtains of eyes, men with beards or masks, a surreal landscape of sloping roofs, with a discarded bent wheel and a giant bird flapping overhead. His description over, Peck is suddenly disturbed by a glimpse of bright snow in the street outside; he cringes away. Aha! says Dr Petersen's expression and aha! swells Miklós Rósza's music. This may be the key!

However arresting and famous its images, the *Spellbound* dream sequence is oddly banal and literal, one of the less effective evocations of the psyche onscreen because it feels so stagey and contrived. What it demonstrates, though, is cinema's devotion to a reductive version of psychoanalysis. As seen onscreen, this is a primitive practice. As the doctor explains in *Spellbound*, 'Once the complexes of the patient are uncovered and inter-preted, the illness and confusion disappear.' Psychiatric problems onscreen are routinely traced back to one key event via flashback; catharsis follows and then complete recovery. One fact, one incident, one association can unlock a patient's misery. This in turn becomes the model for screenplays from romantic comedies to thrillers. If the hero or heroine only knows *that*, then all of *this* that has gone before suddenly makes sense and the plot is resolved – all, as Orson Welles said of *Citizen Kane*, 'dollar-book Freud'.

People who undergo analysis offscreen soon realise that the one secret is unlikely to prove the psychologically curative key; there will rarely be the 'aha!' moment. Cinema audiences, though, constantly have that idea before them; it has since fed through into confessional television programmes which deal in the currency of closure (sometime after the last advert break and before the credits).

In films of the mid-forties, the psychiatrist is usually pretty close to divine. The paragon may be gorgeous Dr Mark Kik (Leo Genn), the doctor charged with treating confused housewife Virginia Cunningham (Olivia de

Havilland) in *The Snake Pit* (1948), directed by Anatole Litvak. The film was sensational at the time for its depiction of brutal treatment in hospitals: legislation changed in seven states shortly after, possibly as a result of the attention the film brought or, more likely, the filmmakers were timely in their choice of theme. The benign agent of Virginia's recovery is the omniscient Dr Kik. His conversations with his adoring patient are often framed so that an image of Freud hangs between them on the wall and in his gentle way he finds the incident that triggered her anxiety. (Funnily enough, her mother is to blame.)

The year before, however, an American film by British director Edmund Goulding which is sometimes described as the *noir*est of the *noir*, had flung caustic acid at the whole business of healing the mind. In *Nightmare Alley* (1947) Tyrone Power plays a fairground chancer-turned-society mindreader, The Great Stanton, who fools the rich in expensive hotel performances with his slickly professional act as a Mentalist. One night the trickiest question is posed by a beautiful woman with an authoritative manner. This leads Stanton to the elegant modernist offices of Dr Lilith Ritter, Consulting Psychologist (Helen Walker). She is apparently a cool professional, both insightful and *femme fatale* (her office boasts the most sleekly seductive couch).

> 'You ever been psychoanalysed?' she challenges.
> 'No,' retorts Stanton, 'I saw one in a murder movie once. A good Mentalist could have straightened the whole thing out in five minutes.'

Stanton and Dr Ritter join forces in a con, using her professional notes and his charisma to play on the anxieties of the suggestible rich, creating facsimile dream sequences in which, most cruelly, they conjure up apparitions of dead relations – a satire on the 1940s resurgence in spiritualism but a bucket of icy water, too, for all those soothing celluloid wraiths. Perhaps unsurprisingly, *Nightmare Alley* failed to impress 1947 audiences and 20th Century Fox boss Daryl F. Zanuck (who had tried to prevent Power from taking such a dirty, dismal role) withdrew it – only for twenty-first-century audiences to applaud it on its DVD release in 2005.

Many *films noirs* have a dream-like or hallucinatory feel as protagonists in the thrall of sexual attraction stumble into absurd and dangerous situations. Sometimes, as in *Out of the Past* (1947), directed by Jacques Tourneur, who also made *Cat People*, the whole narrative may feel like a dream. The action of *Out of the Past* is almost entirely in flashback as Robert Mitchum's character, Jeff, is literally dazzled when he meets Kathie (Jane Greer), a gangster's girlfriend who has run off with a pot of his money. ('And then I saw her, coming out of the sun, and I knew why Whit didn't care about that forty grand.') Later, as he waits in a bar, she walks in 'out of the moon-light, smiling'. The persistent association of attraction and light is hardly original, Juliet, after all, was the sun and other luminous sources to Romeo, but here, combined with Mitchum's fatalistic voiceover, it makes you wonder if Kathie exists at all and if the whole labyrinthine plot might instead be a relief map of Mitchum's character's mental state. Or, as the *film noir* hero might put it: you look like I might be in trouble. *Out of the Past* was, incidentally, one of the key films that Martin Scorsese recommended to his lead actor Leonardo DiCaprio as preparation for the mindbending thriller *Shutter Island*.

Dream sequences may also be more than illusions or codebreakers. An early low-budget experimental film by the Swedish director Ingmar Bergman, *Prison* (1949), deals with a young prostitute who recalls an abusive relationship and a lost child in conversations with a journalist with whom she has become involved. It also uses the film-within-a-film device, so the film set itself becomes a kind of psychiatric consulting room. At one point the girl wanders (Bergman acknowledged the influence of Hitchcock's use of long continuous shots in *Rope* the year before) through a dream/nightmare landscape which, far from 'solving' the character's problems, powerfully evokes her distress. After *Spellbound*, Hitchcock himself took the neurosis out of the mental hospital and put it right into the *mise en scène*, that alchemy of design, cinematography and storytelling, to convey psychic confusion or pathology – most sensationally and obviously in *Psycho* but even more disturbingly in *Vertigo* and *Rear Window*.

Writing in 1947, in *Magic and Myth of the Movies*, the critic Parker Tyler maintained it was not science 'that makes psychiatry adaptable to the screen; rather it's the photogenic character of the dream'. Anticipating the work of therapy-averse David Lynch thirty years later, as well as that of Bernardo Bertolucci, Tyler concluded that 'the happiest function of the psychoanalytic trend in movies would be to focus attention on the dream world as a place; that is, a three-dimensional theatre like the physical world held in common by everyone but individualized like artistic vision itself and holding another mental dimension, that of the fabulous and impossible'. That depiction of a dream world begins with Méliès, right through Lynch's *Lost Highway* (1997) and *Mulholland Drive* (2001), both of which are arguably pure dream from beginning to end.

Lynch himself insists that the process of watching a film in the dark of the cinema is close to dreaming. Your mind is alert, he says, your heart is open. The philosopher Colin McGinn argues that the process cuts both ways. Watching a film may be like having a dream since films are constructed in a similar way – scenes intercut, an actor is two people simultaneously (both Nicole Kidman and Virginia Woolf in *The Hours*, for example) – and dreams themselves are put together like films with scripts, stages and shooting sequences.

In his book *The Power of Movies: How Screen and Mind Interact*, McGinn claims films are the dreams we dream of having. Movies exert such a hypnotic hold because we are already familiar with the cinematic experience in dreams. Both involve emotional immersion where small objects take on huge symbolic significance and 'the eye and the heart are locked intrinsically together'. They are expressions of our fears, anxieties and desires; wish-fulfilment is an essential element of both, allowing protagon-ists to defy physics to beat odds and enemies; they don't just play with our emotions, they give them form. Films are even edited like dreams – we can skip from one location to the next, from Tooting to Timbuktu, in a heartbeat. In the cold light of day, neither dream nor movie narratives are entirely plausible; in the dark they persuade. We are wired to understand the rules.

But surely – to adopt Gregory Peck's initial scepticism in *Spellbound*, as Ingrid Bergman gives him the Freud-for-beginners prescription – this is all too simplistic? Watching a film, unlike dreaming, is a conscious act. McGinn, though, compares watching film to a light sleep state of lucid dreaming; an audience can 'forget' itself, flinching or jumping as if the experience in front of them were direct rather than mediated.

Even as we sit in the *Spellbound* consulting room, as Ingrid Bergman pursues truth through analysis, the simple act of watching a film may actu-ally in itself be therapeutic. The Iranian director Abbas Kiarostami believes watching films is more effective than psychotherapy. In a speech delivered in Paris for the celebration of the centenary of cinema in 1995, he described how the dark gives us safety while the image lifts us out of ourselves and allows for self-scrutiny. One of his later films, *Shirin*, consists entirely of shots of women watching a romantic epic (or at least pretending to). Onscreen each appears to bring her own experience to the same narrative and images appearing before her. As Kiarostami put it, 'The cinema is a window into our dreams and through which it is easier to recognize ourselves. Thanks to the knowledge and passion thus acquired, we transform life to the benefit of our dreams.'

Psychoanalysts and psychotherapists may endorse this approach. Cinematherapy is offered by certain contemporary practitioners like John and Jan Hesley whose 1998 book *Rent Two Films and Let's Talk in the Morning* was a bestseller. They prescribed specific titles for certain psychological issues: mostly, these were startlingly obvious – *Ordinary*

People for troubles with offspring, or Woody Allen's *Hannah and Her Sisters* for infidelity and family troubles, or *Dolores Claiborne* for suppressed childhood trauma. Occasionally, though, the connection was more oblique: in the introduction the Hesleys cited clients of theirs, a couple who rediscovered intimacy after a viewing of *The Bridges of Madison County* revealed to the wife that she still had not forgiven her husband for an earlier affair. Other psychotherapists keep DVDs in their consulting rooms as a resource and tool; clients describe their feelings by reference to scenes in films. Rather than providing a guide to behaviour, film does seem to have this ability to trigger insights and shifts in perception. Academic Madelon Sprengnether was unable for a long time to deal with her father's death, instead shutting it away. Only years later, while watching a young boy grieve for his sister in Satyajit Ray's *Pather Panchali* (1955), she herself broke down in tears, although the circumstances onscreen were very different from those of her father's death. In her 2001 book *Crying at the Movies* she argues that cinema has a uniquely therapeutic power among the arts. Like Abbas Kiarostami, she believes the act of watching places us in a trance-like state, with defences lowered and emotions high.

Spellbound is more intriguing than trance-inducing, however. In the January 1946 edition of *Hollywood Quarterly*, Franklin Fearing, Professor of Psychology at the University of California, noted in an article, 'The Screen Discovers Psychiatry', that Gregory Peck was by no means alone in his predicament: Hollywood films featured an abnormally high incidence of amnesia. Without proper clinical grounding its use was 'merely spectacular or a device . . . to escape from an impasse in the plot'. So much was wrong with the practice of psychiatry as seen in *Spellbound*, beginning with the opening claims that Freudian psychoanalysis had been validated by science: the psychiatrist (Bergman) allows herself to be in love with her patient (as if *that* never happened); she fails to investigate Peck's character's social background or, indeed, his sex life; she confuses the ideas of 'head' and 'heart', finally protesting her conviction of his innocence because her heart tells her it is so.

The real joke, though, is that Professor Fearing really enjoyed the film, citing in particular a 'beautifully directed' scene in which Bergman's character, Dr Petersen, uses psychological techniques to talk a man out of using a gun. It was, wrote the professor, 'hair-raising'.

Aha!

1950s

BEST NOT TALK ABOUT IT

Joe Gillis: You're Norma Desmond. You used to be in silent pictures.
You used to be big.
Norma Desmond: I am big. It's the pictures that got small.

Sunset Boulevard (1950)

illy Wilder's cynical portrait of a struggling writer's entanglement with the magnificent ruin of a silent film star, Norma Desmond, begins like *film noir* and then turns into (among other things) a satire on films and filmmaking. Swanson delivers an exaggerated silent-era performance that screams for attention; William Holden as the writer is a modern rootless, disillusioned loser – if he dies, no one will weep.

As a portrait of Hollywood, *Sunset Boulevard* is lacerating. Louis B. Mayer furiously accused Wilder of biting the hand that fed him in its depiction of a system laced with greed, opportunism and deception, where every declaration is underscored by irony. As a further twist, Norma Desmond's grand statement about the pictures was about to be overturned. In ways spectacular and elaborate, the films were about to get big again. If not necessarily deeper (or better), they would at least become wider, challenging the spectators' peripheral vision in an age of Cinerama, Cinemascope, Vistavision and Super Panavision.

The aim of governments in the 1950s was stable recovery from global conflict with an increase in material comfort. The world was shaking down into two blocs around the United States and the Soviet Union. Confrontation was terrifyingly impossible so the opposition of capitalism and Communism was played out covertly – in espionage, national favour-buying, posturing, proxy wars and technological competition. Suspicion and mistrust drove foreign policy. Arm's-length and indirect aggression began with conflict in Korea, ran through the Suez crisis and on towards the Cuban revolution.

Proxy hostilities continued in the United States via the HUAC investigations which ran until 1958; there was particular concern lest Hollywood should give any succour to the red foe. The novelist and vociferous witness against Communism, Russian-born Ayn Rand, had published a pamphlet, *Screen Guide for Americans*, in which she laid out a dozen commandments: don't denigrate the profit motive, don't glorify failure or depravity or 'the common man' and so on. Producers and audiences alike should be on their guard, she observed: 'The purpose of the Communists in Hollywood is *not* the production of political movies openly advocating Communism. Their purpose is *to corrupt our moral premises by corrupting non-political movies* – by introducing small, casual bits of propaganda into innocent stories – thus making people absorb the basic premises of Collectivism *by indirection and implication*.' Rand herself promoted libertarian values and rugged individualism, qualities displayed onscreen in the 1950s in Westerns. Standing tallest among the western heroes was John Wayne. In 2005 the conservative Los Angeles Liberty Film Festival celebrated the centenary of Ayn Rand's birth alongside a screening of Wayne in *The Searchers* (1956).

Since the world's most powerful governments had adopted diplomacy by metaphor with their Cold War, it was hardly surprising that filmmakers would, too. The first overt reference by Hollywood to HUAC in a mainstream film only came towards the end of the investigations in the Bette Davis vehicle, *Storm Center* (1956), in which she played a librarian with some pinkish titles on her shelves. Two years earlier, a group of blacklisted filmmakers had defiantly made a documentary, *Salt of the Earth*, about unions on strike in New Mexico (tagline: Banned! The Film the US Government Didn't Want You to See!). The film was really only seen by audiences outside the USA; at home influential critic Pauline Kael denounced it as communist propaganda. Overall, the film industry's ambiguity and shame about this period has meant that it has provided few explicit plots for features, although later exceptions include *The Way We Were* (1973), Woody Allen's *The Front* (1976) and *Guilty By Suspicion* (1991).

Old empires were collapsing – the British and French were gradually decolonising and their troubles made their way into Hollywood melodramas set in Africa or Ceylon. Toga epics such as *The Robe* (1953) or *Ben-Hur* (1959) depicted the evils of British-accented empiricist Romans intent on crushing the individualism and principles of American-accented protagonists. New prospects for colonisation opened up. One of the legacies of warfare technology was a sophisticated system of rocket propulsion: the man who had devised the V2 rocket for the Nazis, Wernher von Braun, had surrendered to the Americans in May 1945 and began to work for the US Army. In 1950, von Braun gave an interview triggered by a spate of science fiction films, among them *Destination Moon*, produced by George Pal, whose next film was the spectacular *When Worlds Collide*. Von Braun suggested that rocket flight to the moon was indeed possible. Five years later, he collaborated with Walt Disney on a series of television broadcasts, the first of which, *Man in Space*, attracted record audiences. The Russians launched the first Sputnik satellite in 1957 and the space race began in earnest.

In the West, the bright new atomic age promised cheap, unlimited power; Ford would disclose plans for a nuclear-powered automobile by the end of the decade. Despite the recent experience of war, the development of weapons was presented as progressive with both the United States and the Soviet Union proudly testing. Mushroom clouds from the Pacific and Nevada Proving Grounds could be seen a hundred miles away and the explosions did not go underground until 1962. In Bikini Atoll in Micronesia, tests had began in 1946 (when the itsy-bitsy two-piece swimsuit, so prominent in comedies of the later 1950s, took its topical name from being even smaller than a tiny one-piece called the Atome). From Japan came growing evidence of the long-term effects of radiation after Hiroshima and Nagasaki.

In Hollywood, too, old orders were crumbling. Persistent attempts by legislators over two decades to impose anti-trust measures on the Hollywood studios finally succeeded when block-booking, where studios set the package of films they released to theatres, became illegal. The golden age of the five conglomerates – MGM, Fox, Paramount, RKO and Warner Brothers – plus a trio of the smaller United Artists, Columbia and Universal, came to an end with ties severed between the studios and the exhibiting theatres. The model of vertical integration established in the film industry for more than thirty years was now broken.

Television had proved the catalyst. By the end of the fifties, there were fifty million sets in American households and cinema attendances had fallen by a third. The invasion was not unexpected: industrial production of television sets had begun at the end of the 1930s but the second World War delayed both the broadcasters' and the manufacturers' development. In the 1950s, freed from the privations of war, more affluent Western audiences were starting to face a delicious dilemma: for their entertainment they could venture out or stay at home in increasing comfort. Daytime and weekend programmes increased. The television set, as the radio before it, became a new place of congregation – whether for families at home or groups in bars or clubs – but, unlike the wireless, it demanded full attention to the exclusion of other activities. It might be an educator: public service broadcasters had a remit to improve quality of life – BBC Television, for example, began an alliance in 1946 with the Council of Industrial Design to promote aesthetic awareness. The set could also be a salesman: in the United States, the billings to Madison Avenue advertisers for television spots grew from $12.3 million in 1949 to $128 million in 1951.

Sometimes the advertisements were more arresting than the programming. Vance Packard's bestselling 1957 book, *The Hidden Persuaders*, identified the secret manipulators of modern society, the advertisers, publicists, fund-raisers, politicians and industrial personnel experts, what Packard called 'the depth boys'. The apparatus around the pursuit of material happiness – apparently the greatest prize of all – began to develop tiny cracks. What if the Hollywood arc of struggle and achievement, where the protagonist succeeds to riches or recognition – the compact of *A Star Is Born*, say, now getting its second outing, this time with Judy Garland and James Mason, in 1954 – were a false trail to a questionable goal?

The challenge for studios to tempt people back into the cinemas was to find spectacle and hyperbole – situations and predicaments that were bolder, more lachrymose or tuneful than the small screen could contain; an experience more stimulating, dazzling, exhausting or cathartic delivered in a way no domestic television yet could – and in colour.

Moreover, cinema could also provide the curious connection of people watching together in the dark. As director Michael Mann, son of one of the great 1950s directors, Anthony Mann, has observed, 'a 65-foot screen and 500 people reacting to the movie, there is nothing like that experience'. In his autobiographical films, including *Distant Voices, Still Lives* (1988), Terence Davies recreates the wonder of a small boy's experience of picture-going in Liverpool in the late 1940s and early 1950s. Davies places his camera at the end of the projector's beam of light, as if it hovers just before the screen, where it gazes lovingly down on the upturned, transported faces of the audience.

In the local picture houses, they might be bewitched by a lush melodrama by Douglas Sirk or startled by a coolly stylish thriller by Hitchcock – *Rear Window* (1954), *Vertigo* (1958) or *North by Northwest* (1959) – which placed dark psychology in striking architecture. They might be dazzled by a musical: director Vincente Minnelli might take them into the streets of Montmartre or old Baghdad or up into the misty Scottish Highlands; Stanley Donen's *Singin' in the Rain* (1952) fair bursts out of the screen with blithe exuberance. The following year, Daryl F. Zanuck announced that 20th Century Fox was to broaden its output, in the most literal sense, concentrating on Cinemascope. For MGM, Donen's *Seven Brides for Seven Brothers* (1954) matched the two sets of siblings across the widescreen format (Seven Songs! In 70 Millimetre! declared the trailer) with the golden-haired couples lined up to raise barns, cradle animals and generally advertise, from flowered meadows beneath cornflower blue skies, the milk-fed glory of the American backwoods – like a Soviet realist poster minus the borscht . . . and the Russian soul. The great Cecil B. DeMille directed, produced and narrated *The Greatest Show on Earth* (which duly won Best Film at the 1953 Academy Awards), one of the first films to display new, improved Technicolor. Set in a travelling circus, it promised thrills and 'real' risk as 'real' stars learned the skills of the ring – Betty Hutton on the trapeze, Gloria Grahame on an elephant and James Stewart behind the make-up of a clown! DeMille's introduction didn't spare the martial metaphors: 'a mechanized army on wheels that rolls over any obstacle in its path . . . where disaster and tragedy stalk the Big Top, haunt the backyards, and ride the circus rails . . . where Death is constantly watching for one frayed rope, one weak link, or one trace of fear. A fierce, primitive fighting force that smashes relentlessly forward against impossible odds: that is the circus.' Three years later, DeMille raised the odds still further and parted the Red Sea for Charlton Heston's Moses in *The Ten Commandments*; for this lavish remake of his original 1923 silent picture his team reversed footage of water tumbling from giant tanks to create the effect of the parting of the Red Sea, and won a Visual Effects Oscar for their trouble.

The technique of 3-D projection, first shown in public in 1922, now returned with the weight of the studios behind it. It might be an African adventure (with man-eating big cats) in *Bwana Devil* (1952) – tagline: The Miracle of the Age! The Lion in Your Lap! The Lover in Your Arms! The following year's 3-D offerings included the rollercoaster thriller *Man in the Dark* and the horrific flaming museum of *House of Wax*. The attack on the senses went further with another chiller, this time about a spinal parasite, *The Tingler* (1959), in which buzzers were attached under selected seats in a few movie houses to shock unsuspecting members of the audience. Screams and general hysteria ensued – but not for long. More threatening were other screen infiltrations by creatures, aliens or zombies – horrifying visions of everyday life subverted and destroyed as in *Invasion of the Body Snatchers*.

Television was not only feared by the film industry as its greatest threat, it was denigrated as a repository of the safe and the mediocre, the refuge of the lazy or the defeated. The chilling final sequence of the magnificent Douglas Sirk melodrama *All That Heaven Allows* (1955) shows attractive widow Cary, played by Jane Wyman, who has suffered disapproval and social exile for her relationship with hunky gardener Rock Hudson, being presented with a television by her stuffy children and plonked in front of it, ready for retirement. The image recalls an earlier exchange about Egyptian widows, walled up with their husband's possessions. Cary's desolate expression as the children unveil their gift, demonstrated by a salesman, is reflected in the screen: 'All you have to do is turn that dial and you have all the company you want, right there on the screen . . . drama, comedy, life's parade at your fingertips!'

Yet far from being a bromide, television was actually a fizzing brew of new talents and types. The Oscar-winning Best Film of 1955, which also carried off the Palme d'Or at Cannes, was *Marty*, starring Ernest Borgnine as an unprepossessing Bronx butcher drawn to a plain teacher – or, as Marty puts it, 'She's a dog and I'm a fat, ugly man'. It was an adaptation of a live television play, in which Method actor Rod Steiger had played the lead. Other small-screen dramas would make the same successful transition over the next decade, among them *Twelve Angry Men* and *Days of Wine and Roses.*

The Method and the alumni of the Actors Studio founded by Elia Kazan and Lee Strasberg introduced self-expression and psychological experiment into film acting. Kazan directed Studio graduate James Dean in *East of Eden* (1955); later that year director Nicholas Ray more or less invented the troubled teenager with Dean's performance in *Rebel Without a Cause*. Method actors growled and scowled and roared their way into films – Marlon Brando in *A Streetcar Named Desire* (1951) and *On the Waterfront* (1954), but also Montgomery Clift, Eli Wallach and Dennis Hopper. These were actors whom the lighting did not 'find' in the classic Hollywood way: they might be squinting into the sun or lurking in the shadows. Earlier stars, like Dietrich or Garbo, had been in part 'created' by design and direction. While all those arts would continue to play a vital supporting role, the 1950s were increasingly the age of the apparently 'raw' actor. Outside the United States, the Egyptian director Youssef Chahine brought Omar Sharif to international attention in *The Blazing Sun* (1954). And Japan had its volatile maverick, the wildest of the *Seven Samurai*, the wiry, sensual fighter of *Rashomon* – an actor of almost supernatural speed of expression, Toshiro Mifune.

While the Motion Picture Production Code was still in force in the USA – and in 1951 there was a move to stiffen it even more in the face of a perceived wave of celluloid immorality from abroad – a series of court rulings loosened its hold. Films from abroad offered a more varied culture, more eccentric characters and even the odd flash of nudity. As directors from Fellini to Kurosawa would prove in the 1950s, there were methods of storytelling and characterisation outside the dominant Hollywood models. Politics – rarely approached directly in American films – was the spur to filmmakers abroad. In Eastern Europe, in particular, directors had either to find inventive parables that might get around political repression or to take their creativity into exile. Domestic situations or relationships were scrutinised in realistic detail, without the romantic conventions of Hollywood.

Japanese director Akira Kurosawa first attracted international recognition with *Rashomon* (1950). His *Seven Samurai* (1954), with a running time of 207 minutes, was the longest popular film in America since *Gone With the Wind*, although most audiences initially saw it with fifty minutes cut. Set in the sixteenth century, it concerns a band of mismatched warriors who come together across class divisions to save a village from predators. The plot has since been pillaged, referenced and reworked, from the western *The Magnificent Seven* (1960) to the cartoon *A Bug's Life* (1998) and any heist movie in between, whether *Ocean's 11* or *The Italian Job*, where each member of the gang, despite his or her flaws, is shown to have a particular skill or brand of heroism.

In India epics blended political ideals with fantastical set pieces; *Awara* (1951) directed and produced by Raj Kapoor, found huge audiences not only in the subcontinent but in Turkey, China and Russia where there were reportedly fifty-four million admissions to see it. India's first entry to the new Academy Award for a film not in the English language was the monumental *Mother India* (1957) in which statuesque star Nargis struggles against poverty, labouring in the fields, literally pulling the plough herself and refusing immoral offers from a moneylender in order to raise her children without shame.

Nargis as an onscreen force may have been an emblem of her country but she was also an early example of that earthy, particular character that would emerge in the 1950s – more elemental energy than actor. For women in cinema beyond Britain and America were stronger, more sensual, battling oppression and abuse to some kind of free choice. In Europe they were attractive but contrary: this might range from the blatant, Roger Vadim's showcasing of Brigitte Bardot's pout (and the rest) in *Et Dieu . . . créa la femme* (1956) to perhaps the most subtle and brilliant film of the French *Nouvelle Vague*, written by a woman, Marguerite Duras, and directed by a man, Alain Resnais, in genuine synthesis, weaving documentary with the fictional romance of a French woman and a Japanese man, both survivors of war, in *Hiroshima Mon Amour* (1959).

The attraction of many of these figures was their complexity onscreen: they did not always do the right thing. They worked, they might visit brothels, for example, or they might even work in them. Neo-realism in Italy had made an international star of the elemental Anna Magnani, the 'living she-wolf', but the country also produced, by contrast, another leading female character as far removed from a Hollywood star as she could be, an idiosyncratic, naive anti-heroine played by Federico Fellini's muse and wife, Giulietta Masina, in the circus tale *La Strada*. It is a story that is at once post-war documentary, humanist tragedy, allegory, realist polemic and fantasy. All these elements combine in a distinctive universe – most definitely not Hollywood.

. . . .

LA STRADA (1954)

Director: Federico Fellini
Cast: Giulietta Masina, Anthony Quinn, Richard Basehart
Black and white

Strongman Zampanò (Anthony Quinn) visits a poor widow who lives by the sea. One of her daughters once worked with him in his act; he tells her she has died, but gives no further explanation. Zampanò then pays the mother to take away a younger daughter, Gelsomina (Giulietta Masina) who, the mother admits, is 'not right in the head'. He drags her on the road with him and teaches her the rudimentary skills of clowning. When he treats her roughly, she tries to escape. They meet other circus performers including The Fool (Richard Basehart) who falls out with Zampanò and fascinates Gelsomina. Violence, abandonment and death follow.

Federico Fellini's *La Strada* was his first international success, released in Italy in 1954 but abroad two years later, when it was awarded the inaugural Oscar for a film in a Foreign Language; Fellini and co-writer Tullio Pinelli were also nominated for their screenplay. With its central duo and minimal action – a shambling journey in a three-wheeled vehicle through central and southern Italy – it was a far remove from the flashy, globe-trotting, star-studded Hollywood version of Jules Verne's *Around the World in 80 Days* that won the Best Picture Oscar that year. By comparison, David Niven, Noël Coward, Frank Sinatra, Marlene Dietrich and other seasoned Hollywood veterans swanning around in nineteenth-century costume represented a rather desperate attempt by the old order to cash in on their fading allure.

La Strada's spare plot hangs largely on the performance of Giulietta Masina, who had been married to Fellini since 1943. Her pale face and round eyes, often exaggerated by clown's make-up, her shaggy, fair crop and flat-footed walk, sometimes resolute, sometimes dawdling like a toddler, make her a tragi-comic presence in an often sordid environment. Illumination or despair do not so much pass across her features as radiate from within. What she feels is so evident that the audience does not even have the distance to empathise; *La Strada* is experienced and felt through her. Terrible things happen – beatings, rape, abandonment – but for much of the film she endures, often trotting like a little dog back to the master's side, as if trying to find the world anew in each moment. Like a primitive theatre character or a card in a Tarot pack, she is a powerless victim just as Zampanò is the brute.

By casting Anthony Quinn and Richard Basehart – established Hollywood actors – Fellini was participating in a wider kind of artistic borrowing between the American way of entertainment and the European search for truth in drama. Ingrid Bergman had appeared for her husband Roberto Rossellini in *Stromboli* and *Viaggio in Italia*, while Anna Magnani would star opposite Burt Lancaster in *The Rose Tattoo*. American actors were valued for their naturalism, yet Quinn and Basehart were used in an entirely different way from a Hollywood role. There was nothing heroic about either of their characters. The strongman is ultimately pathetic and the charming high-wire artist insubstantial. There is no magic Hollywood logic to the story, either: as demonstrated in the early scene where Zampanò instructs Gelsomina how to introduce him in the ring. She must perform a drum roll and declare '*È arrivato Zampanò!*' ('Here comes Zampanò!'). An American film might show Judy Garland or someone similar struggling for a moment or two. Perhaps she would mess up the announcement or the drumming but then, however miserable, she would pull out a winning performance. In *La Strada*, Gelsomina mumbles, gets the words in the wrong order and fails to put the act across. Yet still she has to do it. All her suffering must – according to conventional storytelling – lead to some form of redemption. But will it? What if there is no goal?

In 1954, when the film was made, the period of neo-realistic filmmaking in Italy had all but ended – Vittorio De Sica's story of an elderly man living by the sea, *Umberto D*, seemed to take to the limits the use of non-professional actors on location filming deprived lives. Fellini, by contrast, introduced unreality into his characters' situations, preferring to make the analogy with dream. Interviewed by Gideon Bachman, he explained the direct link: 'In dreams there is nothing without significance. Every image also has significance in the film.' The circumstances in which the protagonists act are real enough – the locations with their non-professional actors, the locals used as extras – but what happens might easily be supernatural. At one point, having been temporarily cast aside by Zampanò, Gelsomina waits for him on the kerbside. Hours pass, then a horse trots by with no harness or rider, a moment of grace and beauty in banal surroundings. On another occasion, she encounters a brass band trio by the roadside. Although they are in the open countryside, the sound is studio-pure. Fellini liked sound to be post-synchronised precisely because it was unreal and allowed him complete control over the world of the film, his world.

Fellini had not yet moved on to the stage where his films would be entirely about filmmaking and his life as a filmmaker, such as *8½*. *La Strada*, though, marks a further shift towards the reign of the all-powerful director, a God-like figure who creates the screen universe and pushes around the figures within it. The final news of Gelsomina – what would have been a moment of melodrama in a more conventional film – is delivered almost casually by a young woman hanging out her washing; her face is obscured by a sheet and Zampanò and the audience only catch her words in bursts.

The film Fellini had made the previous year was *I Vitelloni*, which translates literally as 'young bulls' but also carries the idea of idlers or slackers, as a group of young men in a seaside town dream of escape. Martin Scorsese has acknowledged the film's influence on *Mean Streets* (1973), in particular. Like Scorsese's Johnny Boy and Charlie in New York, these boys are not sure where they belong – church or bar, round the family table or with the mob. Fellini shot the film in his hometown, Rimini, which he had left for Rome in 1938, aged eighteen; the young men are loosely based on the slightly older boys he had watched kicking around town. Awarded the Silver Lion at Venice, the film shows them to be well dressed and ambitious but bored, tied variously by economic circumstances, family, Church and romantic complications. The greatest fear is that of making *mamma* cry. They chat about filmstars but live in barely furnished houses. As the evening wears on, we see them variously prepare for the night and the narration intones the disparity between their ideas and their achievements: 'Leopoldo, after eating the supper his aunts prepared, works on his new play' – no surprise, then, when Leopoldo abandons his work after a few seconds to flirt through the window with the maid upstairs. Overall, the five segments of the film, vivid as they may be, lead nowhere much – which is the whole point. These scenes from the lives of the young men, including a mournful trip to a deserted beach on an autumnal Sunday, are ghosts of recollection. If you want a Hollywood-type narrative, Fellini is saying, look elsewhere.

'Watch out, girls! Here come *I Vitelloni!*' The original Italian trailer for the film explains its success not just with critics, but with the paying public. Every viewer could recognise in the characters a little of themselves or their friends and family. Yearning for a more glamorous, comfortable life was something everybody felt – like characters in the film, the audience might sit in the cinema and covet the refrigerator used by an actor onscreen. A film actress from Rome judging a beauty contest in a provincial town was still a big deal, likewise a portable record player. There might be fifty million sets in the United States but no one in *I Vitelloni* or *La Strada* has a television. National broadcasting had yet to start in Italy – and parts of the country would not be able to receive a signal until 1957.

The denizens of *La Strada* seem to belong to an even earlier age – Gelsomina and Zampanò sometimes sleep in derelict buildings and they look unwashed and exhausted (Fellini apparently demanded a degree of authenticity in this). This impression was far from the understated heroism of neo-realism, and politicians of the left accused Fellini of providing a debased image of working people that brought shame on the country. Critics were divided, too. What did it all mean? If it was a metaphor, what for? Fellini himself was resistant to the idea that his films could be neatly understood, arguing that everyone would bring their own experience to their emotional reaction to the film and so many different interpretations were equally valid. And in any case, he argued, why should film improve on life where nothing turns out quite the way we would have written the script? 'I think it is immoral (in the true sense of the word) to tell a story that has a conclusion. Because you cut out the audience the moment you present a solution on the screen. Because there are no "solutions" in their lives.'

There are moments of revelation, though. Gelsomina can glimpse a crucifix in a procession or a high-wire artist above the street and be transported; Zampanò can be aware at night on the beach, with only the sea and sky around him, that there may be some force other than his own senses at work, that the unquestioning way in which he has been living has come at a cost.

Self-questioning turns up in contrasting and yet strangely echoing forms across the world in the 1950s. A contemporary Japanese film with its own dream-like setting, *Ugetsu Monogatori* (1953), directed by Kenji Mizoguchi, stressed the dangers of materialism as a potter neglects his wife and child to make more money at local fairs, eventually falling prey to a seductive and glamorous woman who turns out to be a voracious spectre. Odd as it seems, this situation may not have appeared so fantastical.

In shiny, affluent America two bitter satires questioned the acquisitive, profit-driven rat race – Alexander Mackendrick's knife-sharp portrait of the burgeoning PR business *Sweet Smell of Success* (1957) and, from the same year, the colourful, acidic lampoon of advertising and celebrity *Will Success Spoil Rock Hunter?* This second film features an opening sequence of television advertisements for products that go horribly wrong while the smiling demonstrators resolutely carry on. The ludicrous centre of the picture is the preposterously endowed Jayne Mansfield, spoofing Marilyn Monroe as a breathy starlet. She mesmerises all around with her breasts (men drool, women envy) and her private life is manufactured for public relations.

Mansfield's character occurs in a surprisingly subversive comedy that stresses her alluring pointlessness. The role anticipates by three years the outsize blonde icon played by Anita Ekberg in Fellini's *La Dolce Vita* (1960) who frolics in the Trevi Fountain with the director's screen alter ego, Marcello Mastroianni. Mastroianni/Fellini may mock American culture but he cannot entirely resist it.

In the United States many critics commended *La Strada* despite the film being, as one put it, 'heavily artistic'. A distributor and producer, Irving Levin, organised an Italian film festival in San Francisco where *La Strada* took three of the top prizes. The next year, despite grumbling from the Hollywood studios about further threats to the home-grown product, San Francisco established an international festival to join those founded in the 1930s and 1940s in Venice, Karlovy Vary (Czechoslovakia), Edinburgh, Cannes and Berlin. The international film as artistic expression, which had hovered on the edges of cinema since the days of *Dr Caligari*, was now recognised in California itself. The greatest show on earth, in twentieth-century terms, was not the only attraction.

THE SEARCHERS (1956)

Director: John Ford
Cast: John Wayne, Jeffrey Hunter, Natalie Wood
Colour

In 2008, *The Searchers*, directed more than half a century earlier by John Ford, was dubbed the Greatest American Western of All Time by the American Film Institute. Its central figure is monumental, Ethan Edwards (John Wayne), a veteran of the civil war so taciturn he appears carved from the rock of northern Texas. When he visits his brother on a remote farmstead, a torch still burns faintly for his sister-in-law. Her subsequent murder and the abduction of his nieces by Comanche Indians sets him on a coldly furious pursuit across harsh terrain through changing seasons. This search is fuelled by his hatred of the Native Americans and a visceral fear of miscegenation; as the years pass, he resolves that when he finds his niece Debbie – who has by now been taken as a wife by a Comanche warrior – he must kill her.

For twenty-first-century audiences, the overt racism of *The Searchers* is hard to take. John Ford's own attitude was ambiguous at best. He may have been intending to alert white Americans to injustices inflicted by them on their country's indigenous people. He may have been intending to justify genocide as a weapon of revenge, in the way the Comanche chief, Scar, does later in the film. Whatever the motivation, the result is the same: this is a widely revered film narrative, imitated in such popular and apparently innocuous forms as *Star Wars* (from 1977) and the fishy animation *Finding Nemo* (2003). Ford's 1956 film was certainly not the first art form to employ the seek-and-destroy narrative – classical literature is rich in it – but its influence spreads far beyond the cinema.

The biggest film industry in the world regards the western as its very own genre; those saddlebags are heavy with ideology. Ayn Rand, scourge of the left, may have detested in films the 'indirect' or 'implicit' messages supporting collective values but she enjoyed a western with its celebration of the individual. The first narrative film was a simple linear western, *The Great Train Robbery* (1903), twelve minutes long, which employs cross-cutting to show an outlaw band holding up a train. The film ends with one of the bandits pointing and firing a gun straight into camera. Extremely popular as a representation of frontier derring-do, it was actually filmed in New Jersey. Hollywood itself, with its establishment of the breakaway band of filmmakers on the West Coast, dodging union and patent laws, was a sharp-shooting frontier town of another kind.

In 1893, when film was in its infancy, Frederick Jackson Turner argued in his essay 'The Significance of the Frontier in American History' that 'the colonization of the Great West' was the exploit that gave the United States an identity distinct from its European origins. He eulogised frontiersmen like Daniel Boone who 'helped to open the way for civilization, finding salt licks and trails and land'. The frontier allowed for a Darwinian selection of the self-reliant and adaptable; social status was unimportant compared to survival skills or resistance to the Indians, described as 'a common danger, demanding united action'. Violence was justified at this 'meeting point between savagery and civilization' to ensure progress to democracy – more than that, the frontier was 'a military training school, keeping alive the power of resistance to aggression'. His call to arms in 1893 was provoked by what he considered to be the end of that frontier era and a resultant loss of identity and purpose in the nation.

Republican President Theodore Roosevelt, in office from 1901 to 1909, claimed to be a genuine Cowboy President. A sickly child from a wealthy family, he entered politics in New York before having a taste of real frontier experience, a brief interlude on a ranch he bought in the Dakota Badlands, where he raised stock and administered rough justice to thieves. He exploited this link to the mythical West to great effect in his subsequent political career.

Turner's thesis about the West and national identity was pervasive, according to *Virgin Land*, a critical study of the pioneer ethos by Henry Nash Smith published in 1950 – 'it revolutionized American historiography and eventually made itself felt in economics and sociology, in literature and even in politics'. In 1939 an audit on the effect of Turner's thesis found more than a hundred citations in public life of 'The Significance of the Frontier in American History' including a speech by FDR in 1935.

A film released in 1939 – made with the same combination of director and leading actor as *The Searchers*, John Ford and John Wayne, in their first collaboration – changed the perception of the western. *Stagecoach* was the first cowboy picture to be filmed in Monument Valley, Utah, close to the border with northern Arizona. Ford was impressed by the iron-oxide-tinged sandstone plugs and cliffs standing like isolated figures up to a thousand feet high in the desert. The angle of the sun cast transforming shadows and the landscape was dappled and darkened by dramatic accumulations of cloud. This was resolute, no compromise landscape – expressionism, pioneer-style. Yet, as film historian Nick Clooney notes of Ford's choice in *The Movies that Changed Us*, the formations of Monument Valley had artistic rather than historical appeal. 'In no way symbolic of the West – they are unique to this relatively small, circumscribed place – they have come to evoke the Western myth created, in substantial measure, by John Ford himself.'

Stagecoach won seven Academy Award nominations, taking the western genre out of the pulp category. Ironically, the western myth originated precisely in that key, in the dime novels of the 1860s (later, in 1992, to be satirised in Clint Eastwood's *Unforgiven* where an eyewitness to an incident debunks the account of it in a cheap novella). The stories became increasingly sensational, with ludicrous accounts of impossible sharpshooting, until, as Henry Nash Smith reports, 'by the 1890s the Western dime novel had come to hinge entirely upon conflicts between detectives and bands of robbers that had little to do with ostensibly Western locales'.

Real cowboys were herders who led poorly paid repetitive lives. The cowboy of popular culture owed more to the circus act of William F. 'Buffalo Bill' Cody, who toured America and Europe with an entourage at times eight hundred-strong, numbering knife and gun acts, horsemen and women (among them incidentally, my great-great-uncle) and parades of Native Americans. Cody even performed for and met Queen Victoria at her Golden Jubilee in 1887. Buffalo Bill had in fact started out as a scout – his reputation as Indian killer and pioneer only came later when a journalist embroidered on his biography for *New York Weekly*.

Political commentators over the years have argued that the frontier myth has infused American foreign policy right through to Vietnam, Iraq and Afghanistan as relatively recent examples of unknown territory to be defeated and 'civilised' through Western notions of democracy and justice. By the 1950s, filmmakers were clearly aware of the metaphorical power of the western as a vehicle for Cold War rhetoric with Indians as communists, the mysterious and implacable threat against which the community unites. By no means all westerns boil down to that crude formula, though. In the classic *High Noon* (1952), directed by Fred Zinnemann, Gary Cooper's marshal gradually realises he must face the enemy alone, when the towns-people he has so long protected fail to support him. Interpretations range from right-wing critique – Cooper's character as an avatar of Senator Joseph McCarthy, who made his first anti-communist witch-hunting speech in February 1950 – to an allegory about America's involvement in Korea. The man who actually wrote the film, Carl Foreman, later admitted that he had believed *High Noon* would be his last screenplay. Subpoenaed to appear before HUAC, he was hurt and no doubt alarmed by his fellow artists' reluctance to stand by him, producer Stanley Kramer in particular, so he put some of that anger into the script. (Blacklisted, Foreman went into Hollywood exile in Britain to work, sometimes under the pseudonym Derek Frye, with Joseph Losey, Carol Reed and David Lean, for whom he co-scripted *The Bridge on the River Kwai* (1957).)

John Wayne spotted *High Noon's* political subtext immediately. In an interview at the time, he said he 'resented that scene where the marshal ripped off his badge and threw it in the ground. That was like belittling the Medal of Honor.' Overall, he declared the film 'the most un-American thing I've seen in my whole life'. His riposte was *Rio Bravo* (1959), directed by Howard Hawks, where an ill-assorted group of townspeople help Wayne's Sheriff John Chance to stand strong against an evil and powerful rancher.

If *High Noon* is a left-wing parable, it is intriguing that, according to a documentary made in 2003, *All the President's Movies*, it was also the film most requested at the White House in presidential screenings between 1954 and 1986. In the 1990s, Bill Clinton apparently watched it twenty times. Among Republicans, Dwight D. Eisenhower saw it three times (although he also watched *The Big Country* (1958) four times on successive nights) but George Bush Jr requested the film only once – despite his rhetoric and his wardrobe, he was apparently no great fan of westerns.

A truly Texan President, Lyndon B. Johnson, was more pronounced in his use of frontier imagery at the beginning of the Vietnam War when he made a comparison with the Alamo: 'Somebody damn well needed to go to their aid. Well, by God, I'm going to go to Vietnam's aid and I thank the Lord I've got the men to go with me.' He told US troops he met on an Asian trip that his great-great-grandfather had died at the Alamo – a casualty, according to a 1968 edition of *Life* magazine, that history does not record. Johnson may even have been more influenced by the 1960 film *The Alamo* than documented fact. John Wayne, who led the cast as Davy Crockett and also directed and produced, was quoted in publicity material as saying 'we must sell America to countries threatened with Communist domination'. Wayne hoped the cry 'Remember the Alamo' would put 'new heart and new faith into all the world's free people'. In a letter to President Johnson on December 23 1965 Wayne made a direct comparison to justify America's presence in Vietnam. Davy Crockett's Tennesseans fought in Texas to prevent the spread of Mexican domination, which Crockett in the film refers to as 'goring our oxes'. Wayne went further: '. . . we don't want people like Alexei Kosygin, Mao Tse-Tung, or the like, 'gorin' our oxes'.

Johnson's successor in the White House in 1969, the Republican Richard M. Nixon, watched five hundred films during his five and a half years in office. Mark Feeney's study *Nixon at the Movies* reveals John Ford as his favourite director and John Wayne as preferred actor (altogether, twenty-five Wayne films were shown in the White House screening room). Nixon wrote the star a fan letter after seeing *True Grit* (1969) and made a congratulatory phone call to Wayne when he subsequently won an Oscar for it. In August 1970, he referred to *Chisum*, the latest film starring the Duke, when discussing law and order with journalists in Denver: 'I wondered why it is that the western survives year after year after year. A good western will outdraw some of the other subjects. Perhaps one of the reasons, in addition to the excitement, the gun play, and the rest, which perhaps is part of it but they can get that in other kinds of movies but one of the reasons is, perhaps, and this may be a square observation – is that the good guys come out ahead in the westerns; the bad guys lose.'

Democrat President Jimmy Carter called Wayne 'a symbol of many of the basic qualities that made America great, in an age of few heroes, he was the genuine article'. General Douglas MacArthur described him as the model of an American soldier and he received honorary military awards, although Wayne himself had never served in the forces; he began and then abandoned law studies and played football before working in silent films. He was, however, a founder member of the Motion Picture Alliance for the Preservation of American Ideals and supported Senator McCarthy as one of 'America's most misunderstood heroes'.

This blending of myth and politics places Wayne somewhere between the showman Buffalo Bill and Ronald Reagan, his old friend who became President a year after the Duke's death. Like Teddy Roosevelt, Reagan was known as the Cowboy President – originally, it appeared, for his roles in B movies. In fact, his best-known big-screen roles were as a football coach and a small-town amputee – the cowboy outfit was mainly worn later in a television series. Reagan, though, was nothing less than a wizard of self-reinvention, and having lived in California since he was twenty-six, played on that western association. Nominally a Democrat throughout the 1950s, he provided names of fellow artists suspected of Communism for HUAC before running for state governor as a Republican in the 1960s, when his rhetoric was tinged with black hat/white hat frontierspeak: 'They say the world has become too complex for simple answers. They are wrong. There are no easy answers but there are simple answers.'

When the Reagans moved into the White House in 1981, they brought with them some of the iconography of the Old West. Publicly off duty, the President wore Levis and cowboy boots and specialised in homilies such as 'there's nothing better for the inside of a man than the outside of a horse'. His speeches carried foreign policy references to 'standing tall'. The Western White House was established in California at the Reagans' Rancho del Cielo, near Santa Barbara, where the President was filmed grooming and saddling his horses in check shirt and immaculate jodhpurs. The First Couple (ex-actors both) posed in jeans and fringed leather, leaning on the bonnet of a pick-up truck, post-and-rail-fenced pasture behind them. The ranch's nameplate, in Old Western script, bore a simple R. Reagan beneath, as if he were just some old fella who had claimed a piece of land there decades back, in this prime area of rural Southern California real estate.

In recent years, the myth of the American West has been invoked in the so-called War on Terror. George Bush Jr's rhetoric about Osama bin Laden was borrowed from the corral; in a speech soon after September 11 2001, he declared, 'I want justice', referring to 'an old poster out West, as I recall, that said "Wanted Dead or Alive"', a concept applied to the search for bin Laden. Al-Qaeda was warned that the US forces would 'smoke 'em out of their holes'. Bush Jr, the wealthy oilman's son, had long traded on a cowboy appeal but he was far from the first (and will probably not be the last) American President to reach for this foundation legend at a time of national crisis.

Despite its patent fakery, the appeal of the western endures. From the late 1960s, a generation of cinephile directors and ex-film students (collectively known as the Movie Brats) set out to dissect the ideological dimensions of the western. There were no swelling scores or bulging cactuses in minor-key elegies such as Arthur Penn's *Little Big Man* (1970) or Robert Altman's *McCabe and Mrs Miller* (1971) or *Buffalo Bill and the Indians*, or *Sitting Bull's History Lesson* (1976). The cruellest and most brilliant debunking of them all came in Clint Eastwood's *Unforgiven* (1992), a film that manages to be at once gripping, cynical and tragic. Eastwood's character has killed 'women, children and just about everything that walked or crawled' and he is set on vengeance at any price.

By the twenty-first century, filmmakers had become more meditative about the isolation and misery of the mythical figures of the West. In 2007, three films – *3:10 to Yuma*, *The Assassination of Jesse James by the Coward Robert Ford* and *There Will Be Blood* took audiences inside the desolate interior landscapes of the gunslinger, the celebrity outlaw and the ruthless prospector successful beyond his wildest ambitions.

But to modern eyes, the weirdest western of all may be Nicholas Ray's 1954 *Johnny Guitar* with Joan Crawford as Vienna, the mannish proprietor of a saloon, an 'outsider' with racy friends. Vienna favours a modernising force, a railroad through the valley, for which you might read leftist leanings. The black-clad townspeople, led by her butch nemesis, Emma, violently oppose this change to the status quo. They set out in a band to track her down: beware the posse, says her lover Johnny, played by Sterling Hayden (who regretted his decision years before to name names to HUAC): 'A posse isn't people. I've ridden with 'em, and I've ridden against 'em. A posse is an animal that moves like one and thinks like one.' So stylised that the characters even strike poses and seem apparently superficial, *Johnny Guitar* is also visually and thematically compelling, a lurid allegory not only of McCarthyism but pyscho-sexual politics. As Vienna's croupier puts it, 'Never seen a woman who was more a man. She thinks like one, acts like one, and sometimes makes me feel like I'm not.' A favourite film of the French *Nouvelle Vague* directors, it was 'canonised' in the American National Film Registry in 2008.

Yet for many modern, sophisticated filmmakers, John Ford's *The Searchers* remains their favourite western. So why should that be when Wayne's character is brutal, racist and misogynist? *The Searchers* is not a film that asks you to emulate its central character. His persistence may be heroic but other dimensions are less admirable. Ethan Edwards is always the outsider; not even a patriot, he may be a mercenary: the film begins with an image of a darkened doorframe looking out to a blinding ochre landscape. Ethan's sister-in-law, the woman who has created the idyllic pioneer interior we are about to be invited into, peers out at the desert where a distant horse and rider emerge from the dust. For all his taciturn strength, Edwards always seems wounded: he has endured a bitter civil war, the woman he loves is married to his brother and there is a potent force out there, the Comanche, that he can neither fathom nor control.

When the audience finally gets to see the much-demonised Comanche chief, Scar, he is not only the best-looking man in the film, but he also lives by a code of honour and revenge not dissimilar – and hardly less moral – than Edwards's own. The search for retribution is long and hard and what Edwards eventually finds is simply a yearning to be home, but for him there will be no welcoming hearth. In the film's final, ambiguous, sequence, he returns his niece (who may even be his daughter) to relatives. He lifts her down from his horse and there, waiting in a darkened doorway, looking out, is not his beloved sister-in-law but another family unit, a homely man and woman. They embrace the young woman and take her inside, silhouetted against the bright landscape beyond the doorframe. Once again, the camera is within the homestead (the girl and her new guardians pass by the lens and on out of shot) and Edwards is without, excluded. He hovers on the threshold but when no welcome is extended he turns hesitantly and limps away, ultimately lonely and useless. The door shuts on him. *The Searchers* is a masterpiece not for its assertion of colonising values but for its portrait of the relative powerlessness of the individual in an indifferent landscape.

INVASION OF THE BODY SNATCHERS (1956)

Director: Don Siegel
Cast: Kevin McCarthy, Dana Wynter
Black and white

'*Listen. Please listen. If you don't, if you won't, if you fail to understand, then the same incredible terror that's menacing me will strike at you.'*
Dr Miles J. Bennell (Kevin McCarthy) appeals to camera
in *Invasion of the Body Snatchers* (1956)

'Who do you think they're really after? Who's next? Is it your minister, who will be told what he can say in his pulpit? Is it your school-teacher, who will be told what he can say in the classroom? Is it your children themselves? Is it YOU who will have to look around nervously before you can say what is on your mind?'

Actor Fredric March, from the radio broadcasts,
'Hollywood Fights Back', an appeal to the public on Behalf
of the Hollywood Ten, 26 October and 2 November 1947

Invasion of the Body Snatchers begins in a sunny Norman Rockwell-style community in California where certain individuals, while outwardly seeming normal, begin to appear to their friends and relatives strangely detached and lacking in emotion or humour. Dr Bennell, a physician, is the first to perceive that these chilly beings are in fact not the original individuals but physical replicants. They have grown in alien pods which have drifted in seed form through space. The invasion is fiendishly ingenious ('Suddenly, while you're asleep, they'll absorb your minds, your memories') and often imperceptible at first; gradually, more of the townspeople are taken over.

The meaning of the 1956 film was likewise not so easy to detect. As a metaphor, the emotionless husks that replace the townspeople could represent an external threat, like the Red Menace of the McCarthy investigations – some have found evidence in the film for fears about the growth of black neighbourhoods in hitherto white middle-class areas – or perhaps an even more insidious invasion: a change in the national mentality that might undermine family, work and community.

Fantasy – from sci-fi to elves – is most persuasive for its recognisable detail. (Bilbo Baggins's house in the *Lord of the Rings* films is recognisably 1930s Middle England; mealtimes on the spaceship *Nostromo* in *Alien* seem like the canteen of a science lab.) The visions of disturbance and invasion that creep into 1950s cinema are the stronger for being set in immaculately lawned, picket-fenced small towns. While plots traditionally rest on this being the place where the heart is, in *Invasion of the Body Snatchers* the very conformity becomes sinister.

Even in the 1950s, the pursuit of material happiness in prosperous peacetime did not go unquestioned. In 1950, *The Lonely Crowd: A Study of the American Character*, by three sociologists led by David Riesman, analysed the effect of large corporations and government on individuals. By 1954, Riesman was on the cover of *Time* magazine. He had identified opposing types: the 'inner-directed' or self-motivated people, like nineteenth century paragons, were confident and even entrepreneurial, albeit stubborn on occasions (in other words, your typical movie hero); from the 1940s, though, the 'other-directed' type had begun to emerge. This new breed sought love rather than respect; they judged their progress by comparison to others – whether their houses, cars or beliefs; in short, they were ideally suited to passive employment in large, paternalistic corporations.

The same year as *Body Snatchers* appeared in cinemas, William H. Whyte's *The Organization Man* was in bookshops. Talking to a series of big business chiefs, he concluded that, benign and approachable as they might seem, they wanted in return not just the hours and the sweat but the very soul of their employees – little people like Jack Lemmon's character at the beginning of *The Apartment* (1960), say, or the eager executive of *Will Success Spoil Rock Hunter?* or maybe even the individuals taken over by the pod people in *Invasion of the Body Snatchers*.

Whyte exhorted individuals to resist the enveloping power of the Organisation and 'turn the future away from the dehumanised collective that so haunts our thoughts'. The alternative, perhaps, would be to end up like Dr Bennell, lurching along the freeway, failing to make his horrific experience understood to the indifferent occupants of cars, and screaming at the audience, 'They're here! You're next . . . you're next!'

Not everyone saw an explicit connection. The source of the film was a novel by Jack Finney which had been serialised in *Collier's* magazine in 1954. Finney denied he was writing about ideology or economic pressures; he claimed his inspiration was a psychological condition known as Capgras Delusion in which individuals believe those close to them have been replaced by clones. (But why might they think that? It is, as delusions go, precise.) Director Don Siegel and the head of production at the studio, Walter Mirisch, also shook off any suggestion their film was an allegory. They believed, said Mirisch in his memoir, *I Thought We Were Making Movies, Not History*, that they were concocting a thriller, pure and simple. American reviewers at the time tended to concentrate on the fantastical storyline rather than its allegorical significance, although the *Hollywood Reporter* saw another kind of resonance altogether, in which 'modern man, tired of facing the mental problems of our intricate age, is prone to welcome the irresponsible life of a human vegetable. This is a sobering and shocking thought.'

Other science fiction films reflected a fear of loss of identity – aliens temporarily 'control' humans in *It Came from Outer Space* (1953) or *I Married a Monster from Outer Space* (1958). These stories are most powerful when something unknowable suddenly appears within a domestic environment. In the UK, John Wyndham's 1957 novel *The Midwich Cuckoos* became *Village of the Damned* (1960), in which the hamlet's womenfolk are impregnated with alien spawn to produce a brood of solemn white-blond super-children. It is a fine example of economy of storytelling and the power of the quotidian. The aliens are never seen; the village is a real location, even if the interior of the manor house looks expansively American. At one level *Village of the Damned* is a warning against fascism (in 2003, director Wolf Rilla explained to Alan Dein and Mark Burman of the BBC, 'I don't think any of us were aware of it then,' says Rilla, 'but of course now they remind you of the Hitler Youth, blond-haired Aryan children and all that. I'm convinced that was an unintentional subtext; after all, the war was still fresh in our memories. But none of us had any idea of the impact it would make.'). This association has since been reinforced by Michael Haneke's *The White Ribbon* (2010) in which children in an early twentieth-century southern German town perform apparently motiveless malicious acts. *Village of the Damned*, though, is also a portrait of intellectual arrogance: the brainy and principled, if misguided, scientist (George Sanders) believes he can guide the children, who include his 'own', to some kind of extraterrestrial detente.

Threats from without and within are hardly surprising preoccupations in an age of ambitious experiments out in space and on earth with atomic power and weapons. A series of ostensibly daft 'creature features' took those concerns to both practical and existential limits. The consequence might be giant ants, resurrected dinosaurs or an outsize irradiated octopus. The king of the bunch was the dignified *Gojira* (1954), later known as Godzilla, whose name derives from the Japanese words for gorilla and whale, a warning rising from the waters made radioactive by Allied bombs. There were terrible distortions in the United States, too, in *The Amazing Colossal Man* (1957) while *The Incredible Shrinking Man* utters perhaps the most poignant, if tiny, cry: '. . . smaller than the smallest I meant something too. To God there is no zero, *I still exist*'.

Apocalyptic visions had, by definition, been around for millennia. Within the previous century and a half, accounts of Drs Frankenstein and Jekyll had warned of the dangers of precipitate scientific advance unmitigated by ethics, and H.G. Wells had brought Martians to earth in *The War of the Worlds*. What was new here, however, was the scale and immediacy – mass destruction communicated by mass media. Looking back on this era from the mid-sixties, Susan Sontag in *The Imagination of Disaster*, felt these visions of disaster were neither cathartic nor useful. Too many scares induce apathy and helplessness. 'There is a sense in which all these movies are in complicity with the abhorrent. They neutralise it.'

After September 11 2001 the depiction of catastrophe onscreen became highly sensitive. Producer John Davis, whose Sylvester Stallone thriller *Daylight* (1996) had depicted explosive attacks on New York, commented, 'once it becomes reality and not fantasy, it's not entertaining'. Robert Altman alleged that popular entertainment had provided a blueprint for terrorists with every thriller that contained detailed scenes of planejacking. A sequence in which Arnold Schwarzenegger strong-armed terrorists on a plane was removed from *Collateral Damage* (2002) and the release date postponed from October 2001 to the following spring.

Avoidance was not the only option, though. *Spider-Man*, released in 2002, no longer carried the images, shot before the attacks, of the Twin Towers, but it did show violent assaults on the city at a time when audiences were reading daily of the possibility of further terrorism in the United States and Europe. *Spider-Man* was a huge box office success, the first film to take $100 million in the first weekend. There was also a sudden, surprising increase in rental demand for a 1998 film *The Siege*, a modestly successful thriller of Islamic extremist terrorism in New York. Asked to account for this renewal of interest, its writer, Lawrence Wright, wondered if the film's happy ending gave audiences a resolution they could barely hope for in real life.

Invasion of the Body Snatchers provides no such reassurance; which might account for no less than three subsequent remakes. It may indicate the richness of the metaphor; it may suggest that ambiguous endings provide an enduring challenge; whatever the cause, each version reflects something of its time.

Philip Kaufman's film (1978) takes the story to San Francisco. Interviewed by *Film Comment* at the time, he was forthright about the significance of the invasion: 'We were all asleep in a lot of ways in the fifties, living, conforming, other-directed types of lives. Maybe we woke up a little in the sixties but now we've gone back to sleep again.' This version came four years after President Nixon left office following the threat of impeachment over Watergate; the secrecy of government departments in the film plays into the cycle of paranoid conspiracy thrillers from that decade such as *The Manchurian Candidate* (1962) or *The Parallax View* (1974). In these films, shadowy organisations usually defeat lone protagonists, destroying along the way their faith in the Land of the Free.

The 1978 *Invasion of the Body Snatchers*, which stars Donald Sutherland, is also obsessed with relationships and their failure (this is the decade of Woody Allen and second-wave feminism). By 1993 Abel Ferrara's *Body Snatchers* is set after the first Gulf War in an army base where aliens have infiltrated, although no one seems that bothered (which may be a comment in itself). The 2007 *The Invasion* – with Nicole Kidman and Daniel Craig – mixes pod-people-as-pacifists urging withdrawal from Iraq with fears about the uses and effects of drugs, a confusing cocktail of metaphors and references that dissipates any sense of threat. The power of the original is that we do heed Dr Bennell. However extreme his predicament, there is something recognisable in the terror he faces and it might, just one day, in another form, strike at us, too.

1960s
....

BREAKING WITH THE PAST

F or filmgoers the sixties are not so much a revolution as an avalanche
of consequences of earlier events, both social and political. Superpower
ambition and aggression led the Cold War's leading players, the Soviet
Union and the United States, into direct confrontation over the incursion
of Communism into Cuba with the missile crisis in October 1962 – a
prospect of global annihilation that, amongst other things, gave birth to
Stanley Kubrick's *Dr Strangelove* (1964), in which the Americans launch a
first-strike nuclear attack on the Russians.

Technological developments in the space race were increasingly intertwined with the military threat. From the moment Sputnik 1 began to orbit
around the earth in 1957, casting its eye down on capitalist and communist
alike, the technological competition between Russians and Americans had
become a race for supremacy culminating in a temporary victory – the
first small (American) steps on the moon in 1969. For a while, a whole

new territory was there for the colonisation: interplanetary, even intergalactic, travel promised a solution to earth's finite resources and – perhaps, one day – man's mortality. Meanwhile, widespread jet travel was shrinking the globe itself as transatlantic satellites beamed continents into the same time zone. The 'conquest' of the moon and beyond and the increasingly unpredictable interdependence of man and machine were all prefigured in Kubrick's next vision, *2001: A Space Odyssey* (1968).

Governments moved to the left across Europe but the United States' promise of progressive leadership was truncated by the assassination of President John F. Kennedy in November 1963, an event captured on film and shown repeatedly over the years on television. Despite sixty years of emancipation, black Americans were still discriminated against; as more of them moved to the northern states and governments around the world became more active in the United Nations, the civil rights movement continued to demand change. Political upheaval came close to Hollywood in 1965 with the Watts Riots in Los Angeles in which thirty-four people died and more than a thousand were injured.

Old colonial influences – whether of slavery or occupation – were breaking down around the world. Vietnam demonstrated a prime example of Cold War territorialism: communist-backed North versus US-backed South, with techniques of warfare – underground, terrorist, nationalist – that were hard to fight in conventional ways. Gillo Pontecorvo's *The Battle of Algiers* (1966) was an historical account filmed in a documentary style of an uprising by FLN guerrillas against French rule in the casbah of the Algerian capital between 1954 and 1960. So alarmingly even-handed was its portrayal of French paratroopers and Algerian revolutionaries that, although widely praised internationally, the film was banned in France for five years. Ironically, in 2003 the Pentagon began to show the film to employees, hoping to inform them of the methods of terrorist insurgency. Why, it asked, did the French forces in the film succeed tactically but fail strategically?

The publication of Betty Friedan's *The Feminine Mystique* in 1963 raised the possibility of another insurrection – more fundamental, if less explosive – as mothers, wives and daughters began to question their deal in life. Friedan argued that, despite better education and opportunities, the insecurities of war, both real and Cold, had encouraged a retreat to highly conservative family structures. Alfred Kinsey's reports on male and female sexuality had been in circulation for a decade or so and, by the early sixties, the contraceptive pill was beginning to be available in the metropolises of the USA and Britain, although films still mostly depicted pregnancy as a pitfall of sex, rather than a choice.

Since such adult territory was completely off limits to television, the ready entertainment in the living room, films began to exploit the relatively permissive possibilities – with a mixture of salacious curiosity and fear of these voracious females. An early opportunistic example is *The Chapman Report* (1962), one of George Cukor's less successful films about women. It is an adaptation of an Irving Wallace novel inspired by Kinsey's findings, in which suburban housewives talk about their sexual experiences. Samuel Fuller, a director who never ducked controversy, took audiences inside a mental hospital in *Shock Corridor* (1963), 'a labyrinth of twisted detours that both sexes stumble along' including apparent cases of 'erotic dementia' and a stripteaser (sic) who is also, coincidentally a 'manic sensualist'. Visions of marriage become more cruelly comic – *Who's Afraid of Virginia Woolf?* (1966) and *The Graduate* (1967) – as insecure men quake before predatory hard-drinking women who demand their rights in the bedroom.

Epic struggles were also in evidence at the big American studios. As film attendances continued to decline, the palatial cinemas closed, giving way to the first multiplexes, making filmgoing another part of the shopping experience. One by one the studios merged with or were taken over by other institutions – banks, industrial conglomerates, even aviation companies. Film production increasingly fell to smaller independents, with the studios handling finance and distribution. Some American companies found it cheaper to produce abroad with Britain as the chief beneficiary. The series of Bond films that began with *Dr No* in 1962, and martial arts films from Hong Kong, were both examples of lucrative franchises that originated outside Hollywood.

Cinema's interplay with radical change on all these fronts was, as ever, oblique. Film was not apparently at the forefront of radical politics in the way that the written word was, or campaign-style folk and rock music had become. It was only towards the end of the decade that films reached for the counterculture audience: Peter Fonda's *Easy Rider* (1969), with its stoned bikers, provided an accessible focus; yet some attempts to address current issues onscreen, like Michelangelo Antonioni's *Zabriskie Point* (1970), an opaque study of student protest and sex in the California desert, didn't work – the film was a financial failure.

Mainstream entertainment seemed, if anything, more conservative. Family films became huge international business. While Audrey Hepburn stole Julie Andrews's stage role for the screen musical *My Fair Lady* (1964), Andrews, through talent and force of character, powered the musicals *Mary Poppins* (1964) and *The Sound of Music* (1965) through suffragette London and the rise of the Nazis in Austria, leaving children and their elders around the world singing.

Blockbuster historical epics became even more pumped up: in *El Cid* (1961), Moors and Castilians had to contend for screen space beside the chiselled features of Charlton Heston and the vulpine curves of Sophia Loren; and the Hollywood romantic soap opera played out between Richard Burton and the last great screen goddess, Elizabeth Taylor, dwarfed the Egypto-Roman drama of *Cleopatra* (1963).

The British director David Lean made epics of a different order. He combined the stunning visuals of designer John Box and director of photography Freddie Young with a certain cool intellectualism in *Lawrence of Arabia* (1962) and the lavish romance *Dr Zhivago* (1965) – both huge box office successes, winning multiple Oscars. Robert Bolt, who wrote the screenplays, also adapted his own 1960 play about the Tudor statesman Sir Thomas More, *A Man for All Seasons*, for the screen in 1966. The theme of all three films – the attraction and traps of power, whether imperial or totalitarian, and the risk of compromising principles – may have had personal relevance for Bolt, with his background as sometime communist and anti-nuclear protester, but they also played to the audience's wider political anxieties.

The baby-boomers were growing into teenagers and young adults with expectations of improving on the lot of their parents. Since servicemen had come back from war to go to or return to university in the 1940s, the studios had begun to notice that regular filmgoing was becoming associated with higher levels of education. The widespread consumption of television – and its increasing commercialisation – pushed certain kinds of cinema, by comparison, into a relatively 'arty' category. Nineteen-sixties college students were deemed a 'film generation' and when they went to the cinema they wanted something different from the kind of drama they might find on the small screen. Film studies departments sprouted in prestigious universities like NYU and Columbia in the USA. Children whose youthful years had been captured by parents with amateur cine-cameras began to start experimenting themselves. In the early sixties, the Kodak-UFA company launched the Teenage Film Awards. Records from their ninth annual ceremony show sixteen-year-old Ron Howard (future Oscar-winning director of *A Beautiful Mind* and *Apollo 13*) winning the second prize of $100 for a three and a half minute short of a boy visiting a western filmset, entitled *Deed of Daring-Do*, commended for its storyline and 'effective use of camera angle'.

The 8-mm cine-camera had become a domestic staple. Amateur footage gained official authority when Abraham Zapruder's film of President Kennedy's assassination in Dallas in 1963 was used as evidence in the Warren Commission's investigation. The enhanced Super-8 format was introduced in 1965; cheaper movie cameras came on to the market from Europe and brought the technology within reach of those on average or lower incomes. People became accustomed to the unmitigated image of amateur footage with its subjective sweep, mimicking the movement of the eye. The difficulty of editing meant that dawdling, informal shots were not always discarded but perused for meaning. With the rise of watching over reading or listening, individuals all over the world, in varying degrees, became observers, even snoopers. When that notion of voyeurism was taken to its artistic conclusion, with Michael Powell's portrait of a killer cameraman *Peeping Tom* (1960), it was shocking. Critics, the professional watchers, felt particularly threatened.

The emergence of the 'auteur theory' of directors with a recognisable style and themes had been first sketched out in the 1950s by French critic André Bazin in relation to directors of the 1930s and 1940s. Its application to 1960s filmmakers increased the column inches of criticism; the longer the critique, the more likely it was that the adjective 'enjoyable' took on a pejorative slant. Film could be treated as art – it need no longer be overly concerned with narrative or character. Early in the decade, in May 1960, Michelangelo Antonioni's *L'Avventura* premiered at the Cannes Film Festival. The story seems to concern a missing girl on a stark Mediterranean island. However, the young woman's lover and friend soon lose enthusiasm for the search and form a kind of attachment of their own even though all that binds them, apart from immaculate tailoring, is a profound sense of boredom with their vacuous existence. *L'Avventura* provoked an unprecedented reaction, according to a report in *Sight and Sound*, '. . . boos and jeers, yawns and laughter, such as I have never heard in a cinema. The film spectacularly exhausted the patience of this audience; and it would probably tax any audience in the world.' Penelope Houston's article continued: '*L'Avventura* sometimes seems *deliberately* monotonous, which the festival audience could not forgive.' The Cannes jury not only forgave, it awarded the film a prize – no doubt enjoying the irony of the Adventure in which Nothing Happens. This kind of stately longform cinema – whether it was judged contemplative or portentous – was dubbed Antonioni-ennui. Slower and longer films followed – some of which might well have played better in a gallery than a cinema, like Andy Warhol's eight hours and five minutes of *Empire* (1964), a silent fixed shot of the exterior of the Empire State Building. There had been documentary films about art and artists since the 1920s; now filmmakers appeared to be challenging the very medium itself. Was a silent fixed shot even a film? After a while (and you do have a fair old time), *Empire* makes you consider not so much the building and its location as the very texture and detail of the image itself.

The new lightweight film cameras – the offspring of the Arriflex hand-held devices that had been used by newsreel photographers in the Second World War – meant that film could capture the changing decade. Documentary makers attracted feature film audiences, although in smaller numbers. The Maysles brothers, Albert and David, followed the Beatles in 1964 and the Rolling Stones in 1969 on American tours, while D.A. Pennebaker captured Bob Dylan's much-derided transition from acoustic to electric music in his 1965 tour of Britain. At the end of the decade a documentary of the 1969 Woodstock festival was edited by, among others, old film school friends Martin Scorsese and Thelma Schoonmaker – the beginning of a long and brilliantly productive collaboration of director and editor.

A documentary sensibility had informed the new waves of filmmaking that swept through Europe at the beginning of the decade, starting in France with the group of intellectuals associated with the critical journal *Cahiers du Cinéma*. France itself, under the leadership of Charles de Gaulle, demonstrated a new confidence: the country's post-war recovery was well under way. The President had a vision of a new Europe that would stand apart from the opposing superpowers. Filmmakers for their part rejected the classical values of traditional cinema (*le cinéma de papa*) in favour of blatant authorship and style. The protagonists of a *Nouvelle Vague* film – whether in France or elsewhere – did not look like film heroes and heroines (although they were, to be fair, usually more than averagely good-looking). They had jobs, which audiences actually learned about onscreen. Often they had ambitions, which might or might not have any chance of success. Like the trio who make up Jean-Luc Godard's *Bande à Part* (1964), they were young, disrespectful of conventions, and hungry for novel sensations to jolt them from their boredom. The British New Wave was imbued with anger against the restrictions of austerity and the rigidity of the class system. Domestic locations that were far from glamorous, kitchens and bedsits from the North of England to the less salubrious parts of London, provided the setting for films such as *Saturday Night and Sunday Morning* (1960), *A Taste of Honey* (1961) and *This Sporting Life* (1963).

In the New Waves of the Eastern Bloc the sense of grievance was more muted, or diverted into humour and absurdity. Before the brief freedom of the Prague Spring in 1968, Czech New Wave filmmakers protested against the weight of totalitarianism on private lives with stories of amorous adventures in real working situations with non-professional actors: railway workers in Jiří Menzel's *Closely Observed Trains* (1967) or in a shoe factory in Miloš Forman's *Loves of a Blonde* (1965) – the film that inspired Ken Loach when he made his groundbreaking television drama in the UK about homelessness, *Cathy Come Home*, and then his first feature, *Poor Cow*, in 1967. A graduate of the Polish film school in Łódź, Roman Polanski's debut, *Knife in the Water* (1962), was a stylish thriller about a couple who pick up a stranger on a weekend yachting trip; the tension derives in part from the restrictions of the system under which they are all living and a sense that, even out on the water, they are all watching one another.

Many of the protagonists of Eastern European films of this period were solemn, their expressions hard to read. They stared. The act of watching was a notable feature of 1960s films. Ingmar Bergman in *Persona* (1966) showed a young woman caring for a taciturn patient in an isolated place. The two women's faces are juxtaposed, often in silence. Intercut with documentary footage of atrocities in South East Asia or Europe in the Second

World War, for some critics it hinted at cinema's impotence in the face of world events.

And men were still watching women, as they had always done, but now with the added suspicion of women's ambitions to compete at work. In 1961, Marilyn Monroe, the breathy, giggly fantasy of 1950s comedy, appeared in *The Misfits* in a role written for her by her then husband, Arthur Miller. At one level the story is an elegy for the lost muscular glory of the West, filmed in stark monochrome. Roslyn (Monroe), a recent divorcee, hooks up with a trio of washed-up cowboys (Clark Gable, Eli Wallach and Montgomery Clift) who are roping mustangs in the desert to sell for petfood. Driving together all four, they spy a mare and foal and suddenly stop. Gable lassos the mare's back legs, Wallach slips a noose around her neck and they pull apart to bring the horse down on the sand while the distressed foal circles, darting in to sniff at its mother's body. The tableau – the prone body with the lines pulling away diagonally, a bleak contrast of dark figures on pale sand – horrifies Roslyn. She throws up her head and turns, running away into the flat, white landscape. 'Killers!' screams Roslyn. 'Killers! Murderers! Liars!' The distant voice is harsh and throaty, the Monroe whisper swept away by the primal energy of her Method acting studies with Lee Strasberg. 'You're only happy when you can see something die!' The little figure in the desert stands with her legs slightly bent, the better to deliver her great pain, but her stance recalls the mare and the composition of the shot seems to draw two lines to the outside of the frame, as Wallach and Gable did with the ropes around the horse. The men watch her – Clift drops his eyes but Gable and Wallach squint steadily. The audience watches, too. 'She's crazy,' spits Wallach, finally.

This being a script by Arthur Miller, the men are at least as pathetic and pitiable as Roslyn and yet there is something particularly disturbing about this sequence of shots. Director John Huston, quoted by Anthony Summers in his biography of Monroe, *Goddess*, said she was in effect playing herself. 'She had no techniques. It was all the truth. It was only Marilyn.'

Yet the weight of humanity in this particular landscape is all on the side of the flawed men; the blonde figure in the centre of that isolated shot in the desert is something tiny, tragic . . . and alien.

The audience watched the men watch the woman. In cinema that was nothing new, but when a director made a dark fable of that relationship, it was denounced as an obscenity.

. . . .

PEEPING TOM (1960)

Director: Michael Powell
Cast: Carl Boehm, Anna Massey, Maxine Audley
Colour

At the beginning of the decade, Britain produced one of the most disturbing portraits of a watcher, a deadly voyeur – Mark Lewis (Carl Boehm), the personable young blond photographer who is the central figure of Michael Powell's film *Peeping Tom*. Lewis has every filmlover's dream job: by day he works on colourful sets where he dreams of making features himself. By night he makes extra money as a photographer in Soho, taking seedy 'glamour' pictures of models, but his real enthusiasm is reserved for nocturnal prowling of a homicidal kind, his weapon a nightmarish modification of the photographer's tripod. The film opens with a gruesome sequence in which he stalks a prostitute down a shadowy Soho street, filming her. Puzzled but obliging, she takes him upstairs. As she prepares for work, he advances on her with the phallic spike of his tripod and fatally pierces her while simultaneously capturing on film her expression at the point of death.

Lewis is a quiet, even reticent, character – the kind of undervalued, thoughtful type, with a burgeoning romantic interest in a nice, intelligent, quietly spoken girl, whom films often reveal as an unlikely hero. (And, of course, the kind of observant, clever chap that film critics might identify with, of which more later.) He is only active, or, rather, aroused, when looking through a viewfinder or at a screen. He creates a cycle of filming a death and then replaying it in the privacy of his own rooms in a respectable house – the second act providing even more excitement than the first. When he is befriended by an unwitting young neighbour, Helen (Anna Massey, whose huge eyes fail to register the danger until almost too late), he shows her another kind of home movie featuring himself as a child, the subject of bizarre psychological experiments by his father.

By 1960, Michael Powell had directed some forty films, among them, in partnership with producer Emeric Pressburger, some of the masterpieces of the 1940s and 1950s. Yet for all that body of work, the scandal and horrified reaction to this film would in effect end his career. Alexander Walker, the youngest of the critics to loathe *Peeping Tom* on its release, described it as 'a vicious work, made in a moral vacuum, unrelated to any wider world outside its own far-too-charming killer's maniacal obsession'. Others found it the 'sickest and filthiest film I remember seeing' (*Spectator*) or 'wholly evil' (*Daily Worker*). What seemed to offend was the sense of identification: *Peeping Tom* keeps the audience, like the psychopath Lewis, focused on the young women who may become his victims. Alexander Walker found precisely this suggestion uncomfortable: 'Compounding this offensiveness was the subjective camerawork – the murders seen through the killer's viewfinder – which made us critics feel accomplices to the crimes. In short, we felt we were being indicted as accessories to murder, however unwilling we were.'

Lewis suffers from scopophilia, literally the 'love of looking', which broadly, although not exactly, conforms to a kind of voyeurism. Freud first referred to it in 1905 in *Three Essays on the Theory of Sexuality*, stating that it becomes a perversion 'if it is restricted exclusively to the genitals or . . . if it is connected with the overriding of disgust . . . or if instead of being preparatory to the normal sexual aim, it supplants it'. The idea that filmgoers might also be voyeurs was not entirely new. Buñuel's *Un Chien Andalou* had made audiences flinch by showing a knife slicing an eyeball, the very organ they were employing to view. The French director François Truffaut would later discuss the idea of mass voyeurism in a discussion with Alfred Hitchcock about *Rear Window* in which the audience identifies with James Stewart as he watches through binoculars the comings and goings in the apartments opposite.

Early concerns about filmgoing were restricted to fears of inflammation whether practical – nitrate film had a tendency to catch fire – or sensual – salacious material onscreen might incite young people in particular to emulate onscreen behaviour, or worse. The longer-term psychological effect of voyeurism itself, however, despite its early identification by Freud, only became a hot topic with psychiatrists in the 1950s.

The voyeur, though, had been lurking onscreen from the very beginning in various guises – all those private investigators and harried professors, inquisitive tourists, probing doctors and less respectable types right back to cinema's earliest archetypes. According to Professor Ian Christie, author of *The Last Machine*, 'one way to "frame" the new moving pictures was to include a proxy viewer in the picture. And if the subject was one likely to cause embarrassment, then the substitute viewer could take the blame.' In Edison's 1901 short *Trapeze Disrobing Act*, a girl on a swing, encouraged enthusiastically by two old gentlemen, removes some garments, performs some acrobatics, and takes off even more clothes until she's down to her underwear. From Edison to Brian de Palma, this is the pleasure principle at the heart of Peeping Tom films: the audience can experience the same spectacle as the onscreen voyeur, while remaining at a safe moral distance as the voyeur's voyeur. The questionable ethics of the audience's position, the contradictory impulses – at once censorious and vicarious – seem to have been understood by early filmmakers; as Christie observes 'how else to explain the little dramas of punishment or frustration that are acted out in so many very early films, as Peeping Toms hiding behind screens and using telescopes are discovered by their indignant victims?' In other words, since the audience knows it is wrong to watch, voyeurs in film must get their comeuppance: early examples include *Peeping Tom in the Dressing Room* (1905), in which a voyeur is discovered by chorus girls who hit him with powder puffs, and *The Inquisitive Boots*, in which a shoeshine boy at a hotel peers through keyholes until he gets one in the eye from a peeved guest. This history of crime and punishment extends to Norman Bates peering through the spyhole behind the picture on the flimsy hotel room wall in *Psycho* and to Mark Lewis in *Peeping Tom*.

This relationship is necessarily frustrating. In an early case study of voyeurism, written between the wars, the psychoanalyst Otto Fenichel described a middle-aged Peeping Tom who rented a room in a bordello to spy on activities taking place next door, but would cry every time as he watched, because, according to the analyst, he wanted the woman to leave her client and comfort him instead. Film fans might be seen to fit this pattern, yearning for intimacy with distant idols.

Since the 1960s was also the decade when censorship laws were finally relaxed, making possible not only the sensation of *Peeping Tom* possible but some nudity in mainstream films, the filmgoer could more easily be accused of voyeurism. An essay from 1975 by the film critic Laura Mulvey, 'Visual Pleasure and Narrative Cinema', identified a wider, more subtle practice, however, that recurred through the history of film. In the light of psychoanalysis, Mulvey argued that classical cinema cast women as objects for men to gaze at. Conventional narrative might be a form of sadism, bending characters to its will, with audiences identifying mainly with the male protagonist as he represents an idealised self. If the male protagonist becomes the audience's avatar, other characters are only ever seen from his perspective; women are often introduced by body parts, a close-up of their legs, a sultry mouth and so on. In Mulvey's words, 'the determining male gaze projects its fantasy onto the female figure, which is styled accordingly'.

Put simply, it is Humphrey Bogart's world and Lauren Bacall is a visitor to it. As identification with the female character is impossible, the cinema of classic Hollywood offers no real pleasures for the female audience. Mulvey signed off her essay with the line: 'women, whose image has been continually stolen and used for this end, cannot view the decline of the traditional film form with anything much more than sentimental regret'. Once extremely fashionable among academics, Mulvey's theory has since been debunked for failing to recognise that many women enjoy the classic Hollywood form, or that audiences have some powers of independent appraisal. The woman can yet subvert the male hero: Glen Ford's plodding detective in *The Big Heat* is no competition onscreen for Gloria Grahame's sparky bad girl.

Still, however mysterious and autonomous their characters may seem, it is not difficult to apply the idea to Hitchcock's women as we gaze on Janet Leigh in the shower in *Psycho*, or Tippi Hedren with seagulls in her hair in *The Birds*, or even the range of large-eyed girls left variously abandoned, pregnant or broke by the sexual revolution in 1960s films. This element of watching women in physical or emotional disarray is one of the awkward realities of post-war cinema (although there were also a fair number of women strapped to railway lines, metaphorically or otherwise, before that). To be so punished, women must have seemed very dangerous indeed.

In *Peeping Tom*, the women – whether prostitute or well-spoken studio stand-in – all lit by a dangerously red light, are stabbed, bundled into trunks and suffer the further indignity of having their final moments replayed in Mark Lewis's compulsive, masturbatory screening of his own snuff movies. Yet, oddly, the most sickening sequence (and one that particularly outraged critics because of the role of real father and son) was deemed to be the one in which the child Mark, played by Columba Powell, is seen in an old black and white home movie with his father, played by his real father – the director himself. The child gazes from the top of a wall at an embracing couple. Then he is asleep in bed. His father shines a light on his eyes. Suddenly a lizard is dropped onto the bed, terrifying the child, part of his father's psychological inquiries into fear and the nervous system. Mark is then seen approaching another bed in which his mother lies dead. And so on, through a nightmarishly kaleidoscoped childhood of abandonment and abuse until he is alone in the frame with the camera his father left him as he departed on honeymoon with his new wife. This torture, captured on film, is at the heart of Mark's own pathology – a life that can only be lived through another medium.

Mark watches the footage of his own childhood, searching for meaning, although, typically, he films Helen's response to the home movies, too. In Antonioni's *Blow Up* (1966), another photographer, another blond blue-eyed Londoner with an unsettling stare, this time played by David Hemmings, also tries to make sense of photographic images. Although *Blow Up* was famous for its definitive portrait of 'swinging London' and glimpses of frontal nudity, it is far more a meditation on the act of looking and the truisms that seeing is believing and the camera never lies. In the key central scene, convinced that he has not so much witnessed a murder as caught it incidentally on camera, the photographer investigates his evidence with the essential tool of the classic detective – a magnifying glass. However, by enlarging the image, the proof he was seeking disintegrates into a grainy blur, and what seemed a simple matter of magnification and scrutiny gradually becomes a question of interpretation. In his lurid home movies, Mark Lewis in *Peeping Tom* never reaches quite that point of illumination – the sensation of watching is too engrossing.

In 1978 Martin Scorsese helped to finance a wider release of *Peeping Tom*. Talking to Ian Christie for the book *Scorsese on Scorsese*, he compared the film to Fellini's fantasy on being director, *8½*, made in 1963, three years later: 'I have always felt that *Peeping Tom* and *8½* say everything that can be said about film-making, about the process of dealing with film, the objectivity and subjectivity of it and the confusion between the two. *8½* captures the glamour and enjoyment of film-making, while *Peeping Tom* shows the aggression of it, how the camera violates.'

The man with the movie camera, once a symbol of the avant-garde, was, by the 1960s, a recognisable film protagonist. He was also probably your dad in the garden at home, recording family history. The watchers and recorders turn up increasingly onscreen from now on, most strikingly in James Spader's character in *sex, lies and videotape* (1989), a more benign, passive descendant of Mark Lewis, whose libido appears to reside within his telephoto lens, a man potent only when watching the screen. Yet he has a kind of romanticism, too. The screen voyeurs are now characters who deserve understanding rather than chastisement. We know them. Like us, they grew up watching sensational events onscreen. What could you expect?

· ·

BANDE À PART (1964)

Director: Jean-Luc Godard
Cast: Anna Karina, Claude Brasseur, Sami Frey
Black and white

Franz and Artur are planning a robbery. They have the attitude – Artur (Claude Brasseur) is muscular and quiet while Franz (Sami Frey) is sharp-suited and quick-witted. They have a target – a house where an apparently wealthy man, Mr Stoltz, allegedly keeps a stash of cash. And they have an accomplice, the lovely Odile (Anna Karina), who lives with her aunt in the house. Franz and Artur meet Odile in an English-language class where the teacher is so carried away with her own reading of *Romeo and Juliet* that all manner of distractions take place. They are outsiders, a little group 'à Part'.

The trio, in various combinations of two and threes, are usually on the move, driving or cycling around Joinville, a suburb of Paris, occasionally venturing into the centre. They flirt with each other and with their criminal plans. They get bored. They move on to waste time somewhere else. Whatever they do, they mostly do it outside or on location in houses or cafés. People walk by, oblivious to the action.

Jean-Luc Godard's *Bande à Part* is, on the face of it, the breeziest and most carefree of the French *Nouvelle Vague* films, as demonstrated by Godard, Jacques Rivette, François Truffaut, Eric Rohmer, Claude Chabrol and the rest, the group of critics-turned-directors who formed a critical mass around the magazine *Cahiers du Cinéma*. The *Nouvelle Vague* shrugs off the formality of the old school *cinéma de papa*, with its traditional values of production, characterisation and storytelling, often based on conventional literary adaptations. Like Godard's earlier *A Bout de Souffle* (1960), it opts instead for 'essential' cinema – at once, back to basics and wildly referential to American films, particularly the gangster genre.

Chabrol's *Le Beau Serge* (1958), about a man who returns to his village in rural France, and Truffaut's childhood memoir *Les Quatre Cent Coups* (1959) were the first discernible ripples of the wave – both stories of everyday life shot on location, with some non-professional actors, a legacy of Italian neo-realism and post-war documentary films in general. Truffaut's film was immediately popular outside France, too. But Godard's *A Bout de Souffle* was the truly galvanising jolt, not just to filmmakers but to the image of France itself. If Paris was already familiar as a Hollywood star, from 1950s musicals, audiences could now see her stripped of her make-up and lying on an unmade bed, like Jean Seberg – another kind of American in Paris altogether – sauntering through the traffic on the Champs Elysées selling the *Herald Tribune*. Here was Paris not as an elegant lady but a delinquent, in debt to America still (look at those plots, those gangsters, those guns) but shrugging and rebelling in her own way.

Artur and Franz in *Bande à Part* are small time: they do not even live in Paris. Godard described the film as a 'suburban Western'; its plot, such as it is, is loosely based on an American pulp novel, *Fool's Gold*, about a 'young punk's caper'. In Godard's film the boys mime cowboy shootouts and jump into their convertible – except it is not so much a sleek American roadster as a shabby European Simca, with dubious suspension. They discuss the robbery but never quite get to the details. Odile herself is even vaguer, almost distressingly so. It is all one big shrug – a wry, subversive joke.

The key to this freewheeling approach was the hand-held camera – in *Bande à Part* the camera travels in the open-top car with Franz, Artur and Odile, bouncing along the road. Like *A Bout de Souffle*, Truffaut's *Jules et Jim* and other key works of the *Nouvelle Vague*, *Bande à Part* was shot by former war photographer Raoul Coutard who had spent eleven years in Indo-China. He only began to shoot moving pictures in 1956; a man who was accustomed to challenge and risk-taking, he did not bother to consult with traditional cinematographers, who were in any case dismissive of his efforts. Godard wanted him to shoot 'reportage' style from the shoulder with no artificial lighting. There was no script, or at least only scraps of dialogue on paper that Godard brought along each morning. The protagonists were not 'stars' requiring favoured lighting or romanticised or heroic settings.

Getting sound in sync with the lightweight camera was sometimes a problem. The playful juxtaposition of effects with image that is so characteristic of the picture, the use of music along with Godard's own voiceover and the sudden withdrawal of sound altogether – all of this was stylistic, certainly, but also a necessary disguise for the unevenness of the recording. The less sophisticated production values and black and white photography, the concentration on situation and the expressiveness of faces (in particular the way the camera lingers on the childlike beauty of Anna Karina, Godard's wife and muse at the time) rather than elaborate plot or elegant dialogue all recall silent film. This attempt to recapture film's early freshness and excitement is also a feature of Richard Lester's work in Britain around the same time, among them the Beatles' feature *A Hard Day's Night* (1964) and *The Knack* (1965).

These films are apparently spontaneous – in Lester's film, the Beatles run suddenly into a field, a moment of youthful freedom sometimes credited with germinating the idea for all the outdoor festivals of music and love that would follow. In *Bande à Part* there is a famous, energetic – literally breathless – sequence in which Franz, Artur and Odile try to break the speed record for running through the Louvre galleries. ('An American had done the Louvre in 9 minutes, 45 seconds,' says Godard's voiceover, 'they decided to do better.') The act breaks conventions and rules, a brilliantly exhilarating dash as the trio skid across the wooden and stone floors. (Martin Creed's art installation with runners in the Duveen Galleries of Tate Britain in 2008 nodded to it.) The trio may be planning a robbery but the film itself can be read as a smash and grab raid on established culture, as Godard and co. snatch what they want from papa's cinema, stamping on the rest as they run off.

Yet, for all its celebration of youth and playfulness, *Bande à Part* was at another level elitist. The *Nouvelle Vague* arose from an intellectual movement among the young critics encouraged by André Bazin. Raoul Coutard described his *Cahiers du Cinéma* colleagues as a mafia: if you were not affiliated to them, then your film could not be described as *Nouvelle Vague*. Despite its apparently popular style, it was hardly a cinema for the people, more one for cinephiles, people who understood how and why conventions were being overturned.

The people, in fact, were mainly going to see more conventional films – particularly comedies like the record-setting *La Grande Vadrouille* (1966) about a British airman making his way through Nazi-occupied France, starring popular comedians Bourvil and Louis de Funes. For thirty years, this strangely entrancing piece of nonsense was the highest grossing film in France, selling seventeen million tickets.

By pointing out the conventions of cinema and then poking fun at them, Godard was shocking audiences out of their unquestioning acceptance of the narratives and characters they saw on screen. In perhaps the most famous scene, the trio are sitting at a café table. If you can't say anything clever, observes Franz, maybe we should have a minute's silence, a real minute lasts an eternity. OK, says Odile . . . one, two, three – then Godard sucks the sound right out of the track. Sixty seconds of 'dead' silence does indeed sound never-ending. The trio fidget and exchange glances: Franz lasts barely thirty seconds before leaving the table. When they get up to perform a little line dance, Godard observes over the music, 'Parenthetically, now's the time to describe the characters' feelings . . .' and goes on to list them, absurdly.

Bande à Part was made a couple of years before Godard started making more overtly political films – the protesting students in *La Chinoise* (1967) anticipate the *événéments* of May 1968, for example – culminating in a complete deconstruction of film narrative in *Week-end* (1967) in which his Marxist disgust at bourgeois decadence results in a tailgating car crash of epic proportions. 'End of Cinema', he wrote on the closing credits. In Britain, Lindsay Anderson's *If . . .* (1968) advocated revolt within the class system as public schoolboys took up arms against their oppressors. British films, though, tended generally to be more concerned with social conditions – unmarried pregnancy still casting a shadow of stigma from *A Taste of Honey* to *Alfie*.

The Greco-French filmmaker Costa-Gavras, whose 1969 thriller *Z* was a critique of the Regime of the Colonels in Greece, maintained that all films are political, whether consciously or not, since they necessarily express an ideological viewpoint with every choice made by the director, writer, actors and so on. His later films also blended commercial entertainment with plots close to factual events – concerning the right-wing regime and the 'disappeared' in Chile in *Missing* (1982) for example. Yet he was cautious about the efficacy of politically committed filmmaking: 'I don't think that when an audience comes out of a theatre, they will have changed completely, but if at least they ask themselves one question then I think that's enough.'

Godard's sly consciousness-raising in an 'entertainment' like *Bande à*

Part was so oblique that it probably only really resonated with those whose consciousness was all but perpendicular already. Fifty years on, *A Bout de Souffle*, *Vivre Sa Vie* and *Bande à Part* among other early Godard films are celebrated primarily for their youthful energy and their cool. They are in fact cooler than cool, downright chilly at times – intellectual films rather than emotional ones where the controlling eye and hand of the director are always in evidence.

The tone of the film may be ostensibly carefree but the circumstances of its making were probably not. According to Colin MacCabe's biography of Godard, filming began just three days after Anna Karina was discharged from a mental hospital to which Godard had committed her after her third suicide attempt. The next year she and Godard were divorced. The three characters in *Bande à Part,* Odile, Franz and Artur, do not develop over the course of the picture; they are pawns in Godard's game.

Yet what makes the film memorable is something unconnected with intellect – the body language, the glances and the barely scripted interchanges between the young actors. They seem in certain, brief sequences to steal back their moment. So what you remember is Odile cycling through the traffic in a sunlit street, wobbling slightly as she manoeuvres across the vans and cars, or the way she reaches for the hands of the two boys as they run down a wide flight of stairs and off between the classical statues in the Louvre, or the absorption in all three faces as they concentrate on getting the steps right in 'The Madison' (which is not really a Madison at all but some quirky little dance of their own concoction). Their lips may move slightly with the counts or there might be a tiny smile of triumph when one of them manages a turn dead on the beat. When Artur and Franz peel off one by one, Odile continues dancing until she notices how exposed she is alone and smiles like a small child.

The next sequence shows Odile and Arthur descending like mythical innocents 'to the centre of the earth' into the Metro. She sits, he stands closely over her. There is some dialogue about the meaninglessness of marriage but that hardly registers. Whatever is being said about bourgeois possession is soon forgotten; what persists in the memory is the way he strokes her cheek or she leans in briefly to his chest for some unspecified reassurance. Many directors who later admired Godard – Quentin Tarantino among them – strove to emulate his 'cool'. Some managed in impressive style but few, if any, allowed space for the erratic flashes of tenderness that keep *Bande à Part* forever youthful.

2001: A SPACE ODYSSEY (1968)

Director: Stanley Kubrick
Cast: Keir Dullea, Gary Lockwood
Colour

It begins in darkness, nearly three minutes of night, accompanied only by the eerie, foreboding, apparently themeless music of György Ligeti. The strings die away for a brief appearance of the studio logo. Then, a trio of ascending notes from Richard Strauss's *Also Sprach Zaruthustra* and the first image, the moon, then the earth and, rising beyond them, the sun. As the moon drops from sight . . . *A Stanley Kubrick Production* . . . as the sun rises into full view . . . *2001: A Space Odyssey*.

The full version of *2001* has an audacious and grandiose opening. There is no specially composed theme of the conventional Hollywood kind. Director Stanley Kubrick used found classical music and employed it as a prelude to any action, like the overture to a grand opera. As he later remarked, 'I intended the film to be an intensely subjective experience that reaches the viewer at an inner level of consciousness, just as music does.' It was a radical decision: he had previously commissioned an original score from Alex North but eventually he became deeply attached to the temporary track of classical music he had used while filming and editing. Directors had often used classical music before but Kubrick's precise placing of Strauss, Ligeti and Khachaturian was different: it did not reinforce or introduce themes or narrative. Rather, as musicologist Irena Paulus pointed out in a paper published in 2009, he let the music *per se* work on the audience, at that 'inner level of consciousness'. He disturbs us and then leaves us to work out what it means.

2001 is a series of acts, each one a meditation on evolution. It begins with 'The Dawn of Man' among apes on a plain. A mysterious black mono-lith appears; the apes learn to employ bones as tools and weapons. Many thousands of years later, another monolith, this time on the moon, is discovered by space scientists. Not long afterwards, two astronauts are travelling with a supercomputer, HAL, on a secret mission to Jupiter. HAL's artificial intelligence proves to be more than passive and a struggle of sorts ensues. The final act takes one of the astronauts 'Beyond the Infinite'.

2001 was Kubrick's contribution to science fiction (as opposed to the classical epic *Spartacus*, the costume drama *Barry Lyndon* or the dozen other genre-testing films in the Kubrick oeuvre). It was partly based on a number of Arthur C. Clarke stories, particularly *The Sentinel* from 1951, which had in turn been influenced by Nietzsche's fictional account of Zoroaster, in which the Persian philosopher finds a strange and massive stone on his journey towards evolution from human to superman. Ideas of eternal recurrence, a universe in constant renaissance and the absence, or even death, of God are in the Nietzschean soup, too.

Kubrick, however, was primarily in the business of making a mind-expanding film. He employed an arsenal of techniques as dazzling as the light show which assaults the astronaut Dr David Bowman (Keir Dullea) as he hurtles through space in the famous Stargate sequence.

So the film begins with a complex appeal to both eye and ear. Rather than nudge the narrative or flesh out individual characters, music in *2001* enriches, questions or gives nuance to the situation. Certain compositions are associated with passages in the film – Ligeti with the great black stone monolith; a Strauss waltz with the movement of machinery through space – but the overall ambition of the music is broader and more abstract.

The choice of nineteenth- and twentieth-century music was daring. Kubrick had rejected the modernist electronic option, wisely surmising that nothing ages faster than the 'futuristic'. The great chords of *Zarathustra* accompany the ape's discovery of the use of a bone as a tool and, in time, a weapon. When he has first murdered another of his kind, the ape stands in the red-gold plain and throws the bone up in the air. Kubrick cuts suddenly from the bone falling against the azure sky to a satellite gyrating gracefully down in orbit against the indigo of deep space and shifts us immediately from the pre-history past, before what we can remember, to the supposed future, beyond what we can know. As the satellite glides, another three ascending notes begin Strauss's *Blue Danube Waltz* – and we are carried with it.

Kubrick also makes impressive use of absence – whether silence or the lack of movement. This is particularly unnerving in the middle sections where man and machine, astronaut and technology co-exist closely, so closely you might think one were evolving into the other. On the mission to Jupiter the astronauts are not loquacious: their conversations are often brief and formulaic, particularly in the exchanges with their supercomputer HAL. This dialogue is frequently delivered in wide-framed static shots, which make it seem even less animated and personal. The most dramatic moments tend to occur in silence, in a kind of dislocation, sometimes literally on the other side of the glass.

Meanwhile, the ambient sounds on the spaceship contribute: the hum of airconditioning, the vacuum of a decompression chamber or breathing inside a spacesuit can all induce a sense of strangeness, particularly once astronauts and computer begin to contemplate eliminating one another. The composer and academic Michel Chion has analysed the way Bowman's breathing within his helmet while he removes the memory cells from HAL is transferred in the editing to the disembodied voice of the failing computer as he comments on his own degradation ('Dave, my mind is going . . . I can feel it . . . There is no question about it. I can feel it . . . I am afraid . . . Good afternoon, gentlemen . . . I am a HAL 9000 computer . . .') Bowman, who seems by this point a machine by comparison, continues with his destruction. The ambient noises of the craft hiss louder before HAL grinds to a halt during a growling rendition of his first simulated voice memory, the children's song 'Daisy, Daisy'. It is an extraordinarily compacted and intense evocation of mortality.

2001 is a science fiction film like no other – it incorporates all the fears of dehumanisation that progress can bring as well as its promise; it depicts the unholy trinity of machine, human and superhuman that goes beyond earlier films from *Metropolis* to *Things to Come* and anticipates a new aesthetic of the imagined 'not-present' (i.e. not specifically future or past) such as Andrei Tarkovsky's *Solaris* (1972).

I first saw *2001* when I was ten. I was in awe at the size of the plain inhabited by the apes, losing all sense of scale when the screen opened up still further into immense velvety space. I was terrified by the speed and violence of the Stargate sequence and the monolith was suspended above my bed in nightmares for months. What was it? A gravestone? An altar? It was clearly powerful yet unknowable – encompassing both mortality and eternity. Could there be God in film?

My experience was neither unique nor precocious. An online archive, The Kubrick Site, has testimonies from people deeply influenced by the film when young and who felt themselves irreversibly changed by it. If they saw *2001* at the time of release, they mostly experienced the 'wraparound' Cinerama screen; one contributor, Geoffrey Alexander, recalled noting at the age of nine, 'a reality (or a depiction of one) bigger, deeper and broader than any I had ever seen, especially when looking at the "adult" world'. Randy Walters remembered 'the first intimation my thirteen-year-old brain had that "non-rational" forms of consciousness and communication were possible'. Seven-year-old Tom Stern, who later became a director, 'came out of the theatre in a heady euphoria, feeling as if I'd just been let in on the great cosmic mysteries of all eternity'. Geoffrey Alexander concluded that *2001* came at a particular time when images of space were still limited. Onscreen was a world unlike anything anyone had ever seen – young people, with fewer preconceptions, were particularly open to its mythical and metaphorical implications. So, in a decade when youth became a desirable state, this was a film about the greatest adolescence of all.

Decades after the film's release I met some of the actor-dancers who had been in those ape suits, including Daniel Richter, who played the lead femur-wielding Moonwatcher. Richter subsequently became friends with John Lennon, who was evangelical about the film, stating that it should be shown round the clock in a specially designed temple.

In his book about the making of the film, Jerome Agel cites a little boy who jumped up at a screening during the Stargate sequence and yelled at the screen, 'This is God! This is God!' before being dragged out. Asked at the time about any religious or metaphysical significance by *Playboy* magazine (in itself a mind-bending idea) Kubrick, ever the rationalist, replied, 'I will say that the God concept is at the heart of *2001*, but not any traditional, anthropomorphic image of God'. Kubrick went on to explain that the god he was interested in was grounded in science rather than belief.

The effects of the Stargate sequence also have a materialist basis. As Bowman is swept through the constellations, beyond time, colours flash at him from an axis that is at first vertical, as if he were sliding between cosmic lift doors, and then horizontal, as though he were bound for an infinite horizon, which he is. 'I tried to create a visual experience, one that bypasses verbalized pigeonholing and directly penetrates the unconscious with an emotional and philosophical content,' said Kubrick. To that end he flings purples and pinks, red, orange and blue towards his spaceman – and his audience. Bowman, in the first of a series of reaction shots, squints against this visual assault. An onslaught of orange shards again bombard us, followed by a burning white before several almost subliminal horrific stills – Bowman apparently unconscious in a green light, his mouth open in a terrible grimace; his eye in reversed colour, blue and ochre yellow. Then the oncoming landscape changes: the galaxy itself becomes an iris, gaseous explosions form something that might be an amniotic sac and in time a recognisably organic landscape unfolds . . .

With the Stargate sequence Kubrick wanted the audience to experience exactly what Bowman is going through. And he succeeded in ways that he was unlikely to have anticipated, with the light show becoming essential viewing for a particular section of the audience. Writing in *American Cinematographer* at the time, the effects maestro Douglas Trumbull observed: 'we all joked that *2001* would probably attract a great number of "Hippies" out to get the trip of their lives. It seems now that what was once a joke is fast becoming reality, and as of this writing, I understand that each showing draws an increasing number of these people, who would probably prefer to just see the last two reels over and over again.'

You hardly need LSD to experience the trip of colour, however. Much of *Peeping Tom*'s energy and danger comes from the film being drenched in a dangerous red, the colour of Soho sex clubs, the lamps in a photographer's darkroom . . . and blood. The films of Michael Powell and Emeric Pressburger had long played on the powerful synaesthesic effect of certain combinations of colour. In *The Red Shoes* (1947), the doomed ballerina's scarlet slippers and her red hair are often set against an aqueous blue, echoed by the contrast of red-rimmed eyes set in pale panstick stage make-up – these visual pairings heighten the sense of hysteria. Colour alone can make you feel queasy. *Black Narcissus* (1948) employs Technicolor in a highly theatrical evocation of a mountain-top convent in the Himalayas ('something in the atmosphere makes everything seem exaggerated', observes one character, in what has to be one of cinema's great understatements). Crazy Sister Ruth, renouncing the veil for a claret-red dress, sits with pale blue moonlight filtered through shutters on the wall behind her and drags scarlet lipstick over her mouth. Like these combinations, the Stargate sequence provokes a physical reaction which simulates Bowman's own journey through space and time. But for what? At the very least, it induces a sensory overload after which, stunned, the viewer is receptive to the final section of the film.

Whatever epiphany younger members of *2001*'s early audience may have had, Kubrick was clear he had no conventional notion of a deity. Others have found film a way to a genuinely religious experience. Before writing *Taxi Driver* and *Raging Bull*, Paul Schrader was a critic; his 1972 book *Transcendental Style in Film* opens with the line 'In recent years, film has developed a transcendent style, a style which has been used by various artists in diverse cultures to express the Holy.' More widely, 'transcendental style, like any transcendental art, strives toward the ineffable and invisible'. Schrader was raised a Calvinist but by the time he came to write this he was, as he explained to Kevin Jackson, a believer in 'spirituality, not any sectarian notion of God', thereby placing himself in a significant category of filmmakers who had lost a once strongly held faith. Schrader had been deeply influenced by the architect Charles Eames who had demonstrated to him that an idea could be an image or an object just as easily as a sequence of words. His study of transcendental style was based on three directors – Ozu, Bresson and Dreyer; their austerity seemed to Schrader to reach beyond the material world. By denying sensual awareness with its 'easy and exploitative identifications' the viewer may be forced into a moment of revelation.

If you follow this argument, films hoping to conjure this transcendental expression should not be cluttered with effects, stylish camerawork, mannered acting or flashy editing. Yet Schrader also admired *2001*, in which Kubrick employed all manner of effects – possibly because Kubrick was treating science, the astrophysics of time and space, like a myth or, indeed, a holy truth. As Schrader said, 'Transcendental style can take a viewer through the trials of experience to the expression of the Transcendent: it can return him to experience from a calm region untouched by the vagaries of emotion or personality. Transcendental style can bring us nearer to that silence, that invisible image, in which the parallel lines of religion and art meet and interpenetrate.'

The key, maybe, is the material we add ourselves. The films of Andrei Tarkovsky and his fellow Russian Aleksander Sokurov, for example, are not necessarily pared down; they may be visually rich or emotionally intense rather than austere. Yet they do not rush. 'For the first time in the history of arts, in the history of culture, man found the means to take an impression of time,' wrote Tarkovsky, in his book *Sculpting in Time*, published just before his death in 1986. This sense of time stretching out (if the viewer can bear it) makes us feel that we live in the picture and in that suspension our personal experience begins to interact with the director's creation.

Sokurov's *Russian Ark* (2002) is a film that at once compresses history and delivers it in real time, in a real place – a single Steadicam shot that lasts over an hour and a half, travelling through thirty-three rooms of the St Petersburg Hermitage museum, formerly the Winter Palace, residence of the tsars. Commentary comes from an unseen, unnamed narrator (in fact, it is the director's voice) – a nineteenth-century visitor to the court and the camera is his point of view. Hundreds of costumed actors play out tiny, intimate moments from an era that spans, although not in chronological order, Catherine the Great, the siege of Leningrad and the eve of the 1917 revolution. The camera appears to wander among them, eavesdropping. Sometimes, this being 'as live', there are barely perceptible gaucheries which give the film a naturalism despite the beauty and formality of its setting. It is real time and compressed time all at once.

Tarkovsky did not believe audiences went to see films for entertainment or drug-like escape. 'I think what a person normally goes to the cinema for is its time . . . for cinema, like no other arts, widens, enhances and concentrates a person's experience – and not only enhances it, but makes it longer, significantly longer.' Too long in some cases, however, although a lack of comprehension, like the overhearing of the conversations in *Russian Ark*, forces viewers to supply their own imaginative material. It may not be a coincidence that many of the films deemed by European critics to have this quality of transcendence are not in languages commonly spoken on the continent.

The Iranian director Abbas Kiarostami, whose films are praised as being transcendental, won the Palme d'Or at Cannes for *Taste of Cherry* (1997), a film about a man who drives around searching for someone to fill in his grave if he succeeds in committing suicide. Like many of Kiarostami's films, there is a great deal of watching (both by the audience and the protagonist – we watch him watching someone or something else) without it always being clear what is happening. Things happen off camera, conversations cannot be heard and so on. Yet, as with the best of such work, after a while something does happen, a shift in perception, a realisation that while you thought you were following one road, you have suddenly found yourself in another place entirely.

Like those odd 3-D puzzles that suddenly reveal a deep-focus dinosaur in a field of flowers, or an Islamic pattern that draws you into contemplation, a chant in meditation or the repetition of a prayer, film can provide the pattern which reveals more than its constituent parts. Kiarostami is also a poet: he believes poems do not tell a story but conjure a series of images. If they click with something in your own memory, if you have the code, as it were – then you have access to the mystery. Film, like poetry, benefits from a little shortfall in understanding, an unfinished quality to reach something like the warp-drive of science fiction, the transcendental shift.

1970s
. . . .

JUST WHEN YOU THOUGHT IT WAS SAFE . . .

I
n 1970 the United States began secret negotiations with its ideological
and physical adversaries the North Vietnamese for withdrawal from
South Vietnam, where the first US military 'advisers' had arrived in
1950. At the same time, they increased hostilities and the war extended to
Cambodia, to the distress of many Americans and American allies.
Hollywood icon Henry Fonda's actress daughter, Jane, was dubbed 'Hanoi
Jane' for her visit in 1972 to North Vietnam. By the time a ceasefire was
endorsed in January 1973, an estimated three million Indo-Chinese (and
57,000 US servicemen) had died as a result of the conflict.

Failure in war – the guilt and shame for deeds both done and unfinished
– was so painful that it took years for the trauma to emerge on cinema
screens. During the war itself, *M*A*S*H* (1970), Robert Altman's dark satire
set around a mobile surgical unit in an earlier conflict, the Korean War,
resonated for the Vietnam generation. Critic Richard Shickel enthused in

Life that *M*A*S*H* was 'what the new freedom of the screen is all about!' It was all too pertinent for American authorities, however, who banned it from being shown on US military bases. When filmmakers began to approach the subject of Vietnam itself, they took widely diverging routes. It might be the realist drama of returning, *The Deer Hunter* (1978), or the fantastic nightmare of *Apocalypse Now* (1979). *Taxi Driver* (1976), while it is not *about* the conflict, suggests that Travis Bickle's isolation and depression arise in the context of his having served in Vietnam. Even this premise is only suggested: he claims to be an ex-Marine and there is a Viet Cong flag visible in his room. This has not prevented people from reading his homicidal rampage as a metaphor for America's 'clean-up' operations in South East Asia.

Economic certainties were questioned, too. Volatile situations in the Middle East confused old Cold War strategists. In 1973, Arab oil-producing countries imposed an embargo on exports because the USA was deemed to be supporting Israel during the Yom Kippur War. Oil prices rose and, at the same time, attacks by terrorist groups began in European cities. No sooner was the situation in Vietnam finally resolved than President Nixon was dealing with low growth and high inflation, a syndrome attractively dubbed stagflation in Britain. When combined with rising unemployment in America, it was known as the Misery Index.

A rare glimpse of life in one of the least privileged parts of the USA was made possible through *Killer of Sheep* (1977), a vivid, impressionistic portrait of life in the Watts area of Los Angeles compiled over a number of years with a tiny budget by African-American filmmaker Charles Burnett. The story concerns Stan, who works in a slaughterhouse and tries to find illumination and joy in moments of a deprived life. The film was a prize-winner at the 1981 Berlin Film Festival.

Nixon did not see out his second term of office. In August 1974, finally threatened with impeachment for the scandal that had been revealed by a mysterious break-in at the Watergate offices of the Democratic Party, the

Republican President resigned. Distrust – which had lurked in *film noir* thirty years earlier – was now expressed as anger at abuses of power by secret, sinister organisations uncovered by unassuming protagonists. It might be a period tale of corruption, like *Chinatown*, Roman Polanski's twisting tale of 1930s Los Angeles, or Francis Ford Coppola's close study of a surveillance expert in *The Conversation*, or Alan J. Pakula's conspiracy of politics and commerce in *The Parallax View*. The full paranoia that ensued from fifteen years of assassinations, wars and corruption found a lurid outlet at the end of the decade in *Winter Kills* in which John Huston, as in *Chinatown*, was cast as a domineering American patriarch, charismatic yet evil, but this time the link with contemporary politics was made explicit.

Women, always a potential threat because of their sexuality, were now establishing legal claims to equality with a series of acts throughout the decade in Europe and the USA. A crucial judicial decision, Roe vs Wade, made it easier to obtain an abortion in many American states. There were female heads of state or prime ministers in countries including India, Israel, Argentina and Sri Lanka and by 1980 in Britain and Norway, too. Cinema was slow to reflect this new order – women were still more likely to be stripped, beaten or generally pushed around than to be seen in films running organisations or being the prime movers in the plot. This situation is not much improved forty years on.

Reviewing an early cinematic venture into tackling feminism, *Stand Up and Be Counted* (1972), A.H. Weiler in the *New York Times* acknowledged, 'The Women's Lib movement must have had some effect practically everywhere on this troubled globe by now . . .' while conceding that this Jacqueline Bissett comedy was not exactly the agent for social change – or even laughs. It did have a song over the titles, though, that became a hit that year. The singer/songwriter was an Australian, Helen Reddy. 'I Am Woman' proved so enduring a feminist anthem that it was played in 2010 when Kathryn Bigelow became the first woman ever to collect a Best Director Academy

Award for *The Hurt Locker*. Whether she found this affirming or patronising is not on record.

The first international Festival of Women's Film was held in New York in 1972 and the programme included many celebrated women-centred films, but from male directors, such as Martin Scorsese's *Alice Doesn't Live Here Anymore* (1974) and Paul Mazursky's *An Unmarried Woman* (1978). Looking back, Jill Clayburgh's character in *An Unmarried Woman*, often cited as a feminist heroine, does seem entirely defined by male expectations and fantasies and, for the most part onscreen, female characters were watching men take action or, once again, being watched as objects of desire: in France Erich Rohmer concentrated on that apex of male longing *Claire's Knee* (1970) with an irony that is almost entirely at the expense of the film's male protagonist, an obtuse middle-aged diplomat; Woody Allen dipped back and forth between proclaimed feminism and apparent scorn for the neurotic, changeable women who mess up his male protagonists' lives (as if they couldn't do it for themselves). The queen of Allen's 'difficult' women is *Annie Hall* (1977), at once admirable and ridiculous, desirable and maddening, a character that seemed to bypass Allen to have a direct effect on female audiences and what they wore. And the prom-queen has to be the telekinetically gifted wallflower *Carrie* (1976) who carries within her slim frame all of female power. She is simultaneously magnificent, sympathetic and terrifying.

The tallest, widest image yet was shown on the first IMAX screen at Expo '70 in Japan. Pictures of the world from space, so beautifully rendered in *2001*, increasingly provided an emotive focus for the growing environmental movement. As the first UN conference on environment convened, James Lovelock's Gaia theory built on the concerns of environmental toxicity raised by Rachel Carson's polemic *Silent Spring* in the previous decade. Anxiety grew with evidence of the consequences of mercury poisoning at Minamata in Japan, the release of dioxins from a chemical plant at Seveso in Italy, the *Amoco Cadiz* oil spill and the release of radiation from the Three Mile Island plant in Pennsylvania. While dramas based on particular environmental disasters would come later, Australian director Peter Weir's *The Last Wave* (1977) suggests ancient forces of retribution behind freakish weather events leading to an apocalypse. Die Grünen, the Green party, emerged in Germany as a coalition of various social groups involved in the 1968 protests. The defence of the planet was a rallying cry.

Global economic shifts were also changing Hollywood; old staple revenue earners like the musicals had faded away. The export market was compromised by home-grown industries like Bollywood in India or action movies in the Far East where the Hong Kong-based Golden Harvest studios emerged to rival the established Shaw Brothers empire. In 1973 Golden Harvest became the first to strike a deal with Hollywood for English language martial arts films, beginning with Bruce Lee in *Enter the Dragon*.

By the 1960s regular film attendances were low; at the beginning of the 1970s they dipped further. To get a film made at all the next generation had to produce something distinctive and novel. What worked in 1967 was the snappy, violent, sexy gangster film *Bonnie and Clyde*, directed by Arthur Penn, which took some of the vitality and irreverence of the *Nouvelle Vague* the dynamism of the action film and a certain American ingenuousness. Television now began to develop a more benign relationship with cinema. The two styles sometimes converged as directors abandoned the conventions of heightened settings and lighting to adopt a flatter, more documentary style, occasionally using hand-held cameras. The New Hollywood movie brats (among them Martin Scorsese, Peter Bogdanovich, Bob Rafelson and Brian de Palma) were not genuine independents, they were operating within the studio system but with idiosyncratic, distinctive scripts. Plot was less important than character or situation. Drifters, malcontents and outsiders were ideal material – whether Al Pacino as the stressed bank robber in *Dog Day Afternoon* or Jack Nicholson as a depressed late-night radio host in *The King of Marvin Gardens* or a refusenik classical musician in *Five Easy Pieces*.

These films were making decent returns on small budgets but the studios needed more. They revived the 'event' film with *Jaws* (1975), *Close Encounters of the Third Kind* (1977) and *Star Wars* (1977), plucking profits from the mandibles of big fish and the maw of space. These blockbusters (the films were booked into multiple 'block' venues) began with ensemble disaster stories such as *Airport* (1970) or *The Poseidon Adventure* (1972) and went on to establish commercial patterns: with *Jaws* – where Steven Spielberg's careful construction of place and character provided an all too plausible setting for the toothy effects – the whole film was pre-sold and marketed on an industrial scale. *New York* magazine in October 1975 reported a conversation between Fidel Castro and Francis Ford Coppola in which the Cuban leader claimed *Jaws* was a Marxist picture because it shows that businessmen are ready to sell out the safety of citizens rather than close down against the invasion of sharks. Coppola's response is recorded as a stunned, 'Oh'.

With *Star Wars* two years later, George Lucas began a long-running franchise with a successful formula – an effects-driven adventure for a youthful audience – that others would emulate. Lucas said at the time, 'Nobody except Disney makes pictures for young people anymore.' *Star Wars* played to the young and their parents, too, by creating a parallel universe of politics and family relationships which would last for years, involving successive generations watching both in theatres and, increasingly, on VHS or Betamax in the home and, what was more, buying the merchandise.

The element of saga over several episodes – as opposed to multiple films with a similar format, like the *Thin Man* or *Road to . . .* series of the 1930s and 1940s – may have been influenced by the audience's familiarity with episodic television drama. In an age of social change and concern over family stability, there was also something reassuring about an epic in which Jedi knights adhered to old values. Quests and loyalties, pursued over long periods or unimaginable distances, were compelling. In another genre altogether, the gangster trilogy that began with Francis Ford Coppola's *The*

Godfather (1972) was at least about an enduring set of relationships, even if they were often perverted into betrayal and bloodbath. A murderous dynasty was better than no family at all. Films became a participatory event. Audiences at *Star Wars* applauded the effects, spaceships in particular, just as at *Jaws* they had shrieked at the shark (or its shadow). *Star Wars* fans continued chanting the lines to one another over the decades – knowing it was not so much high art as irresistibly energetic entertainment and, for them, inclusive. Its occasional hokey-ness only added to the charm. The true fans were in on the joke.

The general direction in this decade, however, was forward to a technical sophistication that would anchor the viewer inside the experience of watching a film, making it more immersive. The experience of being there, whether in space or the South American jungle in Werner Herzog's *Aguirre: Wrath of God* was increasingly important. In an age when music had become a vast consumer market, cinemagoers were keenly listening. Dolby Laboratories had been founded in Britain in 1965 to provide record companies with the technology to reduce unwanted noise; in 1976, the company moved to California. With Dolby, you could hear a pin drop. Better than that, sound, rather than a wide shot, could establish an environment with the picture adding key details. Silence could be more profound or ominous; indistinct noises like the muffled sounds of the spaceship *Nostromo* in Ridley Scott's *Alien* (1979) could be expressive in themselves. Michel Chion notes a scene in the 1978 remake of *Invasion of the Body Snatchers* in which a vegetal pod gives 'birth' accompanied by a small organic sound. He describes it in *Film: A Sound Art*: 'this real and precise sound, so clear in its high registers and so tactile, is heard as though we are touching it, the way the contact with the skin of a peach can make one shudder.'

The conventional way of shooting moving or developing sequences involved elaborate paraphernalia, tracks and trolleys, all of which took time to set up. A stabilised camera, however, that could be held in the hand or on the shoulder, anchored to the body by a harness, gave the director greater flexibility and consistency, even in outdoor locations. The movement was natural, it allowed the operator to go in close, if necessary, yet it was perfectly smooth. After some early outings, this paragon, the Steadicam, made its first starring appearances in *Rocky* (1976) and *The Shining* (1980). It has remained a constant presence in contemporary cinema.

Yet there is potentially also something sinister about these innovations: the motion of the Steadicam camera as it glides, like a predatory creature circling, around the house of a teenage victim in *Halloween* (1978), or sweeps across lakes and mountains towards the Overlook Hotel in Stanley Kubrick's *The Shining* (1980) – or the Dolby sound when the little boy, Danny, rides his tricycle along the hotel corridors over polished floors and rugs. Now muffled, then clattering, now quiet until . . . something very bad indeed happens.

CARRIE (1976)

Director: Brian de Palma
Cast: Sissy Spacek, Piper Laurie, Amy Irving, John Travolta
Colour

Why is Carrie in her prom dress, drenched in blood, still one of the most chilling (and thrilling) sequences in film? The image, a virginal bride dripping carmine like a veil, comes from the film's climax when the girl's telekinetic powers are unleashed in retaliation for the bullying she has received from her high school peers. Carrie the victim has become Carrie the destroyer.

At one level, this is a parable of teenage sexuality. The dramatis personae are well fed, spoilt adolescents among whom shy, nervous Carrie White moves unnoticed, or, if noticed, disparaged. All the girls have women's bodies but Carrie has been kept like a child. Sex is on everyone's mind, except hers: even Carrie's fanatically religious mother is obsessed with denying her daughter's sexuality. Director Brian de Palma opens the film with a teasingly soft-porn wander through the girls' locker room after a sports lesson. Naked young women are showering and the camera comes to rest on Carrie, momentarily lost in the pleasure of the water and her own body. Then, with a nod to Hitchcock's *Psycho*, whose score is referenced on the soundtrack, there is blood. The twist here is that the blood is menstrual and the monstrous behaviour which it provokes comes from the angelic forms of the other girls in the shower room. Carrie, kept in ignorance by her mother of the changes her body is going through, is terrified to find herself bleeding and runs to her classmates for help. They turn on her like a mob, taunting and pelting with her with tampons and towels until she huddles in the corner of the shower. This is the Bates High School, after all.

For much of the film, the tension lies not in the prospect of supernatural terrors as with the social cruelty of the other students. The Cinderella transformation Carrie undergoes on Prom Night, when she is taken to the ball by a permed, blond hockey jock, is underscored with dread. For literally above her head wobbles the bucket of pig's blood that will drench her moment of triumph as Prom Queen.

When it does, though, Carrie is transformed. Her body stance alters, her eyes widen; in profile, her uptilted nose backlit by red light, she looks primal, like a foetus. Her neck juts forward and her head turns slowly on the full extension of her upper vertebrae to look around at her tormentors, like a dinosaur about to strike. The most terrifying aspect of Carrie requires no more special effect than a thin, membranous coating of red liquid.

Puberty – so graphically illustrated in *Carrie*'s opening scene – provides the more or less explicit matter of transformation in many horror movies of the time. Carrie is a potential onscreen consort for another transformed youngster, *An American Werewolf in London* (1981). Director John Landis has likened the onscreen lupine evolution of the college boy David to teenage changes – the sudden growth of hair, the deepened voice and even the extension of the jaw into a long muzzle suggestive of an erection. Teenage boys tend to form the majority of the horror-movie audience, something writer Stephen King believes is significant. He was only in his mid-twenties when *Carrie* became the first of his novels adapted for the screen. 'Sex,' he has observed, 'makes young adolescent boys feel many things, but one of them, quite frankly, is scared. The horror film in general and the Vampire film in particular confirms the feeling. Yes, it says, sex is scary; sex is dangerous.' King, whose novels would provide the basis for many more frighteners, including *The Shining* (1980), *Pet Sematary* (1989), *Misery* (1990) and *The Mist* (2007), also suggested a political context for the relative popularity of horror at certain periods. In *Danse Macabre*, his 1981 book about the genre, he writes that a good horror film locates 'national phobic pressure points' – in other words, it finds the vulnerabilities and anxieties of the moment.

Nineteen seventies films are certainly peopled with scary young women. The dark princess of the genre has to be Regan, on the cusp of puberty so energetically possessed by satanic forces in *The Exorcist* (1973), followed rather weakly by Ivy in *Audrey Rose* (1977). Both of these girls are the virtual nieces of Mia Farrow's character in *Rosemary's Baby* (1968) who has grounds for believing she has been impregnated by the Devil. A low-budget film that subsequently acquired cult following, *Let's Scare Jessica to Death* (1971), introduced a contemporary variation on the eternal vampire girl, a scruffier version of Hammer's coiffed and eye-linered brides of Dracula and Frankenstein. The erotic power of Dracula and his crew was not lost on the Hammer filmmakers; later it would be luridly advertised by Francis Ford Coppola in his fabulously overblown 1992 version. Women seem to respond to this: Brigid Cherry's study, *Refusing to Refuse to Look*, was based on questionnaires handed out to female fans. Not surprisingly, vampires, supernatural and Hammer, were the most popular among women but slasher movies had the least appeal. Vampire movies came out on top, the study suggested, for one basic reason: 'as a form of erotica for women, providing these viewers with sexual fantasy'. Modern horror also occasionally offers women the fantasy of empowerment, with many teenage girls adopting *Buffy the Vampire Slayer*, just as their mothers admired Ripley from *Alien* in the 1970s.

Robin Wood, in an influential essay, 'An Introduction to the Horror Film', wrote, as if of the Undead, of the 'return of the repressed'. Wood identified two forms of repression, benign and perverse: the first tames savages into behaving like civilised human beings; the second is a rigid social conditioning that makes us into 'monogamous, heterosexual bourgeois capitalists'. Anything that appears by contrast primitive, violent or libidinous is Other, often depicted as women, children, homosexuals, ethnic groups or even the working class. Sexual energy may be creative but, faced with its blatant manifestation, the community (villagers or suburbanites or high school heroes) determine that The Beast Must Die. However, as Carrie demonstrates so touchingly, it is not that simple. The avenging goddess is also the sweet prom queen in the white silk dress, a victim but also one of the generation who welcomed the Roe vs Wade decision to give them greater power over their bodies. Brian de Palma never lets us feel too tenderly towards her. After an initial confusion as she discovers her terrifying skills of telekinesis, Carrie turns her fury without discrimination on anyone of reproductive age around her. You may not find consistent ideology in *Carrie* but she does wear a fascinating mixture of references and fears mixed into that pig's blood.

Stephen King believes the genre is inherently conservative, appealing to the 'Republican in the three piece suit' in all of us. He regards horror movies, like sick jokes, as an expression of anti-social, uncivilised emotions that 'demand periodic exercise', feeding our basic instincts and most disgusting fantasies for a fleeting moment before order is restored. 'We make up horrors to help us cope with the real ones.' Slasher movies like *Halloween* and *Friday the 13th* were released at the end of the seventies; Vera Dika, author of *Games Of Terror*, argues that they spoke to an audience who voted Ronald Reagan into power after four years of Jimmy Carter's perceived failures. The plots reflect the conservative morality and traditional values of Reaganomics. Teens who drink, take drugs or indulge in pre-marital sex are invariably skewered, throttled or beheaded. Only the pure survive, the virgin is often the last woman standing. The sixties ideals of pacifism and sexual freedom are ineffective in the face of pure evil; a heroine must resort to violence if necessary.

At the box office *Carrie* returned something like eighteen times its budget and, unusually for a shock picture, garnered Academy Award nominations for Sissy Spacek as Carrie and Piper Laurie as her crazed fundamentalist mother. Horror films had really become popular again from the 1960s onwards. It is not difficult to imagine why audiences might have kept away from histrionic images of threat and suffering during and just after a global conflict. On the other hand, by the 1970s the audience had also become accustomed to gruesome and bizarre images on television. The generation that had watched the Kennedy assassinations and Viet Cong prisoners bloodily despatched, their elected leader growl through revelations of duplicity in the Watergate scandal and the police turn guns on American civilians in race riots or university demonstrations was the same generation that went in appreciable hundreds of thousands to watch *The Texas Chainsaw Massacre* (1974) or *The Hills Have Eyes* (1977), films about zombies and cannibalism, both sensational and nihilistic.

So *Carrie*, set in its 1970s milieu, is not so hard to explain as a parable of frightening feminism, with contrasting examples of all too powerful sisterhood – whether the bitchy, assertive classmates or their cringing victim (but look what happens when she gets angry!). Yet, like all interesting films, its messages are not straightforward – the pure do not necessarily survive: Carrie's 'empowerment' arrives in the same year that *Ms* magazine carried a photograph of a battered woman, the first national publication to lead with domestic violence. The *Time* magazine Person of the Year award for 1975 had gone not to an individual but to American Women, with the citation, 'the women's drive penetrated every layer of society, matured beyond ideology to a new status of general – and sometimes unconscious – acceptance'. Or rejection.

No one who has seen *Carrie* can forget that it is not over until the final frame and even then . . . Carrie's supernatural power may persist regardless of the shortcomings of capitalism or sexual liberation or the Carter doctrine. It may be possible to read political significance into the shock of Carrie's hand, still glistening with blood, reaching through her freshly dug grave and clutching her former classmate's arm, but that would miss the real, visceral appeal of horror. That scene is eerily dream-like as Carrie's classmate Amy glides towards the cemetery with her floral tribute, the whole sequence drenched in soupy strings, although the reveal is only too wet, sticky and alive. Again and again it makes you jump, partly from classic horror timing – leaving the sequence beyond the point where you are expecting the fright and then, just as you start to relax, delivering the fright from an unsuspected source. The politics may date but the shock is fresh.

Is *Nosferatu* (1922) less frightening now for our being able to rationalise the vampirism of Count Orlov (Max Schreck) as a manifestation of inter-war German guilt? The film certainly has ludicrous moments – the plotting and much of the acting is crude – yet Count Orlov's obscenely long finger-nails, his huge darkened eyes, hunched shoulders and oversized hairless head are still unsettling and strangely familiar, at once pathetic and terrifying. Like Carrie with her hair slicked down by the bloody bucketful and her wide eyes, there is something foetal about the Count's appearance.

A step backwards in evolution – or towards the womb – seems particularly to worry us, like Hannibal Lecter in *The Silence of the Lambs* (1991) flicking the air with his lizard's tongue when Clarice Starling is near, an action that is suggestive both of something sexual and of an earlier developmental stage, primitive and almost forgotten. The monster in Ridley Scott's *Alien* (1979) undergoes a gruesome 'birth' from within one of the crew's ribcage – doubly grotesque, being both a male 'pregnancy' and a malignant growth. Subsequent horrific generations in the various *Alien* sequels are either viscous and cartilaginous or fishy and primordial. The sense of what they might feel like is essential to our revulsion. The most memorable visual effect in *The Exorcist* is not Regan's revolving head but her projectile vomiting over a man of the cloth. Body fluids of all kinds (mucus, blood, tears and so on) make the Swedish vampire tale *Let the Right One In* so real and affecting. This organic detail extends to the sound – director Tomas Alfredson used fruit and meat for effects; sound artists have long employed water melons as skulls.

The fact that we still scream or flinch, as if in danger of physical harm, while in the comfort of a multiplex or on the sofa at home, is truly peculiar. Professor Ron Tamborini, analyst of audience reactions, attributes this to a particular form of empathy with those in peril onscreen. He calls it 'emotional contagion'. Jennifer M. Barker, an imaginative film academic with a bold theory about 'tactile' cinema, goes further with a discussion of 'contagious contact'. For her, it is all about skin. She cites the philosopher and critic Walter Benjamin's observation about a certain human aversion to contact with animals: that 'The horror that stirs deep in man is an obscure awareness that in him something lives so akin to the animal that it might be recognised. All disgust is originally disgust at touching.' So the sticky pig's blood running down Carrie's hair and on to her skin is truly repellent: not only is fluid that should be *inside* on the outside, but she looks like an oversized newborn, ripped untimely from the womb.

One of Barker's subjects, a contender for the 1970s weirdest and most effective horror film dwells on the compellingly repellent elements of birth, David Lynch's debut feature *Eraserhead* (1976). From the very first seconds, *Eraserhead* is about things fascinating and/or horrible to the touch, made more immediate by the monochrome in which they are filmed. It is, says

Barker, a film that 'sticks, scratches, slithers and smears itself along the viewer'. It is also about the product of reproduction. The narrative (broadly) follows a fastidious and reluctant young father as he engages, or not, with his literally monstrous offspring. It puts in juxtaposition birth and malformation, dereliction and eroticism, dark fluids and old upholstery, flesh and rusting machines, social niceties and slimiest excrescences – the whole set against a delicate soundtrack of dislocated sounds, at once strange and familiar, organic and industrial. All in all, the film is a magnificently disgusting experience.

The power of the *Eraserhead* baby or the parasitic *Alien* that grows inside the body, or, best of all, interred yet vital Carrie, does not diminish even with repeated viewing. Born out of the specific obsessions of the 1970s, she is ever undead.

AGUIRRE, WRATH OF GOD (1972)

Director: Werner Herzog
Cast: Klaus Kinski, Helena Rojo, Del Negro
Colour

In the sixteenth century Amazon jungle, Don Lope de Aguirre (Klaus Kinski) has broken away from Pizarro's expedition to lead his own search for the legendary wealth of El Dorado. He forges on through the alien forest with a party of overdressed nobles and soldiers; he will not deviate from his course, however hostile the environment. He knows that on a map he has seen El Dorado – he simply has to locate it. The jungle, though, does not submit to organisation by cartographers. It is a mysteriously threatening place. The indigenous population is barely visible but there are signs, occasionally. The Spaniards are stunned by the noises, the humidity, the vegetation; the jungle is not so much hostile as unstoppable. In the midst of it, they – the conquistadors – are incidental.

Werner Herzog's *Aguirre, Wrath of God* is more than the representation of the crazed adventurer's voyage down the Amazon. It is a real journey – an inspired occupation of the events rather than a historical recreation. Herzog took crew and cast to the testing environment of the rainforest. He did have a script but, working together and in conflict with his volatile leading man, Kinski, Herzog allowed improvisations and natural interventions to guide the drama.

Talking to the *Radio Times* in 1976, he said of the film, 'I think its attraction – the advantage it has over Hollywood – is that it is real. The spectacle is real; the danger is real. It is the real life of the jungle, not the botanic gardens of the studio . . . It is easy enough to make a film in your own living room but imagine trying to make one with 500 people in the Amazon tributaries.'

The scale and potential volatility of this project were enormous. The audience watches the conquistadors file like lines of ants over the misty mountains towards El Dorado – and insanity – and gradually comes to feel a parallel unease, partly for the historical subjects and partly also for the actors and extras themselves, who are clearly disoriented by the oppressive landscape. The very real impression of being in a rainforest – the dense greenery veiled in fine rain; the churning chocolate river; the cacophony of bird sounds and monkey cries that suddenly, ominously, stop – wears down the Spaniards and in time the audience too. We are being led by a maniac, be it conquistador or director, who seeks to impose his will on an uncontrollable environment.

Herzog once claimed he sought a landscape 'unembarrassed by men'. Often seeming like a figure from another age himself, he was attracted to the idea of wilderness, as powerful for new reasons in the 1970s – not least fears for the health of the planet – as it was for the Romantics in the nineteenth century. Not that *Aguirre* is romantic about nature; Herzog uses it to show up precisely what *is* so embarrassing about humanity. As he said, 'the jungle is really all about our dreams, our deepest emotions, our night-mares. It is not just a location, it is a state of our mind.'

So Aguirre – whose story is compelling enough in its own right – comes to represent every intruder destroying a natural paradise they do not understand, and every colonising soldier dodging phantoms in the jungle, up to and including the Americans in South East Asia. Herzog's film is not about Vietnam but the dream-like disorientation, the oppressive jungle, the increasingly insane quest and even the memento mori in terms of a boat stranded in the branches – all these things call to mind Francis Ford Coppola's *Apocalypse Now* (1979), which is primarily based on Joseph Conrad's novel *Heart of Darkness*. At one point in the extended redux version of Coppola's epic, a Frenchman, part of the old colonial presence in Vietnam, remarks of the US operations there, 'You Americans fight for the biggest nothing in history.' And Aguirre presses on towards El Dorado. Coppola acknowledged that something of *Aguirre* did find its way into *Apocalypse Now*. He helped Herzog find distribution in America for his next film *The Enigma of Kaspar Hauser*.

All Herzog's films are invested with a strong sense of place, whether in the Amazon, the Antarctic or the Sahara, up on a volcano or in the deep caves of southern France. He takes us there, only we are still actually in our upholstered, padded seats in the cinema or even at home. In some ways, without the leeches at the ankles or the sun burning the back of the neck, this is the best way to travel. Ironically, if you were there, you could not have the time, the energy or the perspective to be 'inside' the experience in the same way.

At one point in their Amazonian nightmare the adventurers find themselves on rafts as the waters jostle them down the wide river. The swell separates the rafts to opposing banks and alarm and confusion is apparent on the faces of the protagonists. Herzog let his drama spring from such moments: having mesmerised us with the accretion of tiny sensations, he

gives us characters *in extremis*. We believe that everyone onscreen is genuinely in danger, although interviews with his assistant from the 1970s suggest
that a certain creativity enhanced his accounts of the terrors of the production. The whirlpool of the river did occasionally have to be stirred up with
ropes and chains to make it seethe and threaten; 350 monkeys captured by
local Indians were purchased to enhance the fauna; some of the Indians
were recruited in a supermarket. As with Robert Flaherty's depiction of
the Inuit in *Nanook of the North* fifty years before, this environment was
shaped by the filmmaker.

To create a hallucinatory effect, Herzog often went out of his way to be
mysterious, sometimes using relatively simple techniques. In his book
Herzog On Herzog he describes how and why he punctuated the film with
still images of faces. In practice, he made an actor run for two kilometres,
then dried his face and asked him to stare at the lens but not to breathe
too heavily. As a result the man's face appears inexplicably disfigured and
we struggle to find an interpretation: 'You really don't know what is going
on with this guy. These kinds of shots are where the film holds its breath.
They feel as mystifying and as intense to me as to any other spectator,'
Herzog explained, attributing *Aguirre*'s mesmerising atmosphere to a combination of 'documentary-style filming and these highly stylized frozen stills
. . . even the bird noise and the silences on the soundtrack have taken on
eerie and illusory qualities'. When a character is killed, there is no blood.

For Herzog, 'cinema per se has a secret hypnotic quality to it' and his
interest in mesmerism surfaced more obviously four years later, when he
hypnotised the cast of *Heart of Glass* (1976). Dismissing accusations of
gimmickry, the director claimed he did it to convey the feeling that his
characters were sleep-walking to catastrophe, 'this air of the floating, fluid
movements, the rigidity of a culture caught in decline and superstition, the
atmosphere of prophecy'. That film was about eighteenth-century Bavaria
but the mood also applies to most of Herzog's features.

He then admitted a further ambition: believing that 'actually it is possible to hypnotize someone from a screen', Herzog had initially planned 'to appear on screen in a prologue explaining to the audience that, if they wanted to, they themselves could experience the film under hypnosis'. The director's plan was to ask the audience to focus on an object, in classic stage hypnotist style. At the end of the film he would appear again and gently stir them from their trance: 'I did not follow through with this plan as it would have been wholly irresponsible to do so'. What he has done over the years instead is to hypnotise us by stealth.

From the early days, scientists had been keen to measure the mesmeric effect of the new art form on enraptured, unsuspecting audiences. Psychologists Toulouse and Mourgue monitored the breathing of those watching Abel Gance's *Mater Dolorosa* (1917), noting a phenomenon of 'the same sort as hypnotic suggestion'. What was particularly of interest was a new way of seeing, akin to hallucination, where viewers knew that what they were watching was not real and yet they reacted as if it were. One of the first psychological studies of cinema, *The Photoplay*, published in April 1916, was by a German psychologist, Hugo Munsterberg, who had been teaching at Harvard since 1892. His intellectual scorn for the popular new medium was dispelled by his first cinema trip, to see a 1912 version of the Ondine myth, *Neptune's Daughter*. At once, he observed the conceits of memory, suggestion and emotion that he had wrestled with in his studies of other forms of art come together in celluloid reality. 'Surely,' he admitted, 'I am now under the spell of the movies'. Munsterberg saw, too, this powerful effect en masse. 'It has even been reported that sensory hallucinations and illusions have crept in; neurasthenic persons are especially inclined to experience touch or temperature or smell or sound impressions from what they see on the screen. The associations become as vivid as realities, because the mind is completely given up to the moving pictures'. Such suggestibility might be exploited, he warned: it might even be used by the unscrupulous to promote immoral or even criminal behaviour.

In 1946, Jean Cocteau had declared, 'The collective hypnosis into which the cinema audience is plunged by light and shade is very like a spiritualist seance. Then, the film expresses something other than what it is, something that no one can predict.' Half a century on, the French critic Raymond Bellour reinforced the link: '. . . hypnosis increases the field of consciousness and allows one to see more than one sees normally with the eye of simple memory. This is something that the cinema has in common with hypnosis and realizes according to its own proper means.' His observation occurred in an article about Jacques Tourneur's 1957 horror film *Night of the Demon*, which, strangely enough, carries within it an argument about the power of auto-suggestion in the form of a slip of paper with a mysterious inscription. When this sinister fragment is glimpsed by someone who knows of its reputation, they become convinced they will die. And so they do.

Recent developments in neuroscience also support the comparison with hypnosis. Drawing upon research in neurology and cognitive psychology, filmmaker and theorist Pia Tikka has identified a cinematic consciousness, a form of immersion akin to being in the middle of a dream: 'a conscious state that relates the cognitive experiences of the viewer to the stream of events of the film in such a manner that she momentarily can be claimed not to be fully conscious about the other events around her'. Tikka concedes that in a cinema, unlike in a dream, we are conscious of the fact that we are watching a film and argues that there are two 'psycho-physiological states' – the emotions that the movie induces and the awareness of one's surroundings. These states oscillate and jostle for position. One can even dominate the other so effectively that it shuts it out, at least temporarily: 'in an immersive cinematic experience, interaction with the real world and the conscious brain becomes disconnected at least partially'.

In 2004, Semir Zeki, Professor of Neuroesthetics at University College London, conducted an experiment. He showed students the opening sequences of the Bond movie *Tomorrow Never Dies*, measuring the various intensities of their brain activity through the course of the scenes. What surprised him was the highly independent activity recorded in different parts of the brain over twenty-two minutes of movie-watching. Asked on BBC Radio 4 about the experiment, he suggested that film is capable of engaging 'your attention so completely you are almost in a trance'.

Traditional film before the digital age may have mesmerised us with its flickering between light and dark as each of the dark borders around the twenty-four frames per second spooled through the projector. This constant oscillation between strong light and pitch black may go some way to explaining the contradiction that has lain at the heart of the cinematic experience, that we are comfortably numb, as René Clair put it, but also highly alert. Though unable to influence the outcome of events onscreen, we might still be deeply moved or agitated by them.

Maybe it also explains the particular openness that we have to travel in the cinema, to the sensation of gliding along as a passenger. Many of Herzog's films delineate a journey, like *Stroszek* (1977), in which Bruno S makes his odd way from Berlin to Wisconsin and North Carolina by way of highways and tow trucks. Herzog's fellow in the New German Cinema, Wim Wenders, in the first of his road trilogy *Alice in the Cities* (1974) has Canned Heat's 'On The Road Again' playing to absurdly melancholy effect in a provincial café in the Ruhr. In the next two films, *The Wrong Move* (1975) and *Kings of the Road* (1976), more rootless people travel through Germany as if on the American highways, for, as one character puts it, 'The Americans have colonised our subconscious.'

In America itself, 1970s road movies can become hypnotic abstractions – people searching, but for what? It is always the quest that matters, not the result. In *Vanishing Point* (1971), a Vietnam veteran who has lost every-thing speeds to a final reckoning. A race impels the monosyllabic Driver and Mechanic along Route 66 in Monte Hellman's *Two-Lane Blacktop* (1971). The duo are played by two celebrated musicians (James Taylor and Dennis Wilson of The Beach Boys) who cast off their fame for this existential journey, which the audience shares by gazing with them through the windscreen of the 1955 Chevy that has more or less the same proportions as a cinema screen.

Former philosophy academic turned film director Terrence Malick's *Badlands* (1973) is a floating meditation on love and death riding on an archetypical American narrative of wild youngsters on the run on the road. A similar drowsy excitement accompanies the journey upriver into Vietnam's heart of darkness in *Apocalypse Now* (1979) or, decades later, a boat's progress through the reeds in Malick's *The New World* (2005) – both films that seem to flow from the dream of *Aguirre*.

Although he would return with another crazed Amazon journey, *Fitzcarraldo* (1982) – this time to build an opera house, requiring the tugging of a steamship over a hill to avoid dangerous rapids – Herzog's wildest, grandest expedition is still *Aguirre*. He compels us to consider the most dangerous human vainglory; Aguirre, lost in the jungle with a diminished band of sickly and dying followers, surrounded (as we feel we are) by silent Indians, gabbling monkeys and encroaching vegetation, with the threat of a poisoned arrowhead a half-second away, can still declaim: 'I, the wrath of God, will marry my own daughter and with her I'll found the purest dynasty the world has ever seen.'

This statement may be ludicrous but the audience is not distanced by it. There is something utterly recognisable and human in the extremes of Aguirre. The film may illustrate the horrors of colonialist ambitions or the madness of messing with an ecology but its enduring effect is an atmosphere, a brooding sensation. Herzog's mother, quoted by Gideon Bachman in a 1977 article, said: 'Werner remembers the slightest details: he knows, sees, understands. But explaining is not in his nature. Everything goes into him and comes out transformed.' That transformation is fascinating to us, even if it remains, like Kaspar Hauser, the boy brought up in the dark in Herzog's 1974 film, an enigma. The director would then feel that his spell had fulfilled its purpose: 'I know that I have the ability to articulate images that sit deeply inside us, that I can make them visible.'

ANNIE HALL (1977)

Director: Woody Allen
Cast: Woody Allen, Diane Keaton
Colour

This wry love-gone-missing comedy was 1978's Academy Award Winner of Best Picture and Best Screenplay, Best Director for Woody Allen and Best Actress for Diane Keaton. It survives well: its gentle New Wave-ish innovations (breaking the fourth wall; subtitling the subconscious beneath conversations) and compassionate observations on human frailty put it up there with Allen's best films. Every halfway original romantic comedy/ drama subsequently has been compared to it. Annie is a standard-bearer for New Hollywood women (she also gets more lines than most of them). The often denied autobiographical element (like their screen characters, Keaton and Allen had been lovers and Keaton's real name is Diane Hall) prefigures the in-and-out-of-reality work of twenty-first-century film-makers like Charlie Kaufman.

Yet its most widespread influence at the time was probably on clothes. As Annie, Diane Keaton sported a range of baggy apparently hand-me-down men's trousers with oversized shirts and waistcoats and/or ties. She peered out through wire-framed spectacles beneath the brim of a cloche or floppy fedora. It was a look apparently assembled from family heirlooms and thrift shops, a subversive counterpoint to Keaton's pretty face and long, straight hair. Viewing the film today, that 'Annie Hall look' actually derives probably from no more than two scenes – the first is the initial crucial encounter with Allen's character, Alvy Singer, when she is suddenly trans-formed from a giggly girl in oversized shorts on a tennis court into a monochrome Chaplinesque cross-dresser; the second is the moment featured on the poster, a mutual, if tentative, declaration of love as she strolls with Alvy by the Hudson, wearing a large tweed jacket, felt hat, long skirt and boots, like some Edwardian explorer. Later scenes, when she wears a selection of those 1970s staples, the shirtwaister and baggy bright boiler suit, are, funnily enough, less memorable.

Annie Hall's distinctive clothes are an indicator of character as much as her trademark (la-de-dah . . .) free associating speech. Films are full of sartorial stereotypes – the stiff-collared solicitor, the polo-necked architect, the poet with long cuffs or the political activist, like Barbra Streisand's character in *The Way We Were*, whose hair gets curlier as their views become more radical – but the strength of Annie Hall's costume is its layered, sometimes contradictory quality. She has a strong family (Grammy Hall gave her that tie) but is not traditional; she wears tailored clothes but may not finish her sentences; her high waisted trousers recall Charlie Chaplin but she yearns to be taken seriously: she has dispensed with that shackle to female liberation, the bra, but is not necessarily sexually available – at least not to Alvy. Her clothes suggest attitude, education and sex appeal and, within weeks, all that was available off the peg.

Although Ralph Lauren was credited for designing the clothes in the film, Annie's look was as much the result of a creative partnership between Keaton and costume designer Ruth Morley, encouraged by Allen. Keaton explained in an interview with *In Style* magazine in May 2004, 'Ruth and I went shopping. We borrowed and bought from Ralph because I loved what he did. But in the end it was the way I normally dressed, and we didn't want to change that.'

It was a smart decision. Morley herself was astounded at the way her designs transferred rapidly from screen to street. She expressed her surprise at the success of the 'Annie Hall' style in *Vogue* in August 1978: 'It's crazy; it's practically a household word!' Morley attributed its sudden success to the growing fashion for thrift-shop chic and also suggested that 'it struck a psycho-logical nerve . . . many women picked up on Annie's vulnerability'. The clothes were assembled to reflect the character's state of mind – apparently a charming, idiosyncratic jumble: 'everyone identified with her, particularly the more unformed, insecure Annie at the beginning of the picture'. As the film progresses, and the romance falls apart, Annie's look becomes more coherent, evolving into long, confident dresses and big sunglasses. *Vogue* had its own explanation of the *Annie Hall* phenomenon: 'women's hard-won independence is reflected by the search for more personal and less dictatorial styles'. Women did not just want to look like Annie Hall, they wanted to be her, although they also liked the fact that the clothes seemed thrown together and easy to emulate: 'somehow Ruth Morley hit a sociological as well as a psychic nerve in her clothes for Diane Keaton, which reflected as well as extended these changes'.

Released in 1977, *Annie Hall* fell into an economic cycle skewed by the 1973 OPEC oil price rise and the subsequent stock market falls. Thrift was good (just as Gordon Gekko's socks in *Wall Street* ten years later spoke of luxury fashion in a financial boom), which might explain the instant appeal of Keaton's clothes to students, who tended accidentally to dress that way but with less effect. The bizarre result of the film's stylistic success with older consumers, however, was not that women went to jumble sales or the attics of relatives. *Vogue* noted: 'In a classic "ripple effect" pattern, designers also reacted to the movie's fashion impact and, in turn, incorporated some of the details and feelings into their commercial designs'. Those ripples are evident in the advertisements within *Vogue*. Ralph Lauren was soon showing women in tweeds while an editorial informed readers that the Brooks Brothers spectacles worn by Diane Keaton were this season's sunglasses shape. Later editions proclaimed a man's shirt as the female look of summer '78, while an advert for Saks Fifth Avenue in March of that year highlighted Anne Klein's 'Unstructured Uninhibited' spring collection, which bore more than a passing resemblance to Keaton's tie and trouser ensemble. Morley's contribution to consumer buying patterns was later recognised with a fashion industry award.

The commercial effect spread down from haute couture to high street and across the Atlantic. The British mass market magazine *Woman's Own* observed in the summer of 1978 that 'the movie *Annie Hall* inspired the Tomboy Look – baggy masculine jackets and pants'. Previous editions featured photo-shoots clearly inspired by *Annie Hall*, though not attributed to Keaton or Morley or even Ralph Lauren. In February the magazine posed the question 'why can't a woman dress more like a man?' inevitably accompanied by photographs of models in man-sized jackets, tweedy waistcoats and 'man-style trousers', all available from high street shops like Dorothy Perkins. The cover girl for that issue was garbed in a by-now familiar combo of trousers, shirt, tie, braces and waistcoat. In July *Woman's Own* recommended different kinds of ties to complement the button-down-collar shirt and masculine trousers – 'the essential finishing touch to the summer outfit'.

There are famous precedents. When Clark Gable undressed in *It Happened One Night* (1934) to reveal that he wasn't wearing a vest, sales of the undergarment plummeted within a year. In the 1950s Marlon Brando in *The Wild One* (1953) and James Dean in *Rebel Without a Cause* (1955) unwittingly helped Levi Strauss take denim out of the factory and field and on to the student campus as, paradoxically, a uniform of individuality and revolt. Faye Dunaway's beret in *Bonnie and Clyde* (1968), while historically faithful to photographs of outlaw Bonnie Parker, also subtly echoed Che Guevara's headwear in the famous poster on thousands of student walls. All three wore the beret pulled down towards the left ear. Jane Fonda's thigh-length boots and hotpants in *Barbarella* (1968) became more popular and enduring than the film itself.

By the 1980s, the influences were blatant or more whimsical. The young Tom Cruise gave Ray-Bans a fillip in *Risky Business* (1983) which apparently increased sales by 55 per cent. Ralph Lauren scored again with campaigns based on 1920s safari wear as seen on Streep and Redford in *Out of Africa* (1985) while Chow-Yun Fat modelled a duster coat in John Woo's gangster action picture *A Better Tomorrow* (1986) – dragging this unfashionable item back into shop windows.

In 1998 I saw a classic case on a well-known editor of American publications when she arrived at a British literary festival. Famous for her immaculate power-dressing, she presented a startlingly understated look of fawn jodhpurs, ankle boots and a white shirt. Puzzled, I sought the opinion of a New York-based friend. Easy, she replied, Kristin Scott Thomas in *The Horse Whisperer* – just released in America, it had yet to reach British cinemas.

Right back to the days of Asta Nielsen underwear or Max Factor Pan-Cake make-up, aspiration and fantasy could be exploited. Buy this product and you will look (or even be) like the star. Garment manufacturers were not necessarily convinced that the frivolities onscreen would walk off the rails in the stores. In her 1940 survey *America at the Movies*, Margaret Ferrand Thorp noted that as late as 1930 the rag trade believed 'the movies had no influence on fashion'. One man made the practical link that brought consumer and star closer and eventually allowed Hollywood to challenge Paris as capital of couture. Bernard Waldman of Modern Merchandising Bureau, Inc., owner of Cinema Fashions and Screen Star Styles, had a method. He would visit a film in production, assess the 'frocks, hats or gadgets worn by the stars the average American woman [was] likely to take to her heart' and reproduce them for the masses. So the pirate movie *The Buccaneer* yielded several blouses, variously titled The Boss, The General and Dominique, each with a label sporting a pirate's face with long moustache and cocked hat and the words 'A Buccaneer Fashion, inspired by *The Buccaneer*', lest anyone should be in any doubt. This pioneering tie-in proved hugely popular, especially in Middle America where the European fashion houses made little impression on small-town styles. Other companies soon piled in, such as the 'fine French fabric house' Colcombet, which manufactured silk dresses inspired by *Snow White and the Seven Dwarfs*. Cinema shops opened up in department stores like Macy's, offering ersatz versions of gowns and dresses seen on the stars, including the white chiffon number Joan Crawford wears in *Letty Lynton* (1932), adorned with an explosion of ruffled sleeves and hem. Half a million copies were reportedly manufactured, making it one of the decade's bestsellers. If true, it would have been difficult to attend social functions without running into one or two at least.

Magazine editors and studio publicity departments colluded in this dissemination of unaffordable luxury in budget doses. Nineteen thirties British magazines like *Film Fare* or *Film Fashionland* claimed 'to bring all the charm and romance, all the beauty and intelligence of the Film World into every woman's life'. Peta, a columnist for *Film Pictorial*, passed on tips on being 'star-smart', including the new art of full make-up. Jean Harlow, for example, could teach you to apply powder around the eyes without accentuating wrinkles. Busby Berkeley's Beauty Commandments included 'a good rub down with a rough towel every morning' and 'a sunbath wherever possible (very "fit-making" this)'. More celebrity advice was proffered in the form of advertisements, like Gracie Fields's endorsement for Potter and Moore's Mitcham Lavender Powder-Cream: 'It's grand for the skin'.

Margaret Ferrand Thorp observed that, by 1940, movies were common points of reference and specific at that – 'I want a sofa like the one in Bette Davis's drawing room in *Dark Victory*' or 'I want my curls to go up on the side like Irene Dunne's in the dinner scene in *Love Affair*'. Hairstyles were at least an affordable way to replicate the movie life. According to Thorp, Shirley Temple's curls were foisted, via the Permanent Wave, by doting mothers on to 'thousands of unhappy infants before they were so much as ten years old'. The term 'platinum blonde' had been coined by the *Hell's Angels* (1930) publicists to describe Jean Harlow's dazzling coiffure. It was soon replicated with varying levels of success in hair salons across Europe and America.

Film fans had to make do with what they could afford, in effect running up ballgowns from the curtains like Scarlett O'Hara in *Gone With the Wind*. Jane Wyman's cardigans might be reproduced give or take a dropped stitch via the patterns in *Bestway's Film Star Woollies*. Peta at *Film Pictorial* was always on hand to bridge the awkward ravine between aspiration and reality. In a piece entitled 'Joan Crawford helps the Spring Bride', stills from *Love on the Run* (1936) show the star in a costume by Gilbert Adrian of MGM – a 'glamorous looking, but practical outfit is the black, light-weight woollen dress with the seal skin cape banded with fox at the wrists'. Realising that this ensemble will be way beyond the pockets of her readers, Peta quickly adds 'you and I don't have to have seal skin for a similar cape; we can get an excellent effect with velvet and piece of nicely dyed "bunny" for the wrists'. Scarlett O'Hara would probably have shot the rabbit herself.

Professor Annette Kuhn, in her 2002 study *An Everyday Magic*, quizzed men and women who had grown up in the 1930s, acquiring much of their wisdom from visits to the cinema. Young working-class men were inspired by Warner Brothers gangster films to slick back their hair like George Raft, or Bogart or Cagney, although they stopped short of the machine guns and the slaughter. Women, though, seemed to pick up on something more fundamental: they identified with female movie stars like Crawford or Claudette Colbert, whose intelligence, wit and ingenuity were so blatant they sometimes eclipsed their co-stars. The sealskin capes with fox trim may have been glamorous but the real allure was the attitude, what Margaret Ferrand Thorp identified in 1940 as 'the belief in the possibility of improve-ment, the conviction that something more can be made of what you've got. The movies cater effectively to that deep-rooted instinct.' Annette Kuhn concludes that 'cinema above all offers new forms of femininity' as Annie Hall did for a generation of young women, battling to incorporate the rhetoric of Second Wave Feminism into their dreams of independence and modern romance. A hat can be more than a hat, sometimes.

*   *   *

If Annie Hall was a free spirit, then the branding association with Ralph Lauren seemed to tie her down rather more effectively than Woody Allen's character Alvy ever could. This specific link of star and label went back a couple of decades to the 1950s. In earlier films of the 1930s, costumes were designed by studio employees like Gilbert Adrian or Edith Head. Gloria Swanson had brought Coco Chanel over from France for one disastrous year but her innovations were too radical for Hollywood. The exemplar of haute couture designer and star in symbiosis began in 1954 with *Sabrina* when Givenchy dressed Audrey Hepburn in, among other outfits, a little black cocktail dress with bateau neckline and bows at the shoulder from his spring/summer 1953 collection. Theirs was a partnership that would endure for two decades. In *American Gigolo* (1980) Richard Gere lays out his toning Giorgio Armani suits and shirts on the bed of his Los Angeles apartment with at least as much care and devotion as if they were his mature female clients.

So integrated has the process become that designer Tom Ford can create a bespoke suit for Daniel Craig as James Bond in *Quantum of Solace* (2008) with a ready-to-wear version available in Harrods. Ford, on the strength of his reputation as a designer and taste maker, then went on to write and direct a screen adaptation of Christopher Isherwood's *A Single Man*. This much praised film also allowed Tom Ford's tailoring to delineate some of the elegant reserve of Colin Firth's character, a British professor at a California university in 1962.

Some critics felt the production over-designed, like an extended advertisement for Ford's aesthetic. It is more likely that Ford simply knew how he wanted to portray Isherwood's Britishness in contrast to his American colleagues and students, and knew he could best design the clothes to do it. With James Bond, however, there is no doubt: product placement is part of the Bond brand, from his earliest preferences (Martini, shaken not stirred) to the watches, cars, computers and other consumer goods with which the plots are now studded. The 1997 film *Tomorrow Never Dies* was apparently the first to cover its total production costs with placement deals.

This acceptance of the marriage of entertainment and marketing is a long way from the watchful reports of *Harrison's*, a Hollywood trade paper founded in 1919, which initially boasted of being 'free from the influence of advertising' and chastised any film that featured a commercial brand. An early example was *The Garage* (1919), which lingered on a particular type of gasoline; later offenders might be guilty of nibbling too long on Hershey Bars. *Harrison's Reports* folded in 1962, ironically, just as the Madison Avenue ad men reached their zenith. These days, product placement is an openly done deal. Ray-Ban's contract with *Men in Black 2* (Will Smith tagline: 'I make this look good') tripled sales of the sunglasses.

In April 2010, the *New York Times* interviewed Jordan Yespe, a lawyer with the firm Manatt, Phelps and Phillips, who advises writers on the best way to slip products into the lines of their scripts before the work has even been sold to a studio. A script with its own in-built advertising or brand potential may well be a more attractive package to studios that constantly seek ways to recoup some of the vast expense of movie-making. One of the many ways in which contemporary films hypnotise us is with the regular glimpses of a certain beer or brand of coffee that may send us out of the cinema with a craving. A car that swishes through rainswept streets on its way to the heist onscreen may well catch the eye in a showroom. So advanced is product placement that methods have been devised to track the areas in a scene or in a screen where the gaze falls most often so that the product may be placed to best advantage. This may actually not be so difficult. In 2009 I sat with director James Cameron on stage and observed an audience in 3–D glasses as they watched preview clips of *Avatar*. The director pointed out to me the perfect synchronisation of head movements, all the comedy spectacles angled at once towards the same spot on the screen and moving as one body to the next development. For all the 3–D depth of image and screenwide detail of setting and action, Cameron had in effect 'directed' the audience precisely where to look.

It does not always work, of course – just as propaganda fails when it is perceptible. *Dick Tracy* (1990) did not bring about a revival in 1930s fashions, nor *Evita* for the 1940s. These days one film is unlikely to spawn a whole 'look' in the way that *Letty Lynton* did. Television, internet and the rapidity of information spread means that people want to wear immediately what the stars wore on the red carpet or on television last night, hence the popularity of websites like ASOS, as seen on screen. The product must be ready and available by the time the film is shown.

With film, though, it is not a question of simply wearing the clothes or looking like an attractive onscreen personality – you have to want, even a little, to be Annie Hall or James Bond. Receptivity works on an emotional level. After the success of loveable pig comedy *Babe*, pork sales dropped significantly in countries that showed the film, while in the USA sales of canned meat hit an all-time low. It only took one line in the Californian winery comedy *Sideways* (2005) – 'I am not drinking any fucking merlot' – for sales of merlot to drop 2 per cent nationally in the United Kingdom, while shops in the United States reported as much as a 20 per cent fall. On the other hand, sales of pinot noir, very much the hero of Alexander Payne's comedy, increased 16 per cent in the UK, with up to a 40 per cent increase in American liquor stores. It might be coincidence, or a remarkably accurate pinpointing of cinephile oenophiles.

Annie Hall was not simply a waistcoat, tie and baggy trousers. The character was an eclectic mixture, referential with a modern spin, reliably contradictory, vague but steely – something even the Madison Avenue wizards might not have dreamed of as a commercial concept, until then.

1980s

. . . .

HIGH CONCEPT

The defining international relationship of the decade was like the collision of two B-movie plots. He was the former cowhand, the decent guy with the strong sense of right and wrong. His age gave him a certain homespun perspective, delivered with that sun-creased, twinkly smile but, be in no doubt, the old timer was tough. No one was going to push him around. She was the hard-working grocer's daughter from the quaint English country town of . . . Grantham. Blonde waves and a peachy complexion barely disguised the iron beneath. With determination and hours of study, she had pushed open the doors to the male enclosures of, first, the chemistry laboratory, then Westminster and then Downing Street.

Ronald Reagan and Margaret Thatcher described their political missions in cinematic terms with the promotion of democracy as the MacGuffin, the notional aim. A lone figure before the tanks in Tiananmen Square or denim-clad crowds swarming over the crumbling Berlin Wall had a cinematic clarity that endorsed this view. As George Lucas's space odyssey continued with *The Empire Strikes Back* (1980) and *Return of the Jedi* (1983), Reagan employed *Star Wars* terminology when he urged Americans in 1983 not to seek a nuclear arms freeze, ignoring 'the aggressive impulses of an evil empire', namely the Soviet Union. His Strategic Defense Initiative, which included space systems to intercept incoming nuclear missiles, was promptly dubbed Star Wars. Like a combination of Bette Davis's Elizabeth I and Greer Garson's Mrs Miniver, both roles from her favourite decades of cinema, Margaret Thatcher determined to take on unions, big government, Europe and even, most spectacularly, Argentina over the Falkland Islands. As it happened, her policies, along with her acknowledged indifference to the arts, fostered a resurgence of material for British filmmakers, among them Ken Loach, Stephen Frears, Derek Jarman and Peter Greenaway, sometimes supported by the film production division of the new Channel 4 television.

A series of assassination attempts, unsuccessful against Reagan and Thatcher but fatal for Indira Gandhi in India and Benigno Aquino in the Philippines, reinforced the idea of the deadly lone operator. John Hinckley, who tried to kill Reagan in 1981, claimed he wanted to impress the actress Jodie Foster, who had played a child prostitute in *Taxi Driver*. Onscreen, however, the hit man was a hero – at least if he could operate in a fantastical environment. Austrian bodybuilder Arnold Schwarzenegger displayed his gleaming physique in the two *Conan* pre-history fantasies before director James Cameron constructed from his robotic delivery and superhuman frame a high-tech avenger targeting delinquents, gangsters, mad scientists and the like in *The Terminator* (1984). In a typical sequence, the action hero – lit by a dangerous red and electric blue – beats off assailants with the help of some firepower and impressive pectorals. Cue explosions, running, kicking and punching, flying bodies, shattered glass and then, violence spent, a preternatural calm in which he surveys the chaos, shakes off a trace of debris, utters a comically understated disclaimer and walks, unscathed, towards the shattered doorframe. In the *Rambo* trilogy (1982, 1985 and 1988) an ostracised Vietnam veteran (Sylvester Stallone) overcomes his trauma to return to South East Asia and fight the war again, but with a 'better' outcome. With the help of Steven Spielberg as director and George Lucas as producer, Harrison Ford cracked the whip in *Raiders of the Lost Ark* (1981, sequels in 1984 and 1989) and put the Nazis down with thrills and laughs.

In the West manufacturing struggled while the financial sector swelled as a result of deregulation and inventive new ways of structuring debt by selling it on as assets. Corporate 'raiders' (the term came by association with the film) like Carl Icahn used bonds devised by investment bankers to finance the acquisition of companies which they then stripped down. By the end of the decade, the language was enriched with a new vocabulary of 'poison pills' and 'golden parachutes' and capitalism had a new maxim, 'Greed is Good', uttered in Oliver Stone's *Wall Street* (1987) by charismatic villain Gordon Gekko, who was based on the nimblest of the arbitrageurs and takeover buccaneers. However stringent a satire the director intended, Michael Douglas's characterisation was so compelling that young financiers began to wear red socks and braces and to sweep their hair back, Gekko-style.

Blue-collar workers fought to keep jobs as manufacturing moved away from the United States and Europe to the dynamic new economies in the East. Bruce Willis's character John McClane in the *Die Hard* movies, although a cop, is to all appearances the working man, slugging it out at all hours in his vest against elegantly dressed European villains played by Alan Rickman or Jeremy Irons.

Imports arrived from the East in celluloid form with the aesthetic of Chinese painting in *Yellow Earth* (1984), which begins as the Chinese prepare to repel Japanese invaders in 1939. The film's brilliant cinematographer Zhang Yimou gave Gong-li her first major role on her route to becoming an international star in *Red Sorghum* in 1987. From Japan,

Kurosawa's spectacular epic of a thief who passes as a nobleman, *Kagemusha* (1980), reached international audiences with support from Hollywood princes George Lucas and Francis Ford Coppola; and John Woo and Chow-Yun Fat began the 'gun-fu' series of Hong Kong gangster movies with *A Better Tomorrow* in 1986.

Despite feminism and changing working patterns, romance was as big business as ever. In July 1981, the wedding of the heir to the throne in Britain, Prince Charles, to Lady Diana Spencer was a costume drama spectacular, attracting gold-braided and coroneted guests from around the world and 750 million viewers on television. Eleven years later the couple separated. Divorce statistics in Britain and the United States reached a peak in the 1980s. Although the rate of marriage dropped slightly, weddings themselves, after a bout of minimalism in the 1960s and 1970s, grew ever more elaborate and monumental. Romantic comedies, even with a feminist or progressive slant, still depended on getting your man. Melanie Griffith aspires to more than Sigourney Weaver's job in *Working Girl* (1988): she wants her boyfriend Harrison Ford, too. Rosanna Arquette may abandon a suburban husband for the New York scene in the 1984 *Desperately Seeking Susan* – a film which, incidentally, the producers rushed out on release because they feared co-star Madonna's moment in the music charts might not last – but she's still susceptible to love. After the agonising of the 1970s, romance makes a determined return – from the teen comedy *Pretty in Pink* (1986) to the most knowing rom-com of them all, *When Harry Met Sally* (1989).

If weddings were becoming more baroque, then there was also a new, richer, aesthetic onscreen after the flatness of some 1970s cinematography. The decade was framed by two extraordinary costume dramas by Martin Scorsese, whose black and white masterpiece *Raging Bull*, about boxer Jake LaMotta, set in the 1940s and 1950s, was released in 1980. Towards the end of the 1970s Scorsese had made what was in effect an experimental 1940s Vincente Minnelli musical, complete with Minnelli's daughter, Liza, in a lead role, *New York, New York*. In 1993, he would direct a painterly heart-rending adaptation of Edith Wharton's novel of 1870s New York, *The Age of Innocence*. Literary adaptations sealed the reputations of producer Ismail Merchant and director James Ivory who began a successful run of period dramas with Henry James's *The Bostonians* (1984), moving on to to E.M. Forster with *A Room With a View* (1985) and *Maurice* (1987). The combination of visual richness and restrained emotion was for some audiences clearly a corrective to the more garish high-concept Hollywood products.

There are the first hints of a new topography altogether in the film landscape with *Tron* (1982), the first feature to employ extensive computer-generated effects (courtesy of the supercomputer CRAY 1-S/1300) and to marry these with animation in sequences of futuristic motorbikes and a deadly high-tech game of what looks remarkably like Frisbee. Ironically, at the time, all this technology rendered the film ineligible for an Academy Award for special effects. There was no doubting the developing relationship of man and machine, though, that had run through the decades from *Metropolis* through *La Bête Humaine* to *2001*. It might be a celebration: see Tom Cruise at the controls of a phallic F14 jet in *Top Gun* (1986) – gasp! whoop! cheer! Or it could be eerie: one glimpse of James Woods in *Videodrome* (1983) engaging in erotic congress with a television that breathes alluringly to him with the voice and mouth of Debbie Harry confirms what he has just heard, that 'the television screen is part of the structure of the brain'. The eighties also saw the dawn of cyberpunk: soon after the term was first used by William Gibson, Katsuhiro Otomo's *Akira* (1988) was an early screen representation of urban cyberpunk gangs. In an ostensibly more traditional setting, Woody Allen's *Zelig* (1983) used the new technology to insert the chameleon-like title character into various historical situations, making him plausibly an associate of both Al Capone and Hitler and pre-figuring the moment when computer-generated images would make anything possible on screen and simultaneously undermine our trust in what our eyes were taking in.

Computer technology was now woven into personal lives with hand-held games and chunky mobile phones. The home computers, Sinclairs, Ataris, Commodores and Acorns, were here to stay; bulky off-white plastic intruders colonised spare rooms and studies. With the increase in information and communication technology, the boundary between home and work began to erode. The opening up of global markets increased labour mobility. Long-distance relationships became more common, perpetuated by phones and computer networks.

The Music Television network (MTV) began transmitting in 1981 with what must have seemed a wittily prophetic pop promo: 'Video Killed the Radio Star'. At first the directors of the short music films were anonymous; once credits appeared, MTV directors were seen to include David Fincher, Spike Jonze and Michel Gondry. The MTV style proved influential beyond the music business, bringing down the average length of a shot, incorporating media and graphics into sliced-up narratives.

Bigger budget films seemed at once bold and nervous. In the USA the promising new directors of the 1970s had often been financed by the studios, but art did not always repay investment. The commercial failure of Michael Cimino's western *Heaven's Gate* (1980) – the film allegedly cost $40 million and returned less than $4 million – terrified the accountants. Financiers took a wide detour to avoid auteurs and for some years it was even tough for any kind of filmmaker to get that staple of Hollywood lore, a cowboy picture, into production.

By contrast, a film that announced what it was about in one pithy phrase and whose plot could be summarised in a couple of sentences at most was deemed high concept and, with luck, high reward – an idea that has been credited to television director Barry Diller back in the 1970s. *Jaws* is an obvious high-concept film, as are *Beverley Hills Cop* (1984) and *Flashdance* (1983). Studio executives sought pitches that were no more than three sentences long – for films that were simple but with a specific hook (grown man in baby's body etc) and mass audience appeal. Disaster films such as

Earthquake (1974) or *Meteor!* (1979) had an instant advantage: you knew what you were getting from the title alone – and the genre continues into the twenty-first century with such offerings as *Snakes on a Plane* (2006) or *Sunshine* (2007) where astronauts struggle to revive a dying sun.

Sequels began to seem more attractive. The best box office bet was a film suitable for the whole family that could deliver a few thrilling effects along the way, perhaps with the potential bonus of a franchise opening up. Hence the success of *Ghostbusters* and *Gremlins* (both 1984). By the end of the decade, the summer of 1989 could boast *Indiana Jones and the Last Crusade*, *Ghostbusters II* and Tim Burton's *Batman* – as well as *Lethal Weapon II* for the dads and older boys.

And the exemplar of the safe but stirring blockbuster, the one that would engage all the family while reinforcing what they held dear, was a film by the supreme master of the techniques that make us smile and gasp through our tears . . . the grand master of the blue light himself, Steven Spielberg. *E.T.* was high concept. Spielberg's film about the alien child who escaped from the mothership carried the tagline: 'He is afraid. He is totally alone. He is 3 million light years from home.' It was high on both effects and emotion – exploring anxieties about fragmented families and neglected children, whilst also being visually dazzling. It was highly, hugely, successful.

. . . .

E.T. (1982)

Director: Steven Spielberg
Cast: Dee Wallace, Henry Thomas, Drew Barrymore (and the many uncredited who made the creature so human)

The oyster eyes of the extra-terrestrial who befriends Elliott, the worried little boy fretting for his absent father and abandoned mother, became the repository for a decade's worth of sentiment. Weeping at performances of *E.T.* became an international pastime as audiences feared for the survival of the wrinkled alien so far from his own planet. In Britain the *Sun* newspaper reported that Diana, Princess of Wales, was openly lacrymose. 'After the film's charity premiere, the Princess told its seven-year-old star, Drew Barrymore: I need my hankies.' The *Daily Express* suggested her mother-in-law might be equally affected, with a cartoon showing *E.T.* arriving at Buckingham Palace, which is awash with tears.

Star writers, despatched by newspapers and magazines, reviewed the phenomenon, all correctly identifying the critical moment when the ailing creature languishes, close to death. From Los Angeles, British novelist Martin Amis recounted his traumatic hours in a cinema: 'Towards the end of *E.T.*, barely able to support my own grief and bewilderment, I turned and looked down the aisle at my fellow sufferers: executive, black dude, Japanese businessman, punk, hippie, mother, teenager, child. Each face was a mask of tears.' Val Hennessy in Exeter, observed, 'when naked little E.T. holds out his wasted hands, and turns beseeching, embryo-like eyes to the temporarily repelled screen mother, the cinema throbs with sobs. "He wants his mum", shriek wet-eyed children everywhere. "Help him. Please help him".' But, instead, Elliott's mother and brother naively open the door to a squadron of monsters in the form of scientists in white suits, eyes obscured by helmets. Elliott's mother's own eyes widen and her jaw drops open in what is a trademark Spielberg pose. Soon E.T. and Elliott are plucked away from the home and strapped into separate isolation tents, hooked up by wires and tubes to machines, unable even to touch fingers, in a nightmare reversal of intensive care. The creature loses vital signs.

Sociological interpretations of the film sprang up. It was a metaphor for a depersonalised and depressed America that languished in arid materialism. A Jewish director had delivered a parable of resurrection. Steven Spielberg explained the film's effect in terms of its intention as a story of compassion with themes of tolerance towards those who are different. So we could learn to love E.T. with his curious waddle and shiny, folded skin, and chuckle at his attempts to understand a world that appears to have been designed for the pleasure of able-bodied, affluent Americans with well-stocked fridges and shiny bicycles. For all E.T. might appear to be from another galaxy, he was instantly, recognisably appealing.

To begin where the film does, there is the blue light which is night but not dark, a recognisably illuminating dusk. This light drenches a forest where a gentle rustling indicates industry in the undergrowth. The movement is made by a party of naturalist aliens gathering botanical specimens on the green planet on which they have landed, for all the world like an Edwardian outing but with latex folds instead of plus fours. So *E.T.* begins with a futuristic image that is also comfortingly nostalgic. When the jeeps with humans arrive to check on reports of unusual lights and activity, they seem by contrast like the barbaric intruders, crushing the plants beneath their tyres as their headlights cut through the soft blue.

Steven Spielberg claimed the idea for *E.T.* came to him when he saw an alien in his 1977 film *Close Encounters of the Third Kind* and felt a certain sadness. He also attributed the evolution of the character to a childhood fantasy about an imaginary friend who supported him when his parents were divorcing. Onscreen, though, these sympathetic if nebulous ideas are honed into an efficient mechanism for eliciting emotions and, more precisely, tears. In a documentary made for the twentieth anniversary of the film, Spielberg spoke of the components of this mechanism and of his frustration that he had failed to 'perfect' the emotion and the possibilities that new technologies allowed him to tweak certain scenes. He then demonstrated how modern computer manipulation of the image allowed the eyes to move to suggest that E.T. feels guilt at having dressed up. This is not simply average guilt, though, but the kind of shy shame a small child might display before an adult.

It hardly requires genius to spot that E.T. toddles like a small child. It did, however, take the features of two prominent American writers, Carl Sandburg and Ernest Hemingway, and of the German-Swiss physicist and philosopher Albert Einstein, to make this alien infant appear both wise and compassionate. E.T.'s physiognomy was constructed to include not only aspects of these faces but those of a pet pug dog, while his gravelly voice emanated from a grandmother, voice actress Pat Welsh, to which sound designer Ben Burtt added attendant intimate sounds including his own wife snuffling with a cold as she slept. Burtt, who has provided many imagined characters' voices, from *Star Wars'* Chewbacca up to little robot *WALL-E* (2008), seemed to have our species' ear, the psycho-audio knack, that packs a whole series of associations into a few decibels.

E.T. was a curiously familiar alien, cute yet acute. On its release this story of a grotesque extra-terrestrial with 'humanity' far outperformed its contemporary, *Blade Runner*, in which a good-looking man who appears human may yet be a cloned replicant. Burtt had worked before with composer John Williams to create the mythic mood of *Star Wars*. In *E.T.* the same partnership marries that jaunty heroism (little Elliott, serious and full of integrity, setting off alone for school on his bicycle) with romanticism (both Elliott and E.T. yearn for a complete and fulfilling home, a lack symbolised by the glowing pulsating 'heart' in E.T.'s chest). Williams's score repeats its motif until the key moment at which Elliott and E.T. lift off the ground on the bicycle.

In the passage of soundtrack music that is helpfully named 'E.T. Is Dying', sweet and sharp are mixed in the slow tinkly picking out of the main theme, minor chords, ominous brass, quivering strings: the effect is both pretty and melancholy, recalling the humour and warmth of the preceding episodes but at the same time building into a musical tension worthy of the composer Bernard Herrmann, who provided Hitchcock with atmospheric scores: Will he die? There is also archive footage of Steven Spielberg on set instructing the child actor Henry Thomas, who played Elliott. Spielberg whispers close to him as they both gaze into the mass of medical paraphernalia where the ailing alien lies, 'It'll be sadder if it's happy-sad.'

So is there something specific about the kind of happy-sad weeping *E.T.* provoked? In some ways, the film itself demonstrates the difference. Immediately after E.T.'s miraculous resurrection, Elliott has to fake hysterical grief, a battery of debilitating sobs that double up his skinny frame, rather than an emotion pulled from him by a series of stimuli.

The tear-jerker is often pleasantly cathartic – a good old weep; it frequently shuffles the same cards as the horror film. *E.T.* is built around a distorted anthropomorphic form, with the characteristics of a foetus; the family is often at threat in the tear-jerker, whether through circumstances or some pathology. Spielberg is clearly a master of setting up the desirability but fragility of the family unit – his films from *E.T.* to *A.I.* to *Catch Me If You Can* show children or child-like adults or even aliens gazing from outside in the cold at a tableau of familial life. Given the trauma of his own parents' divorce, Spielberg's theme comes as no surprise. The audience, anonymous in the dark, can shed inhibitions and join in, expressive and conservative at the same time. In the 1980s, the age of divorce and serial marriage, extended families set against high expectations of happiness and material comfort – the family weepy was the ultimate high-concept film.

How though does Spielberg, or any other director, actually make us weep? Analysts of the cinema audience's tears, like theorists Murray Smith, author of *Engaging Characters*, and Carl Plantinga, author of *Moving Viewers*, observe the same kind of 'emotional contagion' from the screen, explicable because, like primates, we are a species given to mimicry. As football managers kick imaginary balls on the touchline and anxious parents reach for imaginary pedals when teaching offspring to drive, so sitting with a distressed person, even one you barely know, can cause your own eyes to fill.

It may even be more than mimicry. Developments in neuroscience suggest we may even 'feel' the pain experienced by characters onscreen.

The agents here are mirror neurons, nerve cells that fail to differentiate between watching somebody do something, and doing it ourselves. 'Our survival depends on understanding the actions, intentions and emotions of others', Dr Giacomo Rizzolatti of the University of Parma told the *New York Times* in 2006, 'mirror neurons allow us to grasp the minds of others not through conceptual reasoning but through direct simulation. By feeling, not thinking.' Crucially, these mirror neurons work for emotions as well as actions. Dr Marco Iacoboni at the University of California added: 'if you see me choke up . . . mirror neurons in your brain simulate my distress. You automatically have empathy for me. You know how I feel because you literally feel for what I'm feeling.'

When that distress is projected in close-up twenty foot high, the effect may be overwhelming. If a character in a Spielberg film goes slack-jawed with astonishment, so, too, to a degree, does the audience. When Elliott and his siblings watch E.T. prone and feebly gesturing, they are tremulous, biting back the tears, and the audience may blubber, too. Spielberg knew exactly where to employ the latest computer technology to 'perfect' the pathetic movement of E.T.'s eyes for maximum effect.

Directors have to use their powers judiciously, though, if we, the audience, are not all to grimace along with the villain. The mirror impulse can override conscious judgement or upset the dynamic of the film, rendering the Sheriff of Nottingham (Alan Rickman) more attractive, for example, than Kevin Costner's *Robin Hood, Prince of Thieves* (1991). It can even play directly against the intentions of the director. The best-known example of this is Hitchcock's 1942 film *Saboteur* in which a Nazi agent, Fry, is pursued by the police to the Statue of Liberty. The hero, Kane, corners him high up on the gantry around the torch. The camera stays on Fry's face as he retreats and falls back over the barrier to dangle from the Statue's hand, hundreds of feet above ground and sea. Kane climbs after him (cut away to medium shot of the terrified man gazing up), grabs hold of Fry's jacket and asks him if he can get a grip with his feet. Fry, close to tears, shakes his head: I can't. Then a couple of shots later, Fry's face appears in a tighter shot as he offers to repent . . . but the seams of the jacket are beginning to pull apart. The villain's face, shiny with anguish, displays a gradual realisation of what is about to happen. The camera stays on him as he drops to his death.

The effect is so shocking that the hero's subsequent climb back up to the gantry and the embrace of his girlfriend seem banal; victory over the enemy is diminished by the lingering hope that the villain might yet have been saved. According to Murray Smith, 'Hitchcock is reported to have subsequently regretted this effect.'

Some of us in the audience may be more vulnerable than others. Researchers in Taiwan trying to establish if women were indeed predisposed to crying at movies found that the mirror neuron system does differ between genders, evidence to reinforce the observed female preference for melodramas. Some films openly play to this – Barbara Stanwyck in the 1937 melodrama *Stella Dallas* stands aside to let her daughter make an advantageous marriage, only able to watch the ceremony from out in the street, her cheeks shining with tears of selfless joy. In *Love Story* (1970) lovers Ryan O'Neal and Ali McGraw cry constantly after her terminal diagnosis (he in particular), augmented by Francis Lai's theme. So effective was the combination that, nearly forty years later, an American shopping mall ran twenty-four-hour screenings in a Father's Day promotion to see if anyone could withstand the *Love Story* onslaught (the prize being a La-Z-Boy recliner). Anthony Minghella's *Truly Madly Deeply* (1990) reverses the convention by showing Juliet Stevenson weeping at length early in the film before we have any knowledge of the character she mourns, played by Alan Rickman. With little context, it is still moving.

Men also cry at films, at the sacrifices made by hobbits or even the teen-to-dotage romance of *The Notebook* (2004), a romantic saga that spans sixty years. Two twenty-first century animations had tear-inducing moments of almost clockwork precision – *Up* (2009) began with a compressed account of a marriage, ending with the wife's death, that was a miracle of economical characterisation; and *Toy Story 3* appeared to trigger in men in particular regrets for things lost, with the sequence where the toys' owner, Andy, now aged seventeen, departs for college, leaving behind not just his parents but his childhood playthings.

Sometimes the effect is the more devastating for its subtlety. I emerged sobbing into London's Soho after an almost empty screening of Louis Malle's *Au Revoir Les Enfants* (1987), a film based on an incident from 1942 when Malle was at a Catholic boarding school which sheltered Jewish boys among its pupils. The film confines its onscreen tears to a restrained encounter at the beginning as the central character, Julien, leaves his mother at the start of term, and a final shot of Julien's face, with a voiceover from decades later. The intervening narrative involves us, like the central character, in the minutiae of life in the boarding school. The betrayal which ensues arises entirely from those circumstances; it is both casual and unconscious but it is a tragedy in which we are all – viewers and protagonist alike – complicit.

For me, this film did not lose the power to move on second viewing two decades later, although there could be few surprises in the narrative. Critic Roger Ebert even observed Louis Malle in tears after a screening. *Au Revoir Les Enfants* has no flying bicycles, no soaring John Williams score; yet unlike a melodramatic weepy, it is genuinely distressing. Why – for the recognition of the carelessness with which we blithely do damage? Or because it is based on real events which cannot be tinkered with in script editing?

Unlike *E.T.*, Malle's film does not reassure. Like it, though, its effect derives from close association with the characters, intensified by the suspense. Talking in another context about Hitchcock, film theorist David Bordwell suggests tension onscreen may trigger involuntary responses which are so 'arresting and arousing *in themselves*' that 'for some part of you, every viewing of a movie *is* the first time'.

So can it be overdone? Some people (like me) have never cried in *E.T.* although they admire it as a piece of filmmaking. The technique, however skilled, can be too apparent. Bizarre as it may seem, in fact *E.T.* makes me angry. If it is a film about compassion and tolerance, or even a film about minorities, how successful would it have been if it had been about, say, an old person like the heavy smoker grandmother, Pat Welsh, who provided E.T.'s voice? It could even have been a story about someone with different physical characteristics from the norm since inside that extra-terrestrial suit during filming were, at various times, a boy with no legs riding a skateboard and actors Tamara de Treaux and Pat Bilon, both under three foot tall. Might they have been less cute?

Even if you feel you are being manipulated, you may still – to your own embarrassment – cry, a syndrome Carl Plantinga identifies as 'meta emotion' in which you are simultaneously inside and outside the feeling. Or you may get angry and exasperated which is a combination Danish director Lars von Trier appears to seek with his extravagant dark melodramas such as *Dancer in the Dark* (2010), in which Bjork is deceived, betrayed and exploited from trailer park to death row, or *Antichrist* (2009), where a beautifully shot black and white sequence shows the death of a child in slow motion, lingering on the dreadful pathos. Here is a director who acknowledges cinema's power to provoke tears and pushes it to the limit, with considerable skill. His purpose, though, is less clear – catharsis or satire? Inside or outside the experience?

TOP GUN (1986)

Director: Tony Scott
Cast: Tom Cruise, Kelly McGillis, Val Kilmer
Colour

The landing deck on the aircraft carrier, as seen through the windscreen of the incoming F14, fills no more than a tenth of the screen. The jet swings in towards it, lurching out of control. Pilot Cougar is sweating and hysterical, eyes rolling down to the photograph of his wife and daughter. Pulling up alongside him is another jet, with his colleagues Goose and Maverick (Tom Cruise) at the controls. Cool and focused, ever upbeat, Maverick calls across the radio to Cougar and reassures him. He looks to his right, as if seeking eye contact with Cougar, and we hear him talking his friend down into the landing routine. Cougar's plane finally thuds onto its floating home and the restraining cables lock around its undercarriage.

Top Gun is a story of skill, rivalry, love and more than twenty thousand pounds of thrust in each of those jets' twin engines. The tagline said it all: 'I feel the need, the need for speed'. Director Tony Scott thought of it as *Star Wars* on earth: *Top Gun* is doubly a child of that, since it was released four years after President Reagan announced his Star Wars Initiative of anti-missile ground and space systems. The aerial war games of the film gloss Cold War manoeuvres with shiny technology and a sense of urgency – although there is very little jeopardy in the film itself. Maverick and crew skirmish with Russian MiGs over the Indian Ocean in F14 Tomcats. Five years later, F14s will be used in another theatre, in President George Bush Sr's Operation Desert Storm, taking away the breath of invading Iraqis, invaded Kuwaitis and many others caught in between.

Tony Scott considered a number of styles before deciding how to tackle *Top Gun*. In the end he decided the mood was 'rock and roll: the pilots were the rock stars and presumably the sky was the great stadium. He claims he was chosen to direct *Top Gun* partly because of the distinctive style of his vampire film *The Hunger* but mainly for a stylish Saab car advertisement in which the luxury vehicle in question appeared to race a jet.

Jerry Bruckheimer, one of the producers of *Top Gun*, once stated that filmmakers were in the transportation business, 'we transport audiences from one place to another'. In a sense, from the very beginnings of cinema and the oncoming train, this fascination with motion – and man's relationship to it – obsesses all filmmakers and excites audiences. It might be of the stately journey of the rocket to the moon in Méliès's 1902 film, or Keaton on board the train in *The General*, or the opening of *La Bête Humaine*, cattle stampedes and horse versus engine races in westerns, or car chases in police dramas like *Bullitt*, space battles in *Star Wars*, or a train again in *Mission Impossible* but this time lashed to a helicopter – or, indeed, a thousand other combinations in so many action films. Audiences have always felt the need for speed and directors have found ways to make it ever faster and ever more immediate. Tony Scott's own film debut (as an actor in brother Ridley's student film) was on a bicycle, freewheeling through the streets and along the coast at Billingham.

The early period of film coincided not just with the birth of the twentieth century and Freud's adventures in psychoanalysis but travelling at gathering speed in trains and then automobiles. The first carousel opened on Coney Island in 1876 but, by 1895, it was offering the Whirlwind of Death. Within a couple of years, cinema audiences could see *The Haverstraw Tunnel*, the first 'phantom ride' shot by a cameraman strapped to the front of a train.

From *Captain Blood* and *The Prisoner of Zenda* onwards, action cinema delivered regular bouts of clashing swords or galloping horses. Compared to early cinema, *Top Gun* spaces out its action sequences. It begins with a mid-air crisis but there may be ten or fifteen minutes of romantic subplot or homoerotic inter-pilot rivalry before the planes take off again. In *How Hollywood Tells It*, David Bordwell notes that 1920s films were cut to a relatively pacy average of 4–6 seconds per shot. (Even then there are wild variations in the same year between, say, the gliding progress of F.W. Murnau's *Sunrise* (1927) and the First World War fighting drama *Wings*, first recipient of Academy Award for Best Picture with its aerial battle, explosions and spectacular crashes. Even the tagline for *Wings* is pure *Top Gun*: 'Youth, hitting the clouds! Laughing at danger! Fighting, loving, dodging death!') The arrival of sound and the need to lay in dialogue slowed the process down. Between 1930 and 1960, the average shot runs for 8–11 seconds but things speed up again in the mid-sixties and by the 1980s mass entertainment films never push the average into double digits. *Top Gun*, for example, has an average shot length of 3.5 seconds. In the twenty-first century the average is closer to 2 seconds.

The speed with which the film passes through the camera may have a vertiginous effect, too – whether time-lapse or high-speed. Bordwell and Kristin Thompson in *Film Art* describe a fireball in a lift shaft in *Die Hard* which appears to get faster as it approaches the camera. The fire was filmed at one hundred frames per second at the bottom of the shaft, which effectively made it look slower when projected at twenty-four frames per second, with the filming speed adjusted on its way up to simulate fearsome acceleration.

In contrast, slow motion is essential to the fighting sequences in the 'gun-fu' series begun in the 1980s by John Woo's *A Better Tomorrow*. It may seem a perverse way to portray fast events like gunfire but television series had been showing action in slow motion for decades to disguise a lack of dynamism. As David Bordwell points out, sound and fury punctuated by silence and slow motion or even a static staring match – the so-called pause/burst/pause – gives greater impact to the physical contact. The Hong Kong cinema seems to 'ask our bodies to recall elemental and universal events like striking, swinging, twisting, leaping and rolling'.

Woo's kinetic style gives rise over time to the most flamboyant sequence in *The Matrix* (1999), known as Bullet Time. Keanu Reeves, in his trademark long, dark coat, appears suspended in the air – and time – as he dodges bullets in the slowest of motion. He leans back at an incredibly acrobatic angle, arms circling gracefully, to evade the missiles which leave visible traces as though they had been shot through liquid. The digitally manipu-lated effect was created by placing a hundred cameras in a semi-circle around the actor. Each camera captured a single, still image in sequence, which were fed into a computer, and spliced together to produce the effect of movement. The computer filled in the missing information, allowing the production team to manipulate the imagery and to slow down or speed up without judder or jerkiness, enhancing the illusion of fluid motion. It is a brilliant effect, if more dream-like than dynamic, and action directors all over the world promptly imitated it. It also began a crossover between surreal action and the increasingly 'real' look of animation. These days, it can be hard to tell where so-called live action lies. Is it any more related to the laws of physics and observable phenomena than a superhero animation like *The Incredibles* (2004)?

In action films, there is often a clear demonstration of one of cinema's enduring conundrums. Are you, the audience, in or out of the action? Unlike the moment in the highly emotional film when you have to decide to abandon yourself to it or resist the manipulation, action films allow you to be simultaneously a spectator and a participant. From the spectator's perspective there are rules. If a character appears in a sequence in the right of frame, looking to another character offscreen to the left, then they must always in subsequent shots maintain that notional spatial relationship. Otherwise the camera 'crosses the line' and those in the audience, static observers, feel disoriented. This convention of framing has shaped most narrative film. On the other hand, near the beginning of *Top Gun* there is a shot from inside the cockpit of an F14, from the point of view of one of the pilots as he attempts a landing on the carrier, that puts us not only behind the windscreen but behind his eyes.

Experimental filmmakers like Jean-Luc Godard mix up and mess with these conventions to remind us we are only looking at a film. As computer-generated images have become more sophisticated, they, too, demand certain flashy breaks with convention to show the new effects off to their best advantage, whether it is the ability to render liquid metal in *Terminator 2* (1991) or the point of view of a bullet in *Wanted* (2008). That said, in 1902 Méliès shot scenes from the point of view of the space rocket approaching the moon. In fact all formal film logic may be abandoned if the effect is good enough.

Eisenstein saw a practical application to the power of a strong audience reaction: he believed it could 'reforge the psyche'. Physiological reactions to what was seen onscreen set off conditioned reflexes. Before psychologists had traced out the notion of 'emotional contagion', Eisenstein identified a 'physical infectiousness'. Decades before the discovery of mirror neurons, he found that juxtaposition of images – the more extreme the better – could provoke physical response. In the famous *Battleship Potemkin* Odessa Steps sequence, a child is shot and falls. Two close-ups and two mid-shots show him trampled – one foot steps on his ankle, a brogue crushes his tiny wrist, other feet kick him over like a doll and a pair of heels stamp on his torso. The effect is not pathetic but brutal. The shots land like blows, evoking discomfort rather than sympathy.

Eisenstein's purpose was to galvanise his viewers into political action. Other directors have used expressionism to evoke the power and speed of violence – a brilliant example is found at the beginning of the 1980s in Martin Scorsese's *Raging Bull*. When he embarked on the film, Scorsese was not a boxing fan; his interest, and that of screenwriter Paul Schrader, lay with the character's arc from hopeful to victor to vanquished and on, as the film progresses, through the humiliation to a battered yet significant knowledge. The fight scenes, however, are exhilarating and exhausting by turns. Although the actual conduct of the fight is not followed as it might be on television, there is a clear sense of which blows matter. LaMotta's two encounters with champion Sugar Ray Robinson in 1943, fights just three weeks apart, are handled in contrasting styles. The first bout – which LaMotta won – is brightly lit (the entire film is in black and white) with a swooping camera that swings with the boxers' punches. The light bounces off LaMotta's shoulders as he floors Robinson; the floor of the ring is dazzling. In the second fight, which LaMotta lost on a judges' decision, Lucifer has fallen. Infernal smoke drifts before the lens; it is hard to discern features and blows land with a terrible roar (sound editor Frank Warner used animal noises – horse and elephant – to intensify the desperation).

A quarter of a century later, director Paul Greengrass employed a different kind of subjectivity in action sequences to convey the confusion of violence, as if dragging the viewer into the fight – for example, in the Waterloo Station sequence of *The Bourne Ultimatum*. This is not smooth, balletic violence of the shoot-'em-up genre, so common that it has become a form of abstraction. Greengrass opts instead for a sequence that is impressionistic in the way that our perception of fast-moving events would be if they were happening to us. Which, in a way, they are. So when Jason Bourne takes on three CIA operatives, grabbing the arm of one and spinning him into his colleague so that they both lose their footing, Greengrass slices that action into four shots from contrasting angles, exaggerating the dislocation, knocking spies and viewers sideways together as Bourne turns to despatch the remaining assailant.

Twenty-five years after it was made, *Top Gun*'s speed and immediacy look stately by comparison. For the sequences in the air, tight shots of the pilots' heads as they fly are juxtaposed with aerial photography of the swooping and soaring jets. Although the audience is occasionally placed in the cockpit looking out, experiencing the dizzying rush, much of the energy derives from the music and views of the control room where officers and colleagues yell and scowl and cheer at the pilots' exploits.

Top Gun was an immediate and lasting box office hit and a big seller in the fledgling home video market. One way or another it was high-octane entertainment. Maybe, as at the beginning of the century, audiences craved the sensation that would eradicate the complications of modern life, as it put on another of its periodic bursts of speed with the domestic use of mobile phones and computers.

During the 1980s director Kathryn Bigelow was developing a distinctive and thoughtful commentary on action in her films, which were, at one level, effective genre pictures. The key lies back in the 1970s, however, when Bigelow was a film student at Columbia, taught by Susan Sontag. Her debut short, *The Set-Up*, shows two men in a protracted and bloody fight while in voiceover two theoreticians discuss the appeal of violence onscreen. Bigelow has often acknowledged film's ability to create a profound emotional response by placing the viewer in the centre of the action. Her 1991 thriller *Point Break* has a breathless dizzying chase (cop Keanu Reeves after robber Patrick Swayze) down alleys, over the fences between suburban gardens and in and out of the houses. You feel every jolt and lurch and, when Swayze hurls a large dog at Reeves, you duck.

Bigelow's most praised meditation yet on action was not in the context of crime, but war, with the Oscar-winning *The Hurt Locker* (2009), a film of 131 minutes in which a bomb-disposal expert in with US forces in Baghdad simply does his job. There is no back story, no attempt to explain his obsessional behaviour in psychological terms: the audience must simply live through the ordeal of the dismantling of one potentially lethal device after another. The clock is always ticking and, thanks to an episode in the first minutes in which an established star is killed off (a Hollywood taboo) they can never relax. Bigelow told BBC Radio 4, 'Maybe this is a slightly heretical comment but prose has the ability to be reflective. I don't think film can be quite as reflective as prose, but what it can do is create physiological reactions to what you're watching. You or I may not want to travel to the front line of a war zone but film can take you there, give you that experience in as three-dimensional a way as possible.'

The Hurt Locker was written by Mark Boal, who, as a reporter was embedded with US troops in Iraq. The film sought to get close to the experience of reportage without mitigating the experience (although the whole business is a fictional recreation). *The Hurt Locker* has a similar mood to a film by one of Bigelow's influences, Sam Fuller, another former reporter. *The Big Red One* (1980) depicts war as a series of incidents, some gruesome, some absurd. It is deeply memorable – as if it were a personal sense memory – without having any narrative you can recall. In many ways, those films differ from *Top Gun*, which has a conventional storyline interrupted by frenetic episodes of action, the equivalent of song and dance numbers in a musical.

Bigelow by contrast used something of the chaos of war in her production, keeping actors ignorant of the precise placing of cameras, for example. A review by *New York Times* critic David Edelstein is evidence of the efficacy of her methods: 'Here is how I knew I was inside the movie. Under fire, his weapon jammed from the sticky blood of its last operator, James screams at Eldridge to clean the blood off the bullets and panicky Eldridge yells, "How?" and James says, "Saliva!" – and I found myself building up spit, as if maybe I could help before the next onslaught.' Eisenstein would have approved of the effect although possibly not of the cause.

WHEN HARRY MET SALLY (1989)

Director: Rob Reiner
Cast: Billy Crystal, Meg Ryan
Colour

'It Had To Be You'. The song is from 1924, a veteran of several romantic and/or comedy films including *Casablanca* and *Annie Hall*. The singer, though, Harry Connick Jr, was young and his retro soundtrack album sold in the millions. In the decade in which marriage and divorce rates peaked, it was the same old sweet song, with a 1980s twist.

Nora Ephron wrote the screenplay for this peppy romantic comedy of the pursuit of happiness through the years by Harry (Billy Crystal) and Sally (Meg Ryan). It is frank about contemporary negotiations between the sexes: love is possible but probably fleeting; friendship often endures but may not be possible between men and women. So can you take the staying power of one and combine it with the excitement of the other? For all its

1980s modernity, though, this is at heart a formula romantic comedy that begins with a 'meet-cute'. The 'meet-cute' – a term which earns a whole discussion to itself in 2006 romcom *The Holiday* – is the first encounter, always in some unlikely or comic situation, between the two people who are destined for the romance in any film. The more antagonism or hilarity generated by this encounter, the more we feel they earn their eventual happiness. Sometimes this can seem like a demented game of consequences: when diffident palaeontologist meets sparky millionaire's niece on the golf course, there's a mix-up over golf balls . . . and we're into *Bringing Up Baby* (1938).

The cute encounter here occurs when the apparently ill-matched individuals – Sally, the pretty, uptight obsessive and Harry, the wisecracking slob – share a car journey. The screenplay races, despite the diversions and pit stops of other relationships, to an inevitable finishing line, a last-minute dash against the odds at the twenty-third hour of the twelfth month of the year for a declaration of love. 'I came here tonight because when you realize you want to spend the rest of your life with somebody, you want the rest of your life to start as soon as possible,' declares Harry.

Nora Ephron's script is never sappy. It presents spiked observations about sexual politics. The 'deli-orgasm' scene, which famously makes women laugh a lot louder than men, is not a generous joke; it undermines the ideal of intimacy that is the foundation of modern romantic comedies. The story is interspersed with what seems like documentary footage of older couples talking about marriage. Gradually, the audience begins to hope that one day Harry and Sally will be giving a similar testimony. As it happens, these witnesses are also faking it: they are character actors retelling true stories that director Rob Reiner collected from real couples.

The fundamental premise of most romantic comedy, which distinguishes it from drama, is that there is one perfect mate out there, if they can only be found. This is like a variation on Aristophanes's speech in Plato's *Symposium* where he outlines the idea of a divided whole separated by

Zeus that runs around trying to be reunited with its missing half. Or, as Charlie (Kelly McGillis), the civilian assessor checking out the pilots' performance in *Top Gun* presciently observes to Tom Cruise as Maverick, 'So *you're* the one . . .' A decade later, Cruise will rework the sentiment in his famous speech as eponymous sports agent *Jerry Maguire* (1996) when he declares to estranged screen wife Renee Zellweger, as part of a commercial metaphor about emotional vulnerability, 'You complete me.'

The structure of romantic comedy itself often seems to replicate that Platonic notion. Symmetry is important in the resolution of the romantic problem: the apparently incompatible protagonists must find common interest and the 'meet-cute' be offset by a grand declaration. Symmetry also contributes to the appeal of a popular dramatic romance like *The Notebook*. To be satisfying there must be a logic: like a Shakespearean gender reversal mix-up in the woods, it must all be worked through. The bigger the challenge, the more emphatic the emotional payoff. Perhaps the most impressive example (although not strictly a romantic comedy, it does have both romance and humour) is Maria's conversion of icy authoritarian Captain von Trapp into a gentle troubadour, crooning in a moonlit greenhouse in *The Sound of Music*. Somewhere in her youth or childhood, Maria certainly did do something good.

Her experience, sadly, is not typical. How many divorces of the 1980s or 1990s were instigated by those little girls of the 1960s who believed from *The Sound of Music* that you could coax emotion from repressed men if, like Maria, you only tried hard enough and remained cheerful? Psychological studies of the effect of screen romance now suggest that younger people, in particular, develop unrealistic expectations of love and romance from film – which has long been an easier way to gain information or vicarious experience about sex and emotions than asking the parents.

The development of the star system fed illusions from the earliest days of film. Famous offscreen couples from Mary Pickford and Douglas Fairbanks onwards intoxicated their fans with declarations of devotion more extreme than any film dialogue. Film magazines like *Photoplay* reinforced the dazzling image, not only by featuring Pickford and Fairbanks in their glamorous home, but by continually reminding their readers how vital it was to find and keep the right man, calling women 'matrimonial ostriches' who 'refuse to admit that marriage is a competitive game in which getting a husband is merely the first trick'.

The idea that marriage could be played like the stock market, ran through the romantic comedies pioneered by Cecil B. DeMille. Sumiko Higashi, author of *Cecil B. DeMille and American Culture*, has written of DeMille's 'transformation of the sentimental heroine' into 'a clothes horse and sexual playmate', exchanging, in the words of DeMille's early domestic dramas, old wives for new. Comedies such as *Don't Change Your Husband* (1919) and *Why Change Your Wife?* (1920) had been made specifically to capture a female audience, who began to link romance with independence and, crucially, with consumption. Yet for all their racy titles (a nod to the rise in divorce rates after the First World War) these silent comedies are morality tales, in which ungrateful or unfaithful spouses learn the value of a solid marriage in a modern world. In *Why Change Your Wife?* a nagging housewife (Gloria Swanson) nearly loses her man to a modern, flirtatious woman (gorgeous Bebe Daniels who would be more tempting yet to husbands as vamp Satan Synne in *The Affairs of Anatol* (1921)). Swanson eventually reclaims her spouse with the help of, shall we say, progressive clothing ('sleeveless, backless, transparent, indecent – I'll go the limit') and a title card delivers the crucial message '. . . and now you know what every husband knows; that a man would rather have his wife for a sweetheart than any other woman, but ladies, if you would be your husband's sweetheart you simply must learn when to forget that you're his wife'.

Beautiful clothes are key to Swanson's strategy and affluence generally is accounted an aphrodisiac down the decades. The biggest grossing romantic comedy of all time thus far is *Pretty Woman*, which arrives at the end of the 1980s, a well-executed if repellent Cinderella story of prostitution and luxury shopping on Rodeo Drive in which the man literally buys the woman's affections. And ensures box office success, as the producer observes in Vincente Minnelli's knife-sharp satire on Hollywood *The Bad and the Beautiful* (1952): 'Give me a picture that ends with a kiss and black ink in the books.'

Dinner is always a key scene. It allows for glamour but it may also suggest a large wallet since romantic comedy aspires upwards in economic terms, however much the protagonists protest that love conquers all. Tracy Lord (Katharine Hepburn) is never going to end up with reporter Mike Connor (James Stewart) in *The Philadelphia Story* (1940). The man is in awe of the size of her swimming pool, after all. Despite a little intervening amorous quadrille, she is clearly destined for fellow socialite and ex-husband, C.K. Dexter Haven (Cary Grant). The humble carwash guy may yet reveal himself as a European prince and the penniless writer own up to his news-paper fortunes. When there is a mismatch, it may be unsettling – will the world's biggest film star (Julia Roberts) in *Notting Hill* (1999) really find lasting contentment with travel bookshop owner (Hugh Grant)?

There are few blue-collar romcoms – Michelle Pfeiffer and Al Pacino are simply too gorgeous to be plausible cooking and serving in a diner in *Frankie and Johnny* (1991). Going rough in this genre means the rumpled chic of Woody Allen intellectuals in *Hannah and Her Sisters* (1986) or the modestly comfortable Brooklyn Heights of *Moonstruck* (1987) where Cher is a bookkeeper and, although Nicolas Cage is a baker, he adores opera.

Attempts to subvert the genre often end up reinforcing it. *10* (1979) may have been intended as a satire on the Western obsession with bodies, as played out in Dudley Moore's erotic obsession with magnificent Bo Derek, when true love lies with down-to-earth Julie Andrews. The inevitable consequence, however, was the worldwide sale of millions of posters of Ms Derek, shallow and callous as her screen character may have been.

Perhaps the most subversive romantic comedy of all is a double bluff,

Mike Nichols's *The Graduate* (1967). So we cheer when Benjamin breaks free of Mrs Robinson's seductive powers (so jaded, so decadent, so against nature) to wrestle her daughter Elaine from the altar, where she is about to marry a regular classmate, and sweep her on to a bus. But what is their destination? As the adrenaline levels drop, the smiles sink from their features – is this small rebellion a basis for a lifelong partnership? The final shot is of the bus pulling away; just visible through the rear window are Ben and Elaine, already with a gap between them. Silence and darkness await, as Simon and Garfunkel's soundtrack lyrics promised.

(500) Days of Summer is a film from 2009 that has the lovers at the centre of it (Joseph Gordon Levitt and Zooey Deschanel) arguing about the interpretation of this scene from *The Graduate* forty years before. *Summer* offers a series of pastiches of various tropes of the romcom genre but its real bite is the suggestion that romance as portrayed through the movies is purely a thing of the moment, far removed from 'happy ever after'. This is a more radical take on the genre than it first appears. For all screen etiquette may have changed – the classic composed 1940s screen kiss, she with her head flung back, his arm firmly supporting the weight of her body, has been replaced by rumpled hair and squashed features with flashes of nudity – the format is much the same. Spiderman may kiss Kirsten Dunst hanging upside down but his intentions remain old-fashioned, even if she is wearing a rainsoaked vest.

Zooey Deschanel's character though is a neat riposte to the fantasy figure played by Ms Dunst in a number of romantic comedy films – a type, dubbed the Manic Pixie Dream Girl by critic Nathan Rabin in 2007, who 'exists solely in the fevered imaginations of sensitive writer-directors to teach broodingly soulful young men to embrace life and its infinite mysteries and adventures'. Rabin, writing for website The AV Club, later listed egregious examples – among them even icons like Katharine Hepburn in *Bringing Up Baby* or Audrey Hepburn in *Breakfast at Tiffany's*. Truman Capote's novella creation Holly Golightly is by no means the same character as Hepburn onscreen. Literary Holly's eccentricity has both causes and effects. The film, though, blends hooker (by denying what she does) with potential housewife or, as the contemporary trailer put it, 'Audrey Hepburn and George Peppard searching for love in the Big Town, sharing only part of their lives until they find the deep warm moment of truth that can't be hidden even by the oddball antics on the surface of New York'.

There were distinctive films that unsettled notions of romance in the 1980s before *When Harry Met Sally* came along to restore the cinematic status quo. Quebecois director Denys Arcand in *The Decline of the American Empire* (1986) showed parallel conversations about love, romance and infidelity between a group of academics as the men prepare dinner and the women work out at a gym. The hairstyles, fashions and wordiness of the protagonists make it look something of a period piece now but it is still sharp on the entwined roots of sexual and economic politics.

From Spain that same year came a literally lacerating comedy from an increasingly popular director, Pedro Almodóvar. *Matador* threw together in a macabre dance an ageing bullfighter and a female lawyer who can only achieve sexual excitement in proximity to death. Caught between them is an innocent (Antonio Banderas), so artless that in an early scene he fails to rape a woman because he can't find the right blade on his pocket knife. The whole thing is played deadpan in the performances and flamboyant in the design – often grotesque, sometimes excessively romantic – a combination that would ensure Almodóvar audiences and prizes over the next two decades. The film's use of red calls to mind Michael Powell's *Peeping Tom* a quarter of a century earlier (which, for all its horror, has exquisite moments of comedy and even romance). The young voyeur photographer (and murderer) in *Peeping Tom* yearns for connection with the one girl who can comprehend (if not forgive) his obsessions and transgression.

Similarly the bullfighter and lawyer are totally and mutually fulfilled by the final frame of *Matador*; the investigating detective says he has never seen anyone happier, although their union and its circumstances would probably only really appeal to a pathologist. *Matador*, although not one of Almodóvar's best films, does make a pointed observation about our romantic ideals – that in some ways, like a detective story, they are about tidying up the loose ends, matching and symmetry. Perhaps the celebration of difference in love is what really lies at the heart of good romantic comedy – something that even *When Harry Met Sally* nods to in Billy Crystal's big New Year's Eve speech.

The 2002 film *Secretary* concerns a couple who find common interest in sadomasochism. It is funny and tender and odd. The obsessive, controlling boss (James Spader) and the inventively submissive employee (Maggie Gyllenhaal) each have their problems. Their strength is that they both recognise the need in the other and are eager to serve it. Comedies that acknowledge this include the internationally successful account of Gallic Sapphic love starring Almodóvar alumna Victoria Abril, *Gazon Maudit* (1996), the British *A Fish Called Wanda* (1988) and *Sideways*, a comedy about two self-obsessed men who happen to find intelligent women who will tolerate them (not an entirely fair deal, perhaps).

Jack Lemmon, though, proves the dark horse in the romcom race, both with Shirley MacLaine in *The Apartment* (1960) and, even more touchingly, in drag at the end of *Some Like It Hot* (1959) as musician Jerry in disguise as Geraldine on the run from the mob. Geraldine has unwittingly attracted and eventually tolerated the attentions of millionaire Osgood Fielding. With the plot's denouement, seated in a boat with Osgood at the wheel, Jerry finally gets to tear off his wig and with it any lingering illusion of femininity. He growls, 'I'm a man!' Osgood's eyes don't flicker from the water ahead: 'Well, nobody's perfect.'

1990s

HOW FAR CAN YOU GO?

A s cinema reached its centenary, the world was changing again. The twentieth-century alignments of ideology and defence were shifting fast. On Christmas Day 1991, Mikhael Gorbachev was forced out of the leadership of the Soviet Union as one Cold War empire began to dissolve. The process was the logical outcome of the reforms he had himself introduced, hastened by the various revolutions against totalitarianism in the Eastern Bloc, beginning in Poland in 1989 and spreading to Hungary, East Germany, Bulgaria, Czechoslovakia and Romania. Strategists were left grasping for a clear concept of the New World Order. Without the alignment of the USA and allies versus the Soviet bloc, chaos could ensue, as in many ways it did.

The first of the many conflicts that threw up challenges for the New World Order was Saddam Hussein's invasion of Kuwait. This was the first 'real-time' war to be covered by visual media: television audiences watched the first bombardment by US and allied planes in January 1991, with images of explosions and tracer fire that would become staples of news bulletins – whether in the Gulf, or later from conflict in Yugoslavia and Kosovo. Werner Herzog travelled to the Kuwaiti desert in the aftermath of Operation Desert Storm to film a documentary, *Lessons of Darkness* (1992), around the oil spills and wells that continued to blaze seven months after the Iraqi retreat. The film had no political commentary; accompanied by a classical music score, it provided a beautiful, apocalyptic coda to the claim that the war had been an efficient air operation. The unforgettable images were later evoked by Sam Mendes in a surreal section of his Desert Storm drama *Jarhead* (2005). An immediate response to the conflict in the former Yugoslavia was Michael Winterbottom's *Welcome to Sarajevo* (1997), which incorporated real footage into the feature; Macedonian filmmaker Milcho Manchevski's Academy Award-nominated *Before the Rain* (1994) collected thirty international prizes. Blending the narratives of several characters he showed the destruction and deep hatred that characterise ethnic wars in particular. A less nuanced action picture was triggered by the 1993 incident when two American Black Hawk helicopters were shot down near Mogadishu, Somalia, during a mission by US special forces to capture the general (or warlord, depending on your perspective) who had rejected the presence of US and UN troops there. The operation to rescue the trapped soldiers would form the plot of Ridley Scott's *Black Hawk Down*, released in 2001. A triumph of style – exciting, noisy, brilliantly edited – it ends with a caption 'over 1,000 Somalis died and 19 Americans lost their lives in the conflict'. The Americans are listed both by name and rank. Not one Somali is portrayed as a character.

A sense of the links and differences that run through separate nations was an acute concern after the European Maastricht Treaty came into force. From 1993 onwards nations in and around Europe pondered the union of policies, currencies, even armies and the crucial question of boundaries.

Who was in or out? Globalisation and interconnectedness became dramatic subjects for cinema with the rise of international corporations and the movement of migrant workers. Filmmakers in Eastern Europe had struggled with censorship under totalitarian governments. Once forced to make dramas that were political by metaphor, they now had to contend with a new constraint: they could make what they liked so long as it had a market value. Many of them failed to find either funding or audiences. The Polish screenwriter and director Krzystof Kieślowski, for example, secured finance for his last few films mainly from France. His trilogy *Three Colours* (*Blue, White, Red*) nods to the values of the French republic but is also a complex evocation of modern international life, across the borders of work and love.

Political upheavals had been reported from the front line with the use of small cameras and satellite phones. The use of amateur footage in features – as in *Welcome to Sarajevo* – added authenticity, as if the camera could still be relied on to tell the truth. All the evidence in the film business, though, was that images could be manipulated and manufactured. As television prepared for the first broadcasts in high-definition in 1998, effects companies became more inventive. The animation house Pixar set the bar high for a deeply realised animation with the release of the first two *Toy Story* features (1995 and 1999). Not only were the images so real and tactile that you could reach out for them, the script was as well constructed and witty as any on the Hollywood circuit. George Lucas's ILM (Industrial Light and Magic), which had provided effects for *Star Wars* but also for *Indiana Jones, Back to the Future, Who Framed Roger Rabbit?* and *Jurassic Park*, now worked with James Cameron on the first partly computer-generated character in *Terminator 2: Judgment Day* (1991), and on the most successful film of all time (until Cameron surpassed himself in 2009), *Titanic* (1997). With its whirlpool of melodrama, torrential effects, factual poignancy and fire of youthful romance, it appealed across generations and continents, making a whopping $1.6 billion. A feverish enthusiasm for *Titanic* gripped the Afghan capital Kabul, for example, in the autumn of 2000. The authorities were concerned about the degenerative effect of such unfettered Western sexuality onscreen, but copies of the film were smuggled in from Pakistan on VHS. Although hardly the most auspicious symbol for a lasting union, wedding cakes in the shape of the liner were popular. These may have been tolerated but barbers were reportedly arrested for executing a DiCaprio-inspired bob for men – short at the back, long side fringe – and anyone sporting the cut promptly received a corrective trim. Khaled Hosseini's book *A Thousand Splendid Suns* describes a district of Kabul known as Titanic City – the market, situated in a river bed, often floods – where ordinary goods were sold with the prefix Titanic on the label.

The success of *Titanic*, the most expensive film ever at the time, confirmed a number of commercial tendencies: big films could bring massive rewards not just in the domestic market but all over the world; Jack and Rose, otherwise known as Kate and Leo, were a global brand; and young people, who might return to the cinema and would definitely re-view at home, were the audience to chase. Over the decade, the salaries and demands of blockbuster stars such as *Mission Impossible*'s Tom Cruise, *Pretty Woman*'s Julia Roberts, *Lethal Weapon*'s Mel Gibson and the *Terminator* himself Arnold Schwarzenegger had also begun to inflate.

The Weinstein brothers, Bob and Harvey, founded Miramax in 1979 to distribute the sort of lower budget independent films that had languished in the age of high-concept. Their first major success was *sex, lies and videotape* in 1989. They now began to collect awards and recognition for low- to medium-budget, carefully scripted and character-focused dramas. *The English Patient* won the Best Picture Oscar in 1996, *Good Will Hunting* (1997) picked up a Supporting Actor Oscar for Robin Williams, but, crucially, the Oscar for the screenplay went to two young actor/writers, childhood friends from Boston, Ben Affleck and Matt Damon. The next year, the Weinsteins were back for the multiple-Oscar-winning *Shakespeare in Love*.

Languages and accents were shifting along with population. Eastern European accents moved west through the continent to Britain. Spanish, America's second language, was gaining on the first. By the year 2000, there were twenty-nine million Spanish speakers in the United States, an increase of 60 per cent on the previous decade; most of these people were in California, Arizona and Texas, not far from Hollywood. The Mexican film *Like Water for Chocolate* (1992) became the highest grossing Spanish language feature outside its home territory. The inventiveness of a plot like *Nine Queens* (2000) from Argentina demonstrated how tired some of the old narratives from the mainstream producers were starting to look. When Hollywood did produce something ingeniously plotted, like *The Usual Suspects* (1992) or *The Sixth Sense* (1999), it was acclaimed.

Independent directors were once again trying to break down what had become the traditional artifices of film. Lars von Trier and Tomas Vinterberg's short-lived Dogme 95 experiment took the production process back to basics with no make-up, no lighting and no scenery. The excruciating family celebration of *Festen* (1998) all but strips the participants down to the bone with its revelations. It does not even have a director credited although Vinterberg co-wrote. Von Trier's *Breaking the Waves* (1996) is not strictly a Dogme film – there are sets and music and graphics – but it may be his most affecting. Emily Watson plays Bess, an innocent from a Scottish island who falls for a Scandinavian oilworker. When an accident on the rig renders him impotent he demands that she give herself to other men then recount her sexual adventures to him. For love, she does what he asks and comes to be convinced that her mission may even have a sacred dimension. Watson's performance was painfully convincing and von Trier played with chapter headings, expressionism in landscape and hand-held camera to give an emotional intensity that was near unbearable. Like much of his work, it troubled. Did the camera linger a little too long on Bess's distress, even to the point of pornography? *Breaking the*

Waves was the first of von Trier's Golden Hearted Trilogy, about the sacrifices women will make for love – the following films were no more reassuring.

Another ordeal – but with minimal emotional involvement this time – was *The Blair Witch Project* (1999), an ultra-low budget film, deliberately and skilfully crafted to look rough and cheaply made. Its target audience was young horror fans sated with formats and tropes that had been around since the 1950s. This apparent 'home movie' of three film students wandering in the woods with a digital camera, finding evidence of supernatural goings-on, reduced screen trickery to the minimum. The producers even claimed, via a sophisticated internet campaign, that the film was a documentary and all the participants were not actually unknown actors, but 'real' people, missing presumed dead.

In Western countries children and young adults were becoming more powerful and discerning consumers. The generation once 'seen but not heard' was now sometimes the deciding voice in the household. If the *Home Alone* series reinforced the idea that young people could look after themselves, be familiar with technology and generally outwit their slower seniors, it also played into parental neuroses about neglecting children for work. The home, generally, came to be the centre of worries about crime whether against property or person. In 1991 *Home Alone* was only knocked off the No.1 box office position it had occupied for twelve weeks by *Sleeping with the Enemy* in which Julia Roberts flees an abusive stalking husband with a knack for getting inside locked homes. Our nightmares were populated with ever more perceptive and intimate serial killers from *The Silence of the Lambs* (1991) to *Se7en* (1995), although in America at least both property and violent crimes declined appreciably in the 1990s. Our neuroses were putting these monsters onscreen.

Onscreen audiences saw hooded knife-wielding robbers, vandals and rapists. The Austrian director Michael Haneke's 1997 *Funny Games* enacted the homeowners' worst nightmare. Two young men enter the holiday house of a wealthy couple. They imprison and torture them, making them play games for their survival. Haneke has the torturers involve the audience by turning occasionally to wink or smile at a particularly unpleasant development, breaking the fourth wall to invite their complicity. The audience may deplore the violence but they have paid money to see it – why? That knowing tone was also evident in a commercially successful erotic thriller, *Basic Instinct* (1992) – a film so flagrant in plot, characterisation and *mise en scene* that it removed all mystery from the genre.

Attempts were made to replicate onscreen the effects of addiction. Among the more successful were the 1996 *Trainspotting*, directed by Danny Boyle, which evoked the rush and desperation of heroin addiction in a headlong style, mixing naturalistic scenes often recorded in one take with colourful hallucinations. Two modestly budgeted American films with women at their centre – Todd Haynes's *Safe* (1995) and Darren Aronofsky's *Requiem for a Dream* (2000) – depicted their addictive predicament in sensory terms. In *Safe*, Julianne Moore's character has a mysterious syndrome, a total allergy to the modern world; an uneasy hum on the soundtrack suggests the ubiquitous technology may be making her ill. Or maybe it is simply the emptiness of her affluent life: perhaps her addiction is to withdrawal. Ellen Burstyn in *Requiem for a Dream* is a sexagenarian addict – to television gameshows, to diet pills and in time to amphetamines – and also the mother of a heroin addict. Most sensational of all are Mickey and Mallory Knox, the media and celebrity junkies who kill for fame, in Oliver Stone's *Natural Born Killers* (1994). With the Knoxes, the dependence and the highs are depicted in a suitably nauseating array of close-up, differing speeds, split screen and distortion, both direct and subtle.

Production values in music videos continued to influence the mainstream. MTV opened stations around the world and produced the most expensive music video of all time: *Scream* by Michael and Janet Jackson, directed by Mark Romanek, who would later move into features, cost $7 million. A music-driven version of Shakespeare, Baz Luhrmann's

Romeo+Juliet (1997) was inspired by MTV, transposing Verona to Miami Beach.

Moving images were entering the home not just through television but now with recorded material and the internet. The first DVDs went on sale to the public in 1997; the following year Netflix began a postal and download rental service. By the end of the decade rental would bring in twice as much revenue as receipts from movie theatres. Interactive computer games – *Grand Theft Auto* was inspired by the 1977 action feature – simulated film action with the added dimension of the player being able to influence events. Bruce Willis was the first actor to have his 'presence' synthesised in a video game in 1999.

The internet also provided a fillip for Hollywood's less reputable relation, the porn industry in San Fernando, sometimes dubbed Silicone Valley. With an annual turnover in the United States alone estimated at approaching $4 billion a year, it was hardly on a par with the $63 billion of the so-called legitimate side of film and video. Yet pornographic material was finding new channels for distribution, many of them straight into the home; a sense that porn was becoming pervasive and corporatised may have underscored *Boogie Nights* (1997), Paul Thomas Anderson's irresistible take on the industry's apparently more innocent days in the 1970s – post-1960s liberation, pre-AIDS. A variation of the star-is-born myth, it offers the cautionary tale of the rise and fall of a singularly gifted young man with the professional moniker of Dirk Diggler. In the end, though, with an ensemble cast including Burt Reynolds (Hollywood star but also ex-*Cosmopolitan* centrefold in 1972), Julianne Moore, Mark Wahlberg, Philip Seymour Hoffman, William H. Macy and John C. Reilly, *Boogie Nights* is as much about collective living and economic pressures as it is about sex. The real porn was elsewhere – in a mainstream thriller. And audiences were the eager punters.

BASIC INSTINCT (1992)

Director: Paul Verhoeven
Cast: Michael Douglas, Sharon Stone
Colour

Catherine Trammell (Sharon Stone), the deadly mystery writer in the thriller *Basic Instinct* – bold, blonde and bisexual – is hardly an enigma. From the first glimpse of her, gazing out at the ocean from her fabulous beach house, the audience knows Trammell is a woman capable of deceit and even murder. This brazen approach went down well: *Basic Instinct* made more than $350 million.

The film begins with the sensational death of a nightclub owner and former rock star. A police detective (Michael Douglas) gets the call. Recovering alcoholic (no one claims any originality for this plot) Nick Curran's investigation soon takes him to the beachside house of the dead man's lover, the celebrated crime writer Trammell. Money is clearly not a motive but who can fathom the desires of this platinum Amazon?

The screen career of the 1990s most blatant star began in arthouse black and white. Sharon Stone had been cast by Woody Allen in his Fellini parody, *Stardust Memories* (1980). Minor roles filled the next decade until a pneumatic pairing with Arnold Schwarzenegger and some onscreen innuendo in fantasy action film *Total Recall* (1990) indicated to director Paul Verhoeven (and the readers of *Playboy*, for whom she posed nude to publicise her bodybuilding for the film) a modern sexual candour.

Basic Instinct was a glossy product. The script by Joe Eszterhas was bought for a reported record $3 million. It attempted a nod to Hitchcock and *film noir* with its themes, its location and its music but had none of the subtlety or depth. *Basic Instinct* roars along like detective Michael Douglas's car on the coast road to Trammell's lair. Sharon Stone was not a Hitchcock blonde, her beauty shrouded in a mysterious fog like Kim Novak in the early scenes of *Vertigo*. What you saw was what you got and, famously, like the detectives interrogating Ms Trammell in the aftermath of the bedroom murder of her lover, what you saw when she crossed and uncrossed her legs was a brief flash of depilated genitalia. Brief and in its clinicality – a blue-lit interrogation room – lacking in either sensuality or humanity.

Basic Instinct was championed by feminist critic Camille Paglia who praised Stone's performance as 'one of the most indelible, charismatic dominatrixes of all time' in what was a 'pornographic film receiving national distribution'. *Basic Instinct* is remarkable precisely for that crossover, that a mainstream star like Michael Douglas could appear in what was passing itself off as a murder mystery/police procedural drama but was in fact a glossy peepshow themed on the ancient pairing of sex and death. The artificiality of the locations – the first murder victim is a millionaire and all the interiors are interior-designed down to the last sharp-edged glass table or 'Picasso' on the wall – and the shiny, tanned bodies and tossed blonde hair of the women in the athletic simulated sex scenes suggest high production-value porn.

The British Board of Film Classification passed the infamous 'crotch shot' from the interrogation scene because it fell within the censor's guide-lines informally known as ILOOLI. Tom Dewe Matthews in his history *Censored* revealed this acronym, which, unfurled, reads 'inner labia is out but outer labia can be in'. Shots of the former were deemed invasive and intrusive and therefore only available as R18 films in licensed sex shops, i.e., over the counter rather than by buying a ticket to a multiplex. Intrusion has its etiquette.

The previous year, 1991, a film by the Japanese director Nagisa Oshima, *Ai No Corrida* (or *The Realm of the Senses*) had finally been passed for cinema release with an 18 certificate. Originally seen in Britain in 1976 at the London Film Festival, *Ai No Corrida*'s themes include subjugation, both political and sexual; it is based on an incident in 1936 in which a female servant castrated and murdered her master after several days of incarcerated congress. The film is unrelentingly intense: there are no body doubles nor is the sex simulated – the actors obviously stopped short of the mutilation and killing, although that can be hard to believe when you watch it.

Despite *Ai No Corrida*'s festival appearance, the BBFC waited fifteen years before passing it for viewing in cinemas (it had been shown in an edited version, unclassified, in private cinema clubs over the years), but they still refused a video certificate for home viewing. The 1991 decision marked a gradual relaxation of certification and a fine distinction between so-called arthouse fare and films for mass consumption: more than twenty years earlier, Ken Russell's *Women in Love* (1969) had been passed by the BBFC only when the firelight was dimmed to make Alan Bates and Oliver Reed's nakedness less prominent in the wrestling scene. Andy Warhol's *Flesh* (1968), directed by Paul Morrissey, showed the lead character, a hustler played by Joe Dallesandro, with an erect penis. The chief censor of the time in Great Britain, John Trevelyan, admired the film but felt unable to pass it. He did, though, recommend it for a private members only screening at the Open Space Theatre in London, which was promptly raided by the police. Trevelyan protested and during the subsequent prosecution stood as a character witness. The case was eventually dropped but the court still handed out fines – which Trevelyan persuaded Warhol to pay. The following year, however, a film from what was then Yugoslavia, *WR: Mysteries of the Organism*, showed an erect penis and this time it was allowed for viewing in cinemas.

WR was in Serbo-Croat with subtitles, and the sex depicted in the film is part of a metaphor about communist oppression. It was, as John Trevelyan put it in his autobiography *What the Censor Saw*, 'an art film that would have limited distribution'. These films seem always to have enjoyed a parallel existence to the mainstream, available to intellectual Olympians but denied to the masses. Whether comedy or popular drama, films intended for the high street cinema chains were subjected to tighter scrutiny, as if the people could not be trusted. In 1989 (as applications were being prepared for a resubmission of *Ai No Corrida* to the censor) a film about the Profumo affair, *Scandal*, was refused a certificate because a man in the background of an orgy scene appeared, not unreasonably, to have an erect penis. Although Stephen Woolley, the film's producer, claimed the offending shape was in fact a candle, the BBFC insisted that the film be altered. In a neat variation on the *Women in Love* solution, the film was returned to the laboratory so that the light balance could be altered. A lamp now appeared to shed a halo that obscured the alleged organ lest viewers be offended – or worse yet, aroused.

It is an odd distinction. Cinema is a medium that depends on a degree of arousal, if not necessarily the sexual kind; at its flesh-creeping, tear-inducing, toe-tapping, deafening, infuriating best (and possibly also at its worst) it is a sensory experience. Pornography is defined by the BBFC as distinct from art in that its 'primary purpose is sexual arousal or stimulation'. In the 1990s, however, British censors appeared to be taking into account views like that expressed by American academic Linda Williams, author of the study of pornography *Hardcore*, who wrote in *Cineaste* magazine, 'in the U.S., we have grown so used to the separation of pornography from art that we tend to assume – sometimes rather hypocritically – that any arousal response is antithetical to art and any emotionally complex art antithetical to arousal'. As the decade wore on, the British Board increasingly granted certificates without any cuts to films that showed graphic instances of real sex. Catherine Breillat's *Romance* (1999) and Lars von Trier's *The Idiots* (1998) were justified by the BBFC in a statement on their website: ' . . . the comparative brevity of the images, combined with the serious intentions of the films, meant that both films could be passed without cuts'.

Von Trier and Vinterberg's Dogme 95 movement sought reality – or at least the illusion of it, this being cinema after all – mimesis rather than documentary. Flesh in the Dogme films (and European arthouse generally) is not tanned, toned and glowing. It may be dimpled, often mottled by cold and appear blue in daylight or when lit by an unforgiving neon strip. In *The Idiots*, von Trier's Dogme debut about a group of people who pretend to be disabled in some physical or mental way as a form of riotous self-expression, the director wanted to show as much as possible of the graphic detail, including a group sex scene, with extreme close-ups of the action. (*The Idiots* raised suspicions that perhaps it was the high-art equivalent of Catherine Trammell's leg-crossing, just there for the shock value.) Yet, as with French director Catherine Breillat's *Romance* about a woman who seeks sex from other men when her boyfriend turns her down, von Trier still employed porn stars for some of the penetrative sex shots.

Breillat is not interested in showing male psychology; her interest is the female characters and she claims not to influence the way the audience receives the arresting images she presents. However, she might have been less than thrilled by the enthusiastic endorsement for *Romance* from the erstwhile men's magazine *Gear* which adorned some publicity for the film's video release – 'Genius! The sexiest movie ever made!'

Public enthusiasm for nudity or explicit sex scenes soon palled. Patrice Chereau's *Intimacy* (2001), based on Hanif Kureishi's novel, was intended to show two people who meet simply to make love, with little context or back story. Michael Winterbottom's *Nine Songs* (2004) portrayed a series of sexual encounters between two people during the course of a relationship. Although media coverage lingered on the question of how far, exactly, the actors took their involvement, the answer with *Nine Songs* was definitive: there was no faking. Neither film, though, proved titillating or, indeed popular, although *Intimacy* – with a strong cast of Kerry Fox and Mark

Rylance – received good reviews and attracted substantial audiences in France where Chereau's reputation was established.

In the 1990s the film that may best illustrate the art versus pornography debate is Stanley Kubrick's final effort, *Eyes Wide Shut* (1999). Kubrick had turned his talents in many directions: to the classical epic (*Spartacus*), the science fiction film (*2001*), the period adaptation (*Barry Lyndon*), the war film (*Paths of Glory*), the horror film (*The Shining*), the satire (*Dr Strangelove*), and so on. To this canon he now added what some viewed as artistic pornography. A version of an Arthur Schnitzler novella, updated to contemporary New York, *Eyes Wide Shut* starred Tom Cruise and Nicole Kidman, then husband and wife, as a couple whose sexual life has become problematic. News of this casting seeded rampant media speculation during the film's two-year production. Would audiences see two of the planet's most famous stars really making love? Was there an autobiographical element to the performance for them? Every encounter in the film is sexualised; the narrative has a dreamy, unreliable quality. Unlike *Basic Instinct* it is all ellipsis and enigma – even though some of its scenes, in the bedroom, or at a hotel or in a baroque orgy with Venetian masks, are drawn from clichés of erotic fantasy. It is an art film about arousal and deception – and although many felt themselves deceived, finding it opaque and slow, audiences went to see it. Curiosity had been aroused if nothing else.

The outrage over *Basic Instinct* eventually had nothing to do with what could be seen between Ms Stone's legs. What upset gay, lesbian and feminist critics of the film was the psychology not the sexuality. They objected to the implication that no sooner do you get a leading character who escapes the narrow confines of Hollywood screen gender types than they are depicted as a heartless maniac. Catherine Trammell was not so much a pioneer for a new model of female sexuality as that old type, the evil, devouring mantis, so cheerily subverted later by Isabella Rossellini in her *Green Porno* short films – infinitely more engaging, entertaining . . . and even sexy.

NATURAL BORN KILLERS (1994)

Director: Oliver Stone
Cast: Woody Harrelson, Juliette Lewis
Colour and black and white

Mickey and Mallory Knox (Woody Harrelson and Juliette Lewis) are at the counter in a diner. After some equivocation, he orders key lime pie from the waitress. Mallory slips off her jacket, approaches the jukebox and begins to gyrate to a record. Soon, some seedy local guy is dancing suggestively alongside her. The mood shifts. Within seconds, Mallory has punched and kicked him to the ground, Mickey has knifed the guy's fat old friend, shot the cook and – eanie-meanie-miney – Mallory swings the gun between the two remaining people standing, picks off the waitress and orders the survivor: 'Tell 'em Mickey and Mallory Knox did this. Understand?'

Oliver Stone's *Natural Born Killers* (1994), about a couple who become media stars for their gruesome killing spree, was initially refused an 'R' rating in the United States until the director made cuts.

But that same year in another diner . . . another couple, a little older and wirier, Honey Bunny and Pumpkin, are eating pie and drinking coffee at a table. Their conversation ranges over the relative merits of robbing restaurants over banks, a debate turning on the fine points of insurance and employee loyalty. Their discourse neatly sealed with a kiss, Pumpkin and Honey Bunny kick into another life as bandits. They jump to their feet, wave their weapons round the room and scream at the customers to get down on the floor. Quentin Tarantino and Roger Avary's script for *Pulp Fiction* (1994) was rewarded with an Oscar for its wordplay, interlocking stories and knowing references to Howard Hawks, Melville, Scorsese, Sam Fuller and more. The film also won the Palme d'Or at Cannes.

The same man was the source of both scripts. Tarantino's screenplay for

Natural Born Killers had passed through other hands before Oliver Stone happened on it. Stone made significant changes which Tarantino did not like and in the end he is credited only with the story. Both films feature violent lowlifes but Stone's film attracted accusations that it inspired copycat crimes. It became the centre of a hyperventilated public debate reminiscent of the frothing media circus that accompanies Mickey and Mallory's murderous rampage.

In some respects, *Natural Born Killers* does a similar job to Terrence Malick's dreamy *Badlands* or Arthur Penn's *Bonnie and Clyde*. It shows young misfits becoming celebrities through violence, which for a deluded moment or two seems romantic. For the 1990s, though, the age of the fast-zapping remote control, Oliver Stone – the stylist who had made *Platoon* (1986), *Wall Street* (1987) and *JFK* (1991) – piled on the effects to drive home the satire. The film cuts incessantly between eighteen different formats. There is monochrome and colour, spectacular landscape and rough news footage, advertisements and animations. In certain scenes elaborate back projections run behind window frames or through car windshields, like the constant television stations running in the couple's head.

Stone sought to show in Mickey and Mallory two kids desensitised by their families and by constant media stimulus almost from the breast, perhaps in lieu of parental care. So Mallory's adolescence, for example, is shown as a cheesy domestic television comedy complete with canned laughter, even though the events – abuse and incest – are hardly humorous. At this stage, compared to Tarantino, Stone was the more experienced and proficient filmmaker. In the early part of the film as he shows the young Mickey and Mallory, eloping in her father's car with Mickey soon incarcerated for Grand Theft Auto, his skill seems to lend them a vulnerability and insouciant energy that borders on glamour – a less intelligent variation of lovers Sailor and Lula in David Lynch's 1990 *Wild at Heart*. Lynch said his film was about two people finding 'Love in Hell', the hell being the violence of modern life; yet Mickey and Mallory's quest (and Oliver Stone's film) lacks that clarity.

Honey Bunny and Pumpkin by contrast are small beer, no more than comedy bit players and the action in *Pulp Fiction* soon leaves them behind. They are merely pawns in a grand scheme as Tarantino and Avary play with classic crime fiction types. Like all the characters in the film, they are attractive enough to amuse and stick in the memory but the audience does not need to get involved. People may have emulated John Travolta and Uma Thurman's dance, which was in turn a loose tribute to Godard's odd little *Bande à Part* dance sequence, but you rarely love a Tarantino character – there is too much irony in the way and they are unlikely to be around long enough to be worth investing in emotionally.

The furore that blazed alongside *Natural Born Killers* sprang from one issue. Did people so identify with Mickey and Mallory that they might go out and kill in a similar way? Instances of alleged copycat offences were identified by newspapers in particular – ten killings in the United States and one in France. The argument became a *cause célèbre* in itself when the bestselling novelist John Grisham declared that Oliver Stone should personally be held legally responsible for the effects of his film under product liability law used against manufacturers of goods which caused injury or death. Grisham had personal reasons to pursue the issue. An acquaintance in Mississippi had been murdered in a random attack by a young couple, Sarah Edmondson and Ben Darras. In their defence, the couple claimed to have watched *Natural Born Killers*. Grisham felt he knew where the blame lay: 'Troubled as they were, Ben and Sarah had no history of violence. Their crime spree was totally out of character. They were confused, disturbed, shiftless, mindless – the adjectives can be heaped on with shovels – but they had never hurt anyone before. Before, that is, they saw a movie. A horrific movie that glamorized casual mayhem and bloodlust. A movie made with the intent of glorifying random murder.'

In the United Kingdom, the *Daily Mail* promptly called for the film to be banned. It took the British Board of Film Classification several months to grant an '18' certificate, on the condition of three minutes of cuts. On the BBFC website, the reasons for the decision are laid out:

> The idea that ordinary people had been turned into killers by being exposed to a particular film was not one with which the FBI or local police forces in America had any sympathy. In all but one of the American cases linked by the press with the title of the film, the accused or dominant member of an accused pair had been in prison, and, in one case, also in a mental hospital, for serious acts of violence, including in three cases murder . . . the one case in France turns out to be have been politically motivated.

Such alarms go back to the silent era, when, amid fears that films might trigger delinquency, a court in Bingley, Yorkshire, in 1913 attributed 'the gangsterism of a boy of nine' to exposure to screen violence. The Breen Office in the 1930s in Hollywood was on the lookout to prohibit criminals onscreen from corrupting the audience, and in the early-fifties *The Wild One* was released in America but not in Britain until 1968, such was the fear of marauding motorcycle gangs. Allegations that groups dressed like Droogs had attacked and committed rape led Stanley Kubrick to withdraw *A Clockwork Orange* (1971) from distribution.

Direct connections between film and criminal action are hard to establish. John Hinckley's 1981 assassination attempt on President Reagan was an attempt to impress Jodie Foster, the young actress in *Taxi Driver*. In Hinckley's defence a medical expert said that Hinckley had watched *Taxi Driver* repeatedly and came to identify with De Niro's character, Travis Bickle. The prosecution claimed the identification was conscious but Hinckley was found not guilty, by reason of insanity. In some cases, the taint remains even when the evidence has been dismissed. Michael Ryan, who shot and killed sixteen people and wounded a further fifteen in

Hungerford, Berkshire, in 1987 was dubbed the 'Rambo' killer. There was no evidence he had ever seen the film.

With the possibility of home viewing, the question of influence became murkier still. The judge in the trial of Robert Thompson and Jon Venables, convicted of the murder of two-year-old James Bulger in 1993, stated 'exposure to violent video films may in part be an explanation'. He alluded to one in particular, *Child's Play 3*, featuring the evil doll Chucky: Venables's father had rented a copy a month before the murder. Although press reports speculated as to similarities between crime and film, the BBFC subsequently examined the alleged connection and found no link.

In 1984 the Board banned a selection of videos for home viewing, but it could hardly be policed. Following the Bulger case, a report by child psychologist Elizabeth Newson, *Video Violence and the Protection of Children*, found evidence of sadistic behaviour in children partly explained by 'the easy availability to children of gross images of violence on video'. Further legislation followed to require the BBFC to consider the potential for harm when deciding classifications.

For every study that finds a causal link, there would seem to be another contesting the methodology or the logic. Violent behaviour rarely has one cause; complex factors contribute. The BBFC, however, is sensitive to the portrayal of 'imitable techniques' down to such specifics as lock-picking or making recipes for explosives which 'may be cut if the instructional details are sufficient to allow people to copy them'. This sounds like a rerun of the concerns of the 1930s, demonstrated in the Payne study on imitative behaviour, with chapters titled 'Movie-Made Criminals'.

There have been instances of techniques being replicated, probably by experts. Director Jules Dassin, for example, joked that he had inadvertently become a criminal mastermind after the release of his film *Rififi* (1955). The twenty-minute robbery sequence in which thieves use an umbrella to break into a jeweller's was tidily replicated in several countries by cineaste felons.

In the film *Gomorra*, directed by Matteo Garrone two hoodlums who seek to be gangsters ape Tony Montana from Brian de Palma's *Scarface* and recite Samuel L. Jackson's speech from *Pulp Fiction*. The passage, supposedly from Ezekiel 25: 17, proceeds in a crescendo:

> The path of the righteous man is beset on all sides by the iniquities of the selfish and the tyranny of evil men. Blessed is he who in the name of charity and good will shepherds the weak through the valley of darkness, for he is truly his brother's keeper and the finder of lost children. And I will strike down upon thee with great vengeance and furious anger those who attempt to poison and destroy my brothers. And you will know *my name* is the Lord when I lay *my vengeance* upon thee.

And with that, like Samuel L. Jackson and John Travolta, they open fire. Tarantino's purpose in *Pulp Fiction* is satirical but the sang-froid is cool, if repulsive to most. Oliver Stone, in a documentary made to coincide with a DVD release of *Natural Born Killers*, appeared to condemn Tarantino's style, when he said: 'Younger filmmakers – I'm surprised that they think violence is cool and hip. And they play it that way – which is fine, you can make a couple of films like that, but I can't see making a career out of it. Morally, it's a repugnant point of view to me, because I've been in Vietnam, I've seen the effects of guns, and it's pretty terrifying.' Ironically, the updated 1983 *Scarface* – the one in which Tony Montana (subsequently so idolised by the Camorra) blasts his way to eternal damnation in his Florida palace – although it may be based on a 1932 film, was scripted by Oliver Stone.

That confusion between a 'just' cause and violence apparently satirised in the Ezekiel speech in *Pulp Fiction* is what most angers screenwriter and director David Mamet. In *Bambi vs Godzilla*, his series of essays about the 'nature, purpose and practice' of the film industry, Mamet makes a distinction: on the one hand, there are classic murder stories – cathartic tales from *The Iliad* to *Crime and Punishment* – for which the screen equivalent might be a drama of passion and ambition like *A Place in the Sun* (1951) or Kubrick's *Paths of Glory* (1957) where the contemplation or execution of violence is set in a moral framework which acknowledges the potential for human evil. To Mamet's examples, you could add 1990s films such as the Australian *Romper Stomper* (1992), with an extraordinary performance from the young Russell Crowe as a neo-Nazi skinhead, or David Fincher's *Fight Club* (1999). And on the other, adds Mamet, there are films that show violence with impunity.

Mamet reserves his real firepower for war and crime films of the 'bring it on'/'make my day' variety – featuring enforcers both martial and unofficial – which he maintains have not so much an individual effect as a broader cultural one, indirectly influencing American foreign policy by imbuing audiences with 'the false glow of untried (and in the case of the moviegoer) proxy triumph'. Since the audience is at no personal risk, they become addicted to the fiction of 'just' revenge, in effect muttering to themselves: 'I am good, I am incapable of violence and even if I were capable of violence, I know for a fact that my cause would be just and, further, as it is just, that my crime would have no psychological (let alone criminal) consequences.'

So where did Oliver Stone stand in that argument when he made Mickey and Mallory Knox see diabolic or grotesque faces, not unlike Mallory's evil father, on their victims before they kill them? Did that make the killings 'just', even a little bit? The cumulative effect of the film – so lurid, relentless and, in effect, scattergun – could be to give their spurious perspective some weight with the viewer. This ambiguous outcome is rather like another sequence from *Natural Born Killers* (again intended as satire) when college kids are heard opining on television in vox pop about the Knoxes' exploits: 'Killing is wrong . . . but if I were a mass murderer, I'd be Mickey and Mallory Knox.'

· ·

THREE COLOURS: BLUE (1993), WHITE (1993), RED (1994)

Director: Krzysztof Kieślowski
Cast: Juliette Binoche, Zbigniew Zamachowski, Irène Jacob
Colour

Krzysztof Kieślowski's trilogy, named for the French tricolore, comprises his last films. The Polish director died in 1996, aged fifty-five. The funding for the films came from France and Kieślowski took the three tenets of the republic – liberty, equality and fraternity – as the guiding idea for each film; the films were also described by the director as an anti-tragedy, an anti-comedy and an anti-romance. All three themes, all three genres in fact, run through this beautiful trilogy: each film has distinct casts and stories, although recurring elements make occasional appearances in more than one film. A character from the first film walks for a moment into a courtroom in the second, for example. The films are connected by contemporary themes, too. All the characters live and work in Europe either as natives or guests but they are not necessarily settled or secure – they may need to move or be forced to leave. These are films about living in a modern world – a 'united' Europe – where economic and political forces permeate our inner lives, where every action is connected and has consequences.

In *Blue*, grieving Julie (Juliette Binoche) no longer wants to live after her husband and young daughter are killed in a car crash. Through work on his music (he was composing a European theme at the time of his death) and the gradual understanding of their emotional affairs, she changes her mind. By knowing the worst, she is set free. This is neither as trite nor as sentimental as it sounds. She seeks oblivion in a blue pool and there is a blue glass ornament that is precious to her. As with all three films, tiny touches of the colour appear in frame not to signify anything in particular but to keep us alert.

Karol (Zbigniew Zamachowski), in *White*, is a Pole in Paris, struggling to understand a divorce hearing in which his French wife, Dominique, petitions on the grounds the marriage was never consummated. The process leaves him humiliated, penniless and heartbroken. He tries to be reconciled but she is implacable. He meets a compatriot from Warsaw who helps him get home to Poland. Karol cannot stop loving Dominique; he even keeps an alabaster bust that reminds him of her. Back in Warsaw, he devises a way to get equal.

Red is centred on Valentine (Irène Jacob), a model in Geneva with a boyfriend on the end of a phone in London. One day her car hits a dog in the street. She takes the injured animal to the address on its collar, a comfortable book-filled house whose owner is hostile. He tells her to keep the dog. In time she returns and finds that the man, a retired judge, has a phone-tapping apparatus to eavesdrop on his neighbours' conversations, including those of a young lawyer with a red jeep who lives opposite Valentine. Despite her reservations and the judge's apparent misanthropy, an understanding grows between them.

Kieślowski's films never develop the way you anticipate. They can be testing at first: the colour theme, albeit beautifully realised, might seem a touch schematic; the comedy – the fumbling Pole at a loss with the exquisite French girl (Julie Delpy) – too cruelly obvious; the dialogue between Valentine and the judge (Jean-Louis Trintignant) portentously measured – and does she really have to be a fashion model?

Yet there comes a moment in all three when you realise that, while you have been watching, a number of other forces have come into play. These are films about the way public and private lives are affected by technology (everyone is always trying to get through on the phone or fax, missing calls, turning off answer machines, losing coins in the payphone); or politics – Julie's husband was composing a piece on the theme of European unity, while Karol in Poland is on the fringes of the new Europe; or economics – the new frontier of capitalism in the east edges forward through scams and haggling where anything is for sale. When Karol needs a dead body, he is asked if he would accept a 'Russian import', while in Geneva beautiful Valentine makes her living modelling for a chewing gum advertisement, and another character devises the most nebulous of services – a personalised weather-forecasting system. Legislation and the judicial process intrude regularly, often with miscarriages of justice; in their own lives people apply judgement and even sanctions on others.

Three Colours is a multi-strand narrative in which each film has a distinct mood but the cumulative effect is symphonic. Strictly speaking, it is an anthology film rather than an ensemble film because the stories are separate, yet the three acts are more like musical movements, their complementary themes bring them together as one work. The development of several stories in parallel dates back decades. *Grand Hotel* from 1932 weaves together the adventures of guests at Berlin's most luxurious hotel but, given that two of them are Greta Garbo and John Barrymore, the plot is inevitably weighted; the stars give it a certain perspective.

True multi-strand stories do not have heroes. Robert Altman's *Short Cuts* (1993), following ten sets of people in Los Angeles over a matter of hours, took its cue from a series of Raymond Carver short stories. Altman was the master of the ensemble piece from *M*A*S*H* to *Nashville* to *Gosford Park*. Each is a society in microcosm, whether country music festival or country house. Altman was less interested in putting an individual's actions at the centre of the story than in the relationships and other forces that shape his or her behaviour. Rather than adopt the conventional screen-writer's three-act structure, Altman preferred the analogy of a mosaic. He encouraged actors to move away from the script (although the over-arching plan was always important) and to improvise, hoping for a degree of chaos and accident. With several cameras running, the actors never knew if they were in or out of shot. The performance might end up unseen or a tiny gesture could be caught in one of Altman's trademark slow zooms. Only *M*A*S*H* and *Gosford Park* among his films made much money and yet his influence was considerable.

After *Boogie Nights* (1997), Paul Thomas Anderson continued his homage to Altman with an ensemble of characters in *Magnolia* (1999), all of whom in different ways seek companionship and absolution. The refusal to adopt a single individual as the protagonist is a political decision of sorts. John Sayles, as director, writer and actor, has kept faithful in his films to the idea of a collective drama, be it about miners in West Virginia in the 1920s in *Matewan* (1987) or a contemporary story like the despairing *City of Hope* (1991), set in New Jersey. Beneath three intertwining stories of crime and corruption the protagonists (thirty-six characters in all, virtuous and criminal alike) struggle to make their way. Sayles, like Ken Loach in Britain, shows working lives; more conventional cinema only allows characters to talk about their jobs or their overdrafts as a plot lever. There are exceptions, however, like Chris Smith's *American Job* (1997) with Randy Russell in a documentary style moving from one low-wage grind to another.

The ensemble film is the place for the 'little' or overlooked characters to shine. Richard Linklater's independent film *Slackers* (1991) drifts entertainingly between students and other bohemians on the street and elsewhere in Austin, Texas. It can on occasions seem more like hard work (how much more relaxing to have the thrust of the plot handed to you via one character!), and if there are too many storylines, energy can be dissipated and the film lose its charge. Tarantino's *Pulp Fiction* never does that; it resolves its loose ends with typical referential panache. Mike Figgis's *Timecode* (2000) literally multiplied the narrative by dividing the screen into four and having stories unfold in real time in each quadrant. After a minute or two, the eye has no problem following all four pictures at once (the next generation, bred on simultaneous mobile phone/computer/television use could probably deal with more) but Figgis had judiciously mixed the sound to favour one box at a time. It was not impossible to subvert what was in effect a sound edit guiding towards one particular storyline, but easier to go with the loudest option. Interestingly, he also mixed the film live on a number of occasions, presumably delivering a slightly altered narrative each time.

In 2000, an anthology film from Mexico won international prizes and launched a wave of lesser imitators. *Amores Perros*, directed by Alejandro Gonzalez Iñárritu, wound three stories around a central event, a car crash. The dramatis personae ranged from a guy who makes money from dogfights to an affluent magazine publisher to a down-and-out. Car crashes do not discriminate between classes or races. This Latin America success was endorsed at the 2004 Oscars when *Crash*, a Hollywood ensemble film about a chain of events fuelled by racial tension and class hatred, won Best Picture. Yet *Crash* had its critics. Maybe it was simply a whole series of Hollywood narratives (and unlikely coincidences) knitted together, rather than a genuinely new and provocative way of seeing the world?

Kieślowski's *Three Colours*, by contrast, is all about provocation rather than telling. There is a lovely moment of no great significance in *White* when Karol sets off to visit a farmer to discuss a piece of land. The mist lies on the soft green; the little cabin lies alone in the landscape. Karol starts walking across the field. Suddenly, between us and him, right in front of our noses, a truck passes, shattering the bucolic view. Old Poland, new industrial Poland – where are we?

And as for love – the great driver, the great panacea – Kieślowski is tough on love, too. It may be compelling but it is neither the guarantee of happiness nor the answer to any predicament. As god-like as the phone-tapping judge, Kieślowski pulls all the strings of these stories together at the end of *Red* in a resolution so implausible that we are mocked for even half wishing it to be true. Maybe happiness, he suggests, is just down to luck of the thousand-to-one variety. That, in a cinema universe of 'earned' resolutions, of single Hollywood protagonists winning through, would be the most provocative story of all.

2000s

TURNING INWARDS

For all that thriller writers may claim to have written scenarios that would anticipate the events of September 11 2001; for all the cinematic genres that the immediate tragedy would seem to evoke – disaster, conspiracy, revenge – there was little that film could do immediately in response. A period of restraint seemed inevitable given the constant replaying of video footage on news programmes, much of which resembled the faux-naturalist, hand-held style of recent action films.

Cinema has rarely rushed to represent events of national significance, like Vietnam, usually pausing to consider for up to a decade, but on the five-year anniversary of 9/11 the first, finely crafted drama of the events, Paul Greengrass's *United 93*, was released. Shot in a sober, non-judgemental style, the narrative followed four of the hijackers from a hotel room to Newark International Airport and on board the plane. Using official records and in consultation with the families of victims, employing some real air crew and traffic controllers in minor parts, it trod a difficult path between memorial and exposition. The extraordinary thing, in retrospect, was that this was a film entirely caught in the hours of the hijack itself – about the immediacy of the danger and violence, about the humanity of the response of all the people on the plane. What the world had to contend with was everything before and after – the myriad reasons that had led to the situation and the ever-dividing consequences that sprang from it. What fascinated the filmmaker was the moment itself, perhaps because it lay at the heart of everyone's fears: what would it be like?

The visual prefiguring of these events in disaster films or thrillers with mysterious terrorists holding cities to ransom had run through 1990s films such as *The Siege*, *Armageddon* and *Deep Impact*. Did this mean that, in some bizarre way, Western entertainment had 'dreamed' the events? Notions of patriotism and unity, never distant in Steven Spielberg's work, were clearly displayed in the midst of alien cataclysm in *The War of the Worlds* (2005), which also featured a terrible plane crash, the smoking, detritus-strewn fuselage of the craft being proudly displayed as an attraction at the Los Angeles Universal studio tour – something I found hard to stomach when visiting the following year.

It was not hard to find resonances elsewhere. Michael Haneke's *Caché* (2005) is set in Paris among the bourgeois intelligentsia. Georges and his wife Anne (Daniel Auteuil and Juliette Binoche) are both creatures of the written word – he presents a television show about books and ideas of that particularly French kind; she is a literary editor. Their story begins, though, with a visual puzzle: a video tape left on their doorstep that shows their house under some kind of surveillance. All their words are useless against the mysterious power of that image. Eventually, a trail appears to lead to a childhood acquaintance of Georges, Majid. Georges is suspicious – what does the man want? Why is he trying to harm them? – and feels he must take a firm line to protect his family. In fact, underlying this apparent threat is an old guilt; Majid is Algerian and Georges's family were part of the colonial presence there; there was a betrayal of sorts. Since this is a film by Michael Haneke, it cannot simply be read as an account of Georges's guilt; the audience is implicated, too. No character in the film (except Majid, possibly) obviously possesses the kind of morality that audiences rely on to help them out of any puzzle. People onscreen (and off) deny and blame. This is not a film about the events of September 11 2001 but it inevitably invites reflection on the way we judge those whom we find threatening. Above all, Haneke wants to question; he has been quoted, refuting Godard, as saying that a feature film is twenty-four lies a second.

On the one hand, there was the prospect of another hostile international fragmentation along ideological lines; on the other, every aspect of communications and commerce suggested globalisation – the world was increasingly one market. This might mean the simultaneous release of blockbuster films around the world or it might suggest the ease with which people and ideas can slip between one culture and another. Steven Soderbergh pursued the illegal drug trade north and south of the border in *Traffic* (2000), while Alejandro Gonzales Iñárritu with *21 Grams* (2003) and *Babel* (2006) played variations on the theme that a seemingly minor event in one country can trigger a chain of consequences – personal and political – around the globe.

While the news channels spoke of wars and imminent attack, in popular cinema there was a clear flight to franchises and fantastic sagas that kept their own logic and struggles within their confined universes. The 2001–3 *Lord of the Rings* trilogy dealt in brotherhood, sacrifice and battles against evil. J.R.R. Tolkien wrote the books between 1937 and 1949 in the shadow of one global conflict. Filmgoers watched the adaptations in a period of shock as politicians declared another, less defined, war, this time on terror. The first *Harry Potter* film appeared in 2001 and concluded a decade later, having taken a whole cohort of youngsters to adulthood. Superheroes from *Spider-Man* to *X-Men* joined *Batman* in the multiplex in a series of crime-fighting revenge myths.

Mortality was portrayed onscreen in news footage from 9/11 to documentaries about assisted suicide in a changing way. In 2004, the chemical basis of DNA was mapped and registered in the Human Genome Project. Life expectancy in Western Europe grew by an average of two years over the decade although the improvement was far less dramatic in developing countries. Innovations in nutrition and medicine, maybe even in nanotechnology and replacement of body parts by cloning, could well extend average life well into the nineties within the foreseeable future. In Western fiction films, as chances of living longer increased, mortality had become close to taboo. So directors in this decade began to approach it. The Thai director Apichatpong Weerasethakul, created a visual poem, *Uncle Boonmee Who Can Recall His Past Lives* (2010), that was both an ebbing away of human life and an elegy for film as a medium.

Documentary with a political edge was surprisingly successful in the mainstream. Guns and violence were the broader target of Michael Moore's satirical *Bowling for Columbine* (2002), which was inspired by the Colorado high school massacre of the title. Former Vice-President Al Gore's environmental polemic *An Inconvenient Truth* (2006), although popular, was outstripped in revenue terms by a more oblique and anthropomorphic perspective on the natural world, *March of the Penguins* (2005), a documentary of the yearly progression inland to breed by the Emperor penguins of Antarctica. The commentary was provided (for the English language version) by the closest cinema has to the larynx of God, Morgan Freeman. Conservative commentators triumphed the stable family units on show; others pointed out that penguins swing a little, changing partners annually. Yet another contingent found evidence to support ideas of intelligent design. The French version was more scientific and less emotive.

In time documentaries tackled the wars in Iraq and Afghanistan. Errol Morris exposed abuses by US military police in Abu Ghraib, a prison near Baghdad, in *Standard Operating Procedure* (2008), while in *Taxi to the Dark*

Side (2007), Alex Gibney exposed the consequences of extrajudicial detention at Bagram Air Base in Afghanistan.

Stories of individuals captured the imagination, whether the mountaineers of *Touching the Void* (2003) or the high-wire artist of *Man on Wire* (2008), a study of self-belief, dedication and concentration made all the more unsettling and compelling by the beautiful images of the lone walker, Philippe Petit, poised thousands of feet above Manhattan on a thin cord held between the twin towers of New York's World Trade Center in 1974. Biographical feature films were suddenly all over cinemas, too, from Che Guevara to Johnny Cash, Hypatia to the Earl of Rochester, William Wilberforce to Marie Antoinette, Jane Austen to Edith Piaf. Running through the list of biopics released in cinemas, some one hundred and forty are listed, twice the number in the previous decade. This may have been a case of commercial conservatism. A picture is clearly easier to pitch and market if it can be presented as a portrait of an individual (even as impressionistic and 'cubist' a likeness as Todd Haynes's film about the many facets of Bob Dylan, *I'm Not There*).

The image of Philippe Petit on the wire between the Twin Towers was doubly disconcerting – firstly for the obvious reason that the monumental buildings were reduced to zero while the tiny figure endured but, secondly, that nothing in those pictures was a digital invention or manipulation. Petit really was up there, all alone, unlike the scores of action heroes who cavorted before blank screens in the safety of studios even if they appeared to be at the top of a skyscraper. Animation and digital realisation were becoming ever more detailed and persuasive as the studios learned how to render hair, eyes and skin. More sophisticated methods of motion capture brought a new natural vitality to virtual characters. Lara Croft in 2001 became the first game character to be given a film presence in the luscious shape of Angelina Jolie. By the end of the decade the video gaming industry was worth around $12 billion annually; having moved from computer to television screen it was now integrated into a system of home entertainment that might be placed in almost any room of the house. With the use of recording systems like TiVo, time could be paused and shifted, commercials removed.

By 2010, many people admitted that their first action on getting up in the morning was to switch on a computer and check emails and social network sites. Facebook was launched in 2004 and attracted 600 million active users by 2011, with Twitter picking up 200 million. Online there might even be the possibility of an alternative existence in fantasy scenarios like Second Life, launched in 2003, not so much a game but somewhere to live for a while. James Cameron's *Avatar* (2009) caught this dream of a parallel existence and infused it with the most advanced rendition of living beings in what appeared to be three dimensions. This dream, or nightmare, was supported by films like the *Matrix* trilogy or *Inception* which also explored the nature of consciousness and memory. The workings of the brain were of increasing interest both to scientists and the general population – partly as a reaction to concern that, with an ageing population, the incidence of dementia in various forms, most notably Alzheimer's disease, would rise dramatically over the following decades. Onscreen this was manifest in films such as the dramatic study of the life and illness of writer Iris Murdoch, *Iris* (2001), or a more oblique imaginative journey into the process of recall in *Eternal Sunshine of the Spotless Mind* (2004).

The Red One digital camera launched in 2007 supplied an ultra-high resolution picture that approached the clarity and richness of analog film. It was also light, weighing around ten pounds. Steven Soderbergh and Peter Jackson were among early adopting directors, Lars von Trier used it for the disturbingly lyrical slow-motion sequence at the beginning of *AntiChrist* and, appropriately for a film about new technology, David Fincher shot *The Social Network* (2010) with it. The quality, flexibility and cost of the product meant that film's future prospects appeared limited (a glance at the products offered by well-known film stock makers certainly indicates a large number of recently discontinued lines). With digital the image is captured at high resolution and transferred on to a digital file for editing and eventual distribution via DVD, hard drive or even by satellite. But there is an unknown here. Will digital storage also degrade? It may not even prove as durable as film.

Films were increasingly distributed digitally – downloaded from one computer to another in the cinema, removing the need for physical film projectors – no more lacing up and reel changing. Digital downloads allow for the possibility of multiple simultaneous openings since distributors and exhibitors no longer have the physical challenge of lugging a limited number of prints around the country. This, in turn, gives cinemas the option of varying the programme during the week – perhaps a feature one night then a performance from a theatre or even a sporting event the next. With food and drink and comfortable seating, certain cinemas started to regain the 'palace of pleasure and varieties' aspect that they had enjoyed a hundred years earlier.

The two great emerging economies of the decade, India and China, continued to develop films for their own internal markets. But they also exported: India sent films abroad to the diaspora and, by influence, through international hits like *Moulin Rouge* (2001), Baz Luhrmann's kaleidoscopic musical that infuses nineteenth-century Paris with the aesthetics and story-telling of Bollywood, and the Mumbai-based *Slumdog Millionaire* (2008).

The success of Asian martial arts films moved into a new dimension with *Crouching Tiger, Hidden Dragon* (2000), directed by Ang Lee, a Taiwanese-American, whose previous film successes had included a Jane Austen adaptation and a 1970s suburban drama. With a Chinese cast and dialogue in Mandarin, the film's scale and beauty captured a wide range of cinemagoers. It was the highest grossing film ever in a language other than English in the United States. China still held a tight quota on the number of foreign films that could be shown in its domestic market but amidst pressure to relax this, it also announced its intentions towards the international market with the first epic Chinese film featuring a mainstream Hollywood star, Christian Bale, directed by Zhang Yimou, who had had an established international reputation for a quarter of a century since *Red Sorghum*.

In this decade, as new media and technologies developed year on year, the choice of how to watch was constantly changing, whether on huge IMAX screens which wrap around the field of vision, or, at the other extreme, on tablet-sized portables or phones, for which at least one drama, Sally Potter's *Rage* (2009), was designed for episodic delivery. Short films, the format that began cinema exhibition, found a way back via the internet, both on specialist film sites and YouTube, which started up in 2001 and offered aspiring filmmakers an unpaid showcase. It highlighted one of the paradoxes of the innovation of digital filmmaking. Yes, it might be cheaper and allow more people access to make the film they want – but how can they find an audience, let alone make any money from one project to finance the next?

Some of the long-anticipated developments failed to germinate. Early forays into 'interactive' films, for example, remained a minority pursuit. Most filmgoers still wanted to be told a story and, if it was not always a conventional narrative, they wanted to be led into an immersive environment – a fantastical location, this world or the next . . . or even inside someone else's head.

· ·

ETERNAL SUNSHINE OF THE SPOTLESS MIND (2004)

Director: Michel Gondry
Cast: Jim Carrey, Kate Winslet
Colour

Not for the first time in cinema, this is a love story that is also a mystery. Joel (Jim Carrey) wakes up depressed, calls in to work sick and takes a train instead in the opposite direction to idle a February day away on a lonely beach. There he encounters Clementine, also apparently walking aimlessly.

Their tentative first conversations are marked by his reticence and her alter-nation between impulse and defence. When Joel makes an early observation, she snaps back, 'You don't know me – so you don't know, do you?'

The uneasy but undeniable attraction continues with a staple of incipient screen romance, the madcap outing. Clementine takes Joel on a midnight picnic on the frozen Charles River. He is nervous – is she going too far? Will they fall through the ice to the deadly cold water? – but eventually they lie together gazing up at the night sky. In the ice beside them is a spidery fissure, a fracture which underlines the fragility of their moment of tranquillity and harmony.

They return to the city and she asks to sleep at his apartment. While she fetches her toothbrush from her own apartment, a stranger knocks on Joel's car window and challenges him. The film has been running for nearly seventeen minutes and suddenly the credits roll. Joel is still in the car but outside it is now clearly night rather than early morning. He is distraught, in shock and weeping. The audience shares his disorientation. What can have gone wrong? It is now apparent that most of the film is taking place in Joel's mind and, because of the process he is about to undergo – a sci-fi creation called 'targeted memory erasure' – it is a surreal and unreliable location. Incidentally, the title of the film is a quotation from Alexander Pope's 1717 poem, *Eloisa to Abelard,* in which the only hope of relief for the famous separated lovers is loss of memory.

'Targeted memory erasure' is the therapy of choice – in an age of so many therapies available for those with the resources to purchase them – for the broken-hearted as explained to Joel in the cod science of the consultant (Tom Wilkinson) at the mysterious firm Lacuna. In the reassuring tones of a 1940s screen psychiatrist, accompanied by suitably period music, he explains that they must eradicate the 'emotional core to memories'. So they do, with Joel both observing and undergoing the treatment. Various forms of treated film evoke the deterioration of the memory – saturated colour giving way to bleaching, fuzziness, darkness, graininess – and illogical events erupt within a scene, undermining the reliability of the narrative. Childhood recollections have an Alice in Wonderland distorted perspective. Joel's world is literally disintegrating around him.

The couple who began with a romantic-comedy-style absurd encounter on the beach have now run into a more puzzling obstacle than typically challenges screen lovers. They must contend neither with social convention nor guilt nor wars nor deserts, but the simple scarring of their own memories. The filmic recall of these memories, culminating in the conditional blissful oblivion of a 'happy ending' with a snowy whiteout on a beach, plays on cinema conventions about memory. Michel Gondry had experimented with various techniques including splicing fantasy into narrative in his music videos. Writer Charlie Kaufman's script for *Being John Malkovich* (1999) had already introduced themes of consciousness. Their collaboration here brought into the twenty-first century the cinematic depiction of memory so familiar from 1940s psychodrama and *film noir*, to which the consultant's speech about memory refers.

The difference here is that memory and the workings of the mind are generally impressionistic and fluid rather than simple, linear, unchanging and – crucially – explanatory. Love, with its inherent dual perspective, makes a fine vehicle for these more ambiguous explorations of memory. Alain Resnais's *Last Year in Marienbad* (1961) anticipates *Eternal Sunshine* in that a man seeks to persuade a woman that they were lovers the previous year; she has apparently forgotten. The viewer dangles between the two accounts and the slivers of images that each invokes.

In 1916, Hugo Munsterberg's book *The Photoplay* saw 'cutbacks', or flashbacks as they would later be known, as 'an objectivisation of our memory function'. The forward momentum of film ensured that each individual watching would also supply 'our own material of memory ideas' which kept the experience fresh on each viewing. Munsterberg felt the new art form could aid in the mapping of the human mind, the complex interweaving of images and narrative strands being close to the performance of neural pathways.

Six decades later, a Russian director, Andrei Tarkovsky, appeared to fulfil Munsterberg's ambitions. In his films, the protagonists might be in one place one moment, elsewhere (forward or back in time) the next, sometimes in colour, sometimes in monochrome. In *Sculpting in Time*, he claimed that Proust 'spoke of raising "a vast edifice of memories", and that seems to me to be what cinema is called to do.' An astronaut in *Solaris* (1972) may be visited in space by his dead wife – who is apparently real to him in a sensory way, since he can feel her touch and breathe in her scent, while *Mirror* (1975) evokes the thought processes of a man lying sick in bed, recalling childhood and contemporary events, including news footage, in a ramble of synapses.

Solaris was remade in 2002 with George Clooney, the same year that Roman Polanski's *The Pianist* won both Palme d'Or at Cannes and Best Director at the Oscars. This adaptation of the memoir of Jewish Polish pianist Władysław Szpilman – who survived the Nazi invasion and subsequent murderous persecution – is unusual in that the central character takes little part in the action. As played by Adrien Brody, he is typically watching the horrors unfold from a house across the street or other hiding place. Like Polanski himself, although older, Szpilman was a witness to the Holocaust who survived while many close to him died. The whole film – with its almost dispassionate tone – may have a coherent narrative but it is, above all, an evocation of a state of mind, a form of recollection coloured by regret and loss and distance.

But do we really file away our memories like film sequences? Perhaps a whole generation's childhoods can be recalled on Super8 format, introduced in 1965, while their children will remember the framing of camcorder recollections. The question of whether film memory has shaped our own sense of recollection is sharply defined in two controversial areas – false memory syndrome and post-traumatic stress disorder, conditions formally identified in the 1980s and 1990s.

The recovery of sometimes suppressed memories is hardly new, a staple of Freudian psychodramas of the 1940s, like *Spellbound*. By the mid-1960s, though, one mainstream feature, *The Pawnbroker*, directed by Sidney Lumet, was attempting to show more precisely the process of reluctant recall in his character Sol Nazerman, an old man whose family perished in a concentration camp. Lumet, in his memoir *Making Movies*, described how he sought to represent Nazerman's thought processes. He began by observing how his own memory worked, even with minor incidents that he wanted to forget – 'suppressed feeling kept recurring in longer and longer bursts of time until it emerged fully, dominating, taking over all other conscious thought'. Lumet experimented with this effect in the edit, splicing ever shorter images from another scene into a continuing narrative. Eventually, he found he could insert segments of one-eighth of a second (i.e. three frames) which he had previously thought was shorter than the human brain could process. So in the film's 'present' Nazerman passes a chain-link fence, behind which children are fighting. Almost subliminally, the historic image of a relative caught by dogs against a similar fence in the concentration camp pops into view. Lumet found the effect strong enough that he was able to reduce the splice even further to just two frames, a twelfth of a second. The climax of this technique was an underground train ride where the subway carriage becomes that of the wagon transporting his family to extermination. Both sequences were shot on a 360-degree pan so that the arc of the camera could be matched exactly and the move appears to be continuous although it spans events twenty years apart.

So successful and so imitated was Lumet's technique that advertisers soon adopted comparable suggestive techniques. Roger Luckhurst in his book *The Trauma Question* (2008) also believes the film informed psychiatric definitions of traumatic flashbacks, culminating in the term being officially recognised by the American psychiatric profession in 1987. A couple of years earlier, twenty-five Vietnam veterans had been diagnosed as suffering from 'combat-related flashbacks'.

Film may have given more than the framework to our sense of recall; it may also occasionally have supplied the content, too. *Stolen Valor* is a study by Vietnam veteran B.G. Burkett and journalist Glenna Whitley with the stated aim of debunking what they believe is a false stereotype of the traumatised or psychotic ex-serviceman. They claim that reported instances of battlefield horrors are often no more than reproductions of images from films like *Rambo* or *The Deer Hunter*. They support their argument by cross-referencing official records with memoirs of veterans, such as the man who claimed he had gunned down a group of fishermen and their families in their boat after mistaking them for Vietcong. There was in fact no record of this incident but it did strongly recall a scene from *Apocalypse Now*. More specific was the testimony of Donald Liston, a former Green Beret who toured the United States speaking of his harrowing experiences as a POW. Liston claimed that he was held in a bamboo tiger cage suspended chest-high in water, escaping only by chewing through the bars. Digging through official files, Burkett and Whitley discovered that Liston had never been a prisoner of war. His 'escape' was 'straight out of *The Deer Hunter*. In order to feel that his story of Vietnam mattered, Liston had to appropriate the stereotypes and clichés peddled by filmmakers and the media.' The authors believed that the soldier had consciously fabricated his story, yet an acquaintance of Liston's suggested that the veteran had somehow convinced himself that his cinematic escapade was in fact the truth.

After a century of moving images, in a medium that appears to resemble our dreams, it may be inevitable that we confuse films with our own recollections, or, at the very least, recall events as if we were watching a movie. The backlash in the 1990s against the concept of recovered memory and the industry that profited from it used this melding of fiction and experience as evidence. Mark Pendergrast's controversial book *Victims of Memory* claimed that psychotherapists were implanting or suggesting false memories in the minds of their patients during hypnosis, and that patients were mixing these stories with other material, including scenes or plots of films.

For the patients, this process was unconscious. 'Many ritual abuse survivors honestly believe that they never saw a movie, read a book, listened to a talk show, or overheard a conversation that provided the details they bring forth in a hypnotic session.' According to Pendergrast, therapists invited patients to think of their memories in movie terms. Some doctors encouraged hypnotised patients to 'visualize their past abuse on a mental movie screen', so that events can be fast forwarded, slowed down, zoomed in. Other therapists, 'looking for repressed memories, encourage their clients to fill in memory gaps, to put together a movie or script'. He quotes analysts who considered traumatic memories as 'a series of still snapshots or a silent movie' where the therapist provides the words and music. So it was not simply a case of movies providing a handy metaphor for the way our memories work; the narrative process shapes the memories themselves, transforming them into stories, which, perversely, makes them feel more authentic: 'we can summon up fragmentary visual images and edit them into an internal movie of our lives . . . with repeated visualisation, or the verbal repetition of the stories they become more real.'

In any case, neuroscientists have begun to question whether human beings do record and recall in a cinematic way, after all. Visual data may be just one element and, unlike much of modern entertainment, not available on demand. Recall involves a complicated process of neural networks linked to many senses – not so much a video to be plucked off the shelf as a shimmering mosaic, different every time. Psychiatrist Harvey Roy Greenberg and literature Professor Krin Gabbard, discount in their paper 'Reel Recollections' the idea that the brain can 'regurgitate' a complete visual memory, as, for example, Rick does when recalling Ilsa in Paris in *Casablanca*, right down to the details of her clothes and the nightclub. Instead, 'the cerebrum decodes and encodes "bits" of visual information along with bits from other senses dispersed through the frontal cortex. Upon requisite stimulus, the appropriate fragments are then recombined as memories in a complex dynamic involving short and long-term storage sites.'

It is not so easy to dislodge cultural associations, however. The philosopher Henri Bergson had first identified image-memory as a 'pure' form of recall in *Matter and Memory* in 1896 and went on to stress its similarity with cinema. Film might even be able 'to assist in the synthesis of memory', as perhaps it has. The parallel development of these strands of philosophy, aesthetics and the incipient science of psychiatry raise question about who was leading whom. As film academic Professor Maureen Turim has wondered, 'did cinematic style itself . . . give more credence to an image theory of memory than it might have gained otherwise?'

It certainly works powerfully upon us. Martin Scorsese's *Shutter Island* (2010) is a film about a man, Teddy Daniels, played by Leonardo DiCaprio, who obscures his unbearable memories with elaborate and increasingly contradictory false recollections. These include 'flashbacks' to wartime service in Germany and the liberation of concentration camps, sequences which employ certain aspects of the horror familiar from newsreels and dramatic representations. These sequences have variously drawn condemnations of inaccuracy and praise for the impressive rendition of the horror. Yet, like the clunky reveal of the final act, this may not be the point. It is the working of Daniels's mind – and the labyrinth it creates – that is the engine of this film, as it is so often with Scorsese's brilliant expressionist filmmaking. Daniels is constantly creating a narrative of unreliable memories, pulling on tropes and images stored in his memory including, no doubt, ones from films. Likewise, the delusional ballerina in Darren Aronofsky's *Black Swan* (2011) imposes her neuroses on the environment and characters around her. Both directors insert minute cuts that disturb the audience by stealth. A character drinks from a glass that is not there in *Shutter Island* or is seen in an environment that is artificially heightened; almost subliminal shots in *Black Swan* have one or other of the female characters in the clothes and pose of another for a fraction of a second – all contributing to the film's themes of doubling and fracture and the breakdown of the heroine's stability.

*   *   *

Twenty-first-century cinema has drawn much inspiration from the odd functioning of the human brain – whether a thriller about a man with memory loss, *Memento* (2000), or an emotional drama about consciousness and communication following a stroke, *The Diving Bell and the Butterfly* (2007). Sometimes the audience is reassured as to where the truth may lie; they can construct a coherent and to that extent reassuring narrative. A Hollywood example is *A Beautiful Mind* (2001), about a Nobel laureate in economics, John Nash, which collected four Academy Awards, including Best Picture. Nash suffered from paranoid schizophrenia, illustrated by his delusions of working in espionage, and three imaginary characters. (In fact, this was artistic licence: Nash's delusions came in several forms but none of them involved hallucination.) However, the film 'explains' his behaviour and appears to resolve his story.

Other films, though – and *Shutter Island* falls into this category – are confined inside the experience of the protagonist, like *Spider* (2002), David Cronenberg's thriller about a schizophrenic played by Ralph Fiennes, or *Donnie Darko* (2001), Richard Kelly's film about a disturbed adolescent, that has given rise to labyrinthine explanations on the internet of ludicrous rationality as to what exactly is happening and how it all ties up. Sometimes, the perspective is so subtle as to be almost imperceptible, such as the dislocation in *The Assassination of Jesse James by the Coward Robert Ford* (2007) or the mood of the Portuguese *The Headless Woman* (2010), which leaves the audience as bewildered as Vero, the distracted middle-aged woman at the centre of this whodunwhat mystery, who may be on the verge of dementia.

The most seductive – and hard to interpret – of these visions of conscious-ness is David Lynch's *Mulholland Drive* (2001). It is Lynch's achievement to have presented what appears to be a thriller and then to lose the audience in it, acknowledging only that it is a 'love story in the city of dreams'. Two actresses are in love, or maybe one of them is dead or about to be. Which is the true story and which the fantasy? Many found this disorientation

– characters reappear in a slightly different guise; trails peter out – frustrating. Yet the film is by turns lusciously involving and intriguing with a peculiar inexplicable logic. As critic Philip French observed in the *Guardian* shortly after its release, 'It seems to me that it is a collective dream – the clue is in the title. Mulholland Drive is a twisting, turning road that tells a story of the history of Hollywood.' Then again, Lynch, practitioner and advocate of transcendental meditation, may believe that the concentration inherent in the journey to understanding may in itself be exercise enough. After all, he claims it is the only one of his films where the ideas actually came to him during meditation. As he explained in his book *Catching the Big Fish*, '. . . somewhere about ten minutes in, *sssst!* There it was. Like a string of pearls, the ideas came. And they affected the middle, the beginning and the end. I felt very blessed.' For those seeking further elucidation, however, the next chapter heading refers to one of the more mysterious sequences in *Mulholland Drive*, 'The Box and the Key.' The chapter comprises one short sentence. 'I don't have a clue what those are.'

Sometimes the picture only becomes clear when you look from a particular position. Michael Powell and Emeric Pressburger's fantastical wartime spectacular, *A Matter of Life and Death* (1946), is considered one of the greatest of British films – poignant in the prospect of imminent death for its central character, twenty-one-year-old RAF bomber pilot Peter Carter (David Niven), beautiful in the contrast between the lusciously coloured earth and the cool monochrome of heaven where Carter is put on trial to see if he should die or live. The film begins with a crisis as the young squadron leader is forced to abandon his flaming aircraft and jump without a parachute. He falls on to a beach and, by rights, he should be dead, but a celestial bureaucratic blunder means he remains on earth, a confusion explained by a visitation from the inefficient functionary responsible for the situation. This vision is diagnosed by a local doctor as brain trauma, chronic adhesive arachnoiditis, attributed to an old injury. Surgery follows during which, as Carter lies unconscious, the 'trial' takes place. Ironically for a film about the afterlife, *A Matter of Life and Death* came to haunt an American nurse specialising in epilepsy, forty-four years after it was released. Diane Broadbent Friedman caught the film by chance on television. She was immediately convinced that what she was seeing was the elaborate rendition of temporal lobe seizures, accompanied by olfactory and other hallucinations. (Carter claims to smell fried onions and to hear strains of a certain piece of music just before each visionary episode.) In her initial 1992 paper, Friedman wrote, 'this film depicts clinical details in such an accurate way that a clinician might diagnose the probable site of the lesion'. She subsequently made enquiries into Michael Powell's research for the film and discovered he had consulted neurologists at Charing Cross and Ashridge hospitals, observed examinations and studied medical records. Further convinced of the film's relevance she wrote a book, *A Matter of Life and Death: The Brain Revealed by the Mind of Michael Powell*. Reviewing it in *The Lancet* in 2009, neurologist Oliver Sacks praised not only Friedman's work but the film itself, which he acknowledged had a 'minutely worked-out neurological basis' and he urged physicians and neurologists to view a restored version. In 1946, though, no one had eyes to see.

AVATAR (2009)

Director: James Cameron
Cast: Sam Worthington, Zoë Saldaña, Sigourney Weaver
Colour

In the winter of 2009–2010, hundreds of millions of people around the world believed they had seen the future. It was living in 2154, it was three metres high, it had a sinuous swishing tail and it was blue. The humanoid

Na'vi – slim, elegant and athletic with the best physical traits of every race combined – were guides to their planet Pandora, avatars for all of us to a new immersive world.

The biggest selling film of all time so far is an elaborately constructed edifice of our collective fantasies, skilfully designed and executed by director James Cameron. Space scientists and military seek to colonise a resource-rich planet, Pandora. To infiltrate the indigenous population they must adopt the bodies and powers of the Na'vi, putting their brains into another, idealised, body. Pandora is covered in tropical rainforests similar to the Amazon basin, its creatures and plants are exaggerated variations on the most spectacular wildlife or natural history television programme with allusive names like viperwolves or Thanator (a deadly big cat/lizard/hellhound with classical pretensions). The planet glows with phosphorescence like an underwater paradise (Cameron has extensive experience of diving and filming the deep). Pandora works 'like a nervous system', according to a line in a promotional video for the film, narrated like a National Geographic documentary. That is, what happens on each part of the planet affects the whole. Pandora, though, is a nervous system in more than one sense. For millions of people, it became part of theirs. Could they believe their eyes? No. Was it less of an experience for that? Clearly not. At one level, *Avatar* is another exploration of how the unconscious works, as the soldier in a wheelchair discards his body for a 'virtual' identity; at another it is the ultimate realisation of the Second Life/gaming fantasies of internet users for whom the term 'avatar' has a more practical connotation.

In the twenty-first century, computer-generated images became more sophisticated and prominent in filmmaking. Even Werner Herzog, the king of hypnotic reveries onscreen, used it judiciously in his film *Rescue Dawn* (2006), comparing its invention to that of the cannon. Yet he was specific about its use. As he explained to website Movieweb in August 2010, in reference to the real struggle of the extras in *Fitzcarraldo*, 'When I pull a ship over a mountain, I pull a ship over a mountain! I want to have the audience back in a position where they can trust their eyes again.'

That is a crucial distinction. The computer effects of the late twentieth century, such as those in Ridley Scott's *Alien*, *Blade Runner* or *Gladiator*, and even in previous James Cameron films going back to *Terminator 2* or *Titanic*, were, however fantastic the premise, intended to persuade the audience that the events onscreen were real. Gradually, though, came the conjured worlds: the afterlife (as though hallucinated by an art historian) in Vincent Ward's *What Dreams May Come* (1998), Baz Luhrmann's lurid version of Paris, created in a Sydney warehouse, for *Moulin Rouge* (2001), or Roberto Rodriguez's hellish pulp metropolis *Sin City* (2005) – black, white and splashes of gore.

Avatar's Pandora invites the audience into an environment that is more impressive than the story, although one element – the way the mind of the injured soldier can travel beyond the limitations of his body – clearly has relevance for every one in the audience. Although *Avatar* delivered this illusion of immersion with the latest 3-D technology, the principle goes back to 1838 when scientist Charles Wheatstone first recognised that each eye sees a different picture which the brain processes as one image to create depth perception. Wheatstone's discovery of binocular vision made for entertainment in the early days of photography in the shape of stereograms, which sold in their thousands. As pictures began to move, in 1907 William Friese-Green patented a 3-D system with two films projected in parallel and viewed through a stereoscope, but the apparatus was too bulky to be practically or economically viable for mass entertainment. In 1915, Edwin Porter screened tests in stereoscopic imagery for a selected audience, but nothing more was seen of his short experiments, despite a correspondent of the *New York Dramatic Mirror* declaring, 'many in the audience appeared to regard them as the forerunners of a new era in motion picture realism'. Eight years later, the first 3-D feature, *The Power of Love*, was shown to two hundred journalists, scientists and photographers, but not, it seems, to the public, as the film was never released.

Stage designers and artists had long played with *trompe l'oeil*, miniatures and deceptive angles to suggest physical depth. F.W. Murnau's silent film *The Last Laugh* (1924), about an elderly hotel porter, drew the audience in further via the introduction of a moving 'unchained' camera and, incidentally, the elimination of intrusive intertitles which might jolt the viewer out of the drama. In the 1930s and 1940s, the most persuasive innovation was the most aesthetically pleasing – depth of focus as devised by directors and cinematographers working together, as Orson Welles and Gregg Toland did on *Citizen Kane*.

In the 1950s the approach was less sophisticated with a clutch of 3-D shockers, musicals and action films such as *Kiss Me Kate* or *House of Wax*. Producer/director Arch Oboler, who made the 3-D African adventure *Bwana Devil* (1952), was quick to spot that even his own creation had a camp gimmickry that would soon make it an anachronism. He was quoted in *American Cinematographer* in August 1952: 'one of the characteristics of 3-dimensional movies, which made it such a spectacular innovation years ago when first presented to the public is the way that objects can be made to appear coming right out of the screen and into the audience. Today such freak innovations must be avoided.' *Bwana Devil* is hardly an advertisement for this observation but a near-contemporary film was – Hitchcock's thriller *Dial M For Murder* (1954). The director used the perspective to place the viewer deep in the claustrophobia-inducing architecture of the cream and brown apartment in which Grace Kelly lives with sinister husband Ray Milland, visited occasionally by her writer lover. Shots looking up from below the wing of an armchair or down from above a chandelier increase the impression of the location as an elegant trap, more torture chamber than refuge. Hitchcock did permit himself one particularly theatrical intrusion into the audience, however. When Kelly wrestles with the man sent to kill her, her hand reaches out behind her – towards the audience – and gropes for a pair of scissors which she then plunges into her assailant's back. When the man falls, dying, he does so towards the audience – landing on his back, arched over the jutting scissors.

Around the same time, exhibitors were playing with the way images were delivered. The experimental Synchro Screen at the Plaza Theatre in New York removed the black masking and extended the sides of the screen, as if eliminating the boundary between audience and film action. Cinemascope and the short-lived three-projector Cinerama prepared the way for the modern IMAX. If 3-D continued to pop out of the screen sporadically in 1970s and 1980s horror or action films – always more of a joke than a revolution – then the twenty-first-century move into large-scale 3-D formats on huge IMAX screens soon demonstrated that the technology works better for creating atmosphere than depicting action.

The 2006 *Superman Returns*, directed by Bryan Singer, viewed in 3-D at an IMAX, was nauseatingly frantic in its action sequences. Where it worked, briefly, was a meditative sequence with a young Clark Kent in his adoptive guardians' farmyard, watching the sky and listening to the sounds of the countryside. Robert Zemeckis' *Beowulf* (2007) flung spears, body parts and all manner of unlikely missiles at the auditorium but inspired a sense of awe only in its realisation of the echoing cathedral of a cave where Grendel's mother (Angelina Jolie) lurks. It was this sense of place that persuaded Werner Herzog to shoot the Palaeolithic paintings on the curving surfaces of caves in 3-D in *Cave of Forgotten Dreams*.

Yet some critics question whether 3-D does in fact do more to 'place' the audience in a situation than deep-focus photography. Mogul Darryl Zanuck, interviewed by *Time* magazine back in 1953, declared: 'We don't need depth. My brain gives me all the depth I need. I've been supplying my own third dimension all my life.' Even before the first general release 3-D feature had appeared in cinemas, Howard Cricks in the September 1951 issue of *Picturegoer* worried that people would baulk at the special spectacles and, even if they could accept the hardware, it might be wasted on almost half the population: 'according to the latest figures something like 45% of the population of this country has defective eyesight in one form or another. Could this mean that just under half the total number of picturegoers would not be able to appreciate stereoscopic films to the full?' Even for those with perfect eyesight, the cinematic version of 3-D is not an accurate replica of our binocular vision, even in films where objects don't leap out at us. As Dave Kehr pointed out in a January 2010 *Film Comment* article, a void sometimes seems to open up between the foreground and background: 'space in stereoscopic films does not appear continuous so much as it seems to be built out of a series of flat planes stacked one atop another.'

Binocular convergence, interestingly, one of the crucial factors in depth perception by the human eye, is only effective for distances less than ten metres, a fact exploited by director Gareth Edwards in rendering the background effects for his low-budget films like *Monsters* (2010). His argument is that we do not perceive – except through shadowing – depth of vision beyond that point. At the other end of the budget spectrum, James Cameron found a solution to what may sometimes appear an awkward gap between foreground and background. As Dave Kehr explained: 'he's filled in the gaps between objects with a continuous field of moving particles – dust mites, tiny insects, mist – that give a visual density to the ostensibly empty space . . . with this viscous space, Cameron has brought an entirely new element to the game . . . a continuum closer to the way we actually perceive the world'. This suggests that every 3-D movie seeking to emulate human vision would have to be set on Pandora or somewhere foggy.

Yet the lustrous atmosphere of Pandora is effective in more than one sense. Those nine-foot avatars projected in vast detail have the sheen of superior computer rendition. The shine in their eyes, the little pulses beneath their gently gleaming skin, the pores and the lashes have returned to cinema a degree of fetishisation that decades of realism had rubbed off. It restores the kind of diffused light that Josef von Sternberg employed to serve Marlene

Dietrich so well. Now that the so-called 'uncanny valley' – the term coined in 1970 by roboticist Masahiro Mori for the revulsion people feel when confronted with a mechanised simulacrum of humanity – has been bridged with superior rendering, the images are becoming so real that we feel we can touch them. And so attractive that we may want to.

For now, at least, we cannot. Even if filmmakers no longer seek to make us duck while the slavering dinosaur's jaws hang over the auditorium, they will never stop inviting us into the scene. Doubtless the emptiness of that invitation and the frustration it may induce worried guardians of our collective psychic health a hundred years ago. Psychologist Hugo Munsterberg identified in 1916 the crux of the filmmakers' and viewers' conundrum: 'we are never deceived. We are fully conscious of the depth, and yet we do not take it for real depth . . . we are constantly reminded of the flatness of the picture because the two eyes receive identical impressions.' Now that cinema has found a way around the essential flatness that Munsterberg identified in 1916, does it confuse our sense of the world?

Dr Susan R. Barry is a neurobiologist who suffered from crossed eyes. She only gained stereopsis (the ability to see in 3-D) after treatment in her forties. Thus newly equipped, she went to see 3-D *Avatar* on its release and wrote about it in her blog for *Psychology Today* in January 2010. She enjoyed the film, being particularly impressed by the forest receding into the distance and, like many, the way the seeds from the magical tree revered by the Na'vi appeared to float in the space between her and the screen. Yet the experience overall gave her pause: 'what you see contradicts the information you're getting from other sensory systems. When we feel a disconnect between our senses, we need to re-interpret where we and other things are in space, and this confusion may induce bodily discomforts.' So some may experience headaches or nausea but more than that, this mismatch of sensory information could trigger a more serious crisis: as Dr Barry explains: 'our sense of ourselves is rooted in our understanding of where our bodies end and the rest of the world begins and in our interpretation of where we are located relative to everything else in space. If we disturb our spatial sense, not only do we upset our sense of security and our ability to move, but we also challenge a fundamental aspect of our identity.'

This existential nausea was not, funnily enough, unfamiliar to Jean-Paul Sartre, who was ocularly challenged himself. In *Words*, Sartre recalls how each visit to the cinema in 1912 would end with the hero triumphant and the villain vanquished. In the silent era, he experienced a perfect revelation of destiny in the convergence of music and plot, the last knife-stab coinciding with the last chord: 'I was satisfied, I had found the world in which I wanted to live – I was in touch with the absolute. What uneasiness, too, when the lights went on again: I was torn with love for those characters and they had disappeared, taking their world with them; I had felt their victory in my bones, yet it was theirs and not mine: out in the street, I was a supernumerary once more.'

That sense of the absolute – a lurid green, blue and pink absolute – was precisely what appealed to many who went to see *Avatar*, not once, but repeatedly. In extreme cases, according to television channel CNN, it was so seductive that these filmgoers found the real world depressingly drab and grey in comparison. A forum entitled 'Ways to cope with the depression of the dream of Pandora being intangible' received more than a thousand posts, including 'ever since I went to see *Avatar* I have been depressed. Watching the wonderful world of Pandora and all the Na'vi made me want to be one of them. I can't stop thinking about all the things that happened in the film and all of the tears and shivers. I even contemplated suicide thinking that if I do it I will be rebirthed in a world similar to Pandora and then everything is the same as in *Avatar*.' And: 'When I woke up this morning after watching *Avatar* for the first time yesterday, the world seemed . . . gray. It was like my whole life, everything I've done and worked for, lost its meaning.'

. . . .

UNCLE BOONMEE WHO CAN RECALL HIS PAST LIVES (2010)

Director: Apichatpong Weerasethakul

Cast: Thanapat Saisaymar, Jenjira Pongpas

Colour

Boonmee is sick. His kidneys are failing. He lives in a rural area of Thailand near the border with Laos, attended by his quiet sister-in-law, Jen, a nephew and another young man, a nurse who changes his dressings. Boonmee is living out his last days.

This film by Thai director Apichatpong Weerasethakul – winner of the Palme d'Or at the 2010 Cannes Film Festival and favourite of critics internationally – is not a melodrama of impending death in the traditional Western sense; there is no dramatic tension over Boonmee's survival. Life continues in the pasture and jungle around his wooden house. A buffalo grazes; Boonmee and Jen stroll around the farm; he lets her taste the honey straight from the frame. They have dinner with the nephew on the veranda. Beyond the blue electric light, the jungle is dark. Conversation is slow, unremarkable but harmonious. Then a fourth person slowly reveals herself at the table – barely there, a faint outline like the Victorian double exposure 'spirit' photographs. It is Huay, Boonmee's wife who has been dead some years but, as she remarks, 'I have no concept of time any more'. After an initial surprise, the quartet fall back into a domestic murmuring. Another diner soon joins them, emerging from the shadows of the house, red eyes glowing, in a gorilla suit that is comic but at the same time strangely impressive. He is recognised as Boonmee's son, Boonsong, also dead.

The film moves on from reel to reel – including a costume fantasy of a medieval princess carried by bearers to a magic pool where she is made love to by a . . . catfish. Boonmee's consciousness is expanding while gradually shutting down – these visions may be previous or future incarnations – and he eventually expires in a womb-like cave, surrounded by his relatives, his disconnected catheter running gently out on the sand, an ebbing life-force. Some time later Jen and her daughter watch television, passively uniting their experience of ghosts, machines and ghosts-in-machines.

The film had many critics in raptures while other viewers were frustrated by its pace and opacity. In an interview with the *Bangkok Post* published in 2010, Weerasethakul talked of being inspired by a factual account of one old man's precise recollection of past lives. Yet the film's relevance went beyond simple human mortality. 'When you watch a film, it's something that's already happened. It already has a past life,' he said.

> Uncle Boonmee is really about cinema to me . . . When you make a film about recollection and death, you realise that cinema is also facing death. Uncle Boonmee is one of the last pictures shot on film – now everybody shoots digital. It's my own little lamentation, this thing about dividing the six reels into six styles. In the first reel, it's my kind of film when you see long takes of animals and people driving. The second reel is like old cinema with stiff acting and classical staging, then it's a documentary style in the third reel. The fourth reel is a costume drama . . .

And so on.

Uncle Boonmee Who Can Recall His Past Lives is doubly a film about death – both the physical shutting down of a living organism and the obsolescence of a method in a twenty-first-century industry. It was released during a period when death hovered over many films. This was not in the explosive, casual way of lethal action films but as a mood or even a character in itself. It arrived in a decade when death through conflict or natural disaster was always present on our television screens but most of us lived sheltered from its presence. In our daily lives we were unlikely to see the dying or the deceased.

*   *   *

Alexandra (2007), directed by Alexander Sokurov, is a Russian film set in the second Chechen War; it is both engaging to watch and hard to decipher. An elderly woman (played by the soprano Galina Vishnevskaya) visits her grandson Denis who is serving at a military base near Grozny. A formidable presence in a print dress, she wanders barely supervised among the tented barracks and into the town. She and Denis sit in a tank and she holds a Kalashnikov with a sudden steely expertise that speaks of her experiences in the Second World War. She is invited into the devastated apartment block of a Chechen woman. There is much to reflect on about Russia and her values. At one point, her grandson brushes and then plaits the silver curtain of her hair – an image, an icon almost, of unconditional familial love.

But is Alexandra there at all? Or, like Boonmee, is her mind wandering at the point of death? Sokurov's earlier film *Russian Ark* (2002) meanders constantly through the decorative splendour of the St Petersburg Hermitage museum. Our guide tells us from the outset that he is a ghost as he takes us with him to glimpse tableaux from the eighteenth century onwards. More than an hour and a half later, he is as real to us as any other figure onscreen. The camera moves on in its continuous shot, never stopping. Excitement builds as young aristocrats gather for a ball and everyone is swept together into a great hall where the orchestra plays. The momentum carries the noisy crowd out, they chatter and cluster on the staircases down and onwards . . . then the camera floats away. We are no longer with them. They are all dead – a perfectly unremarkable conclusion that feels at once sad and celebratory, conveying both humanity and its vanities. They went to a ball when their world was about to collapse.

In 2010 director Alejandro Gonzalez Iñárritu depicted Uxbal (Javier Bardem) a man with terminal cancer in his film *Biutiful*. Iñárritu, who also wrote the film, felt impelled to do so because of what he described as the 'profound thanatophobia [fear of death]' of modern society. To challenge this, he wanted to depict – in the midst of a complex plot to do with immigration and exploitation in Barcelona – a man whose body is failing and whose consciousness is altering in preparation for the inevitable close-down. As with Jean-Dominique Bauby (Matthieu Amalric) in *The Diving Bell and the Butterfly*, the film's perspective is that of the dying man. 'Locked in', Jean-Do experiences the world as if in a bathyscope. Both these characters fight to retain what hold they can on the living – estranged wives, children – with vivid visions both of memory and association.

In *The Death of Mr Lazarescu*, Christi Puiu's 2005 film from Romania, there is no death, or at least none we know of. Mr Lazarescu is a sick man and a paramedic is trying to find him a hospital bed in Bucharest. They go in the back of an ambulance from hospital to hospital, from one emergency room to another, or a corridor, or worse. The power is all in the details of living. The outcome is not in doubt – nor, indeed, for any of us – but it is the way that life is conducted with all the frustrations of a cynical Romanian bureaucracy that makes it so funny and real. A fascinating film for many reasons – it was actually marketed as a popular comedy in Romania, while it also carried off a major prize at the Cannes Film Festival – it refuses to make an issue of the deathbed scene.

Death is a fetish in film. The lavish deathbed tableaux of melodrama, the piled-up body count of gangster epics, the stylised fatal spins of shot cowboys satirised by the pantomime of Franz and Artur in *Bande à Part*, the vertiginous falls from cliffs, the goring, biting, stabbing paroxysms, the long, languishing farewells – all of these are played again and again. The old film print may disintegrate but, as far as we know, we now have the technical expertise to keep those sequences running forever, caught like Butch and Sundance running out into the open, guns at the ready, that idea of escape to Australia still fresh in their minds. They never actually die on screen, of course, they just fade to sepia, but all those other deaths and all that comes before them can be seen over and over again. Long after the participants – director, actors and crew – are dead, their performances will survive as fresh as the day they were recorded.

Screen images ensure that Jack Nicholson as the grizzled old mobster blasted to eternity in Martin Scorsese's *The Departed* (2006) is just as vital as classical pianist Bobby Dupea in *Five Easy Pieces* (1970). In *The Limey* (1998) Steven Soderbergh spliced his contemporary thriller with footage from a 1967 Ken Loach film, *Poor Cow*, featuring the same actor. Sixty-year-old Terence Stamp was playing beside his own youthful beauty. Which of the two images was more real? What more graphic illustration of mortality and humanity can there be? The fragility of life and its transience becomes the more poignant when the screen actor has died young but is captured perpetually moving in the most recent past imaginable. Heath Ledger's final appearance in the Batman film *The Dark Knight* (2008) drew posthumous awards but the film in which he appears that best evokes the passing of time is *Brokeback Mountain* (2005).

Ang Lee's direction of Annie Proulx's short story about two Wyoming cowboys, Ennis del Mar (Ledger) and Jack Twist (Jake Gyllenhaal), won multiple international awards. The film was praised for its sensitive portrayal of homosexual love in a genre hitherto associated with machismo. Its dominant theme, however, is the inability to seize time. One of the unusual aspects of the film is that the dramatic crisis occurs in the first third. After that, the protagonists must live with the consequences as time seeps away. As for most of us, their innermost ambitions are not resolved – or in some cases even stated – by the final reel. The ending sequence, with middle-aged Ennis in his trailer home, touching the shirt of the dead lover who remains as young as when he wore it, is simply done. This is not a senti-mental tableau but a simple shot of a flimsy wardrobe with a glimpse of sky behind, yet it conveys an overwhelming sense of loss and missed opportunity. The whole film has the sense of being a flashback, a narrative dictated by longing rather than chronology.

Elegy is one of the most powerful moods in cinema. Ingmar Bergman's final film, *Saraband* (2003), reunited a couple of actors (Liv Ullmann and Erland Josephson) who had played the same characters in *Scenes From a*

Marriage thirty years before. Death is present in much of Bergman's work, from the hooded figure in the medieval myth *The Seventh Seal* (1957) to the prolonged passing of a sister in *Cries and Whispers* (1972). It is in his lyrical recollections of the past, though, that loss is felt most keenly – in the holiday romance of *Summer with Monika* (1953) or the dappled countryside of childhood in *Wild Strawberries* (1957) where the dead are still vital. His ghosts are so alive that they live on in the scenes with the bereaved.

Filmgoers understood cinema's potential for resurrecting the dead from the very beginning. An early review of the Lumière Brothers' first séance (the nicely ambiguous French term for screening) at the Salon Indien Du Grand Café in 1895 recognised the advantage that moving pictures had over traditional photography. Films could capture life without freezing their subjects in time, mute and immobile. The critic of *La Poste* sensed profound implications: 'when these cameras are made available to the public, when everyone can photograph their dear ones, no longer in a motionless form, but in their movements, their activity, their familiar gestures, with words on their lips, death will have ceased to be absolute.'

In André Bazin's famous essay, 'The Ontology of the Photographic Image', published in a book of his writings in 1958, he defined the history of painting and sculpture as a prolonged attempt to defeat Death by means of what he called the 'mummy complex', a piece of art as an insurance against mortality. Cinema could go further: not only could it trap the likeness, it could create a simulacrum of life itself, it was 'no longer a question of survival after death but a larger concept, the creation of an ideal world in the likeness of the real, with its own temporal identity'.

This juxtaposition of then and now, ourselves as we were and are now, manages to be a memorial and living thing at once. Sometimes, the simulacrum of living is better evoked not by frantic action but by contemplation. When it might seem that cinema had by now exhausted every stylistic and thematic possibility – excessive, minimal, fast, loud, lyrical or colourful – along comes a series of films, many of them, but by no means all, from the East, that do not seek to compete with the herd rushing to ever faster editing and more mobile cameras. These films do not try to outrun time, they inhabit it. As an example, the Mexican director Carlos Reygadas's *Silent Light* (2007) takes contemplation to a real-time extreme with a continuous unedited shot of a tree on a hillside which lasts more than five minutes as the sky changes from the silvery black of night to orange sunrise. Only bird and animal noises accompany.

The pause for contemplation might be a delayed response across a century to the warning by writer and dramatist Leonid Andreyev, quoted by Yuri Tsivian in his book *Early Cinema in Russia and Its Cultural Reception*, of the power unleashed by the medium. In 1909, Andreyev glimpsed his own face onscreen and was profoundly disturbed by the implications of this capture: 'Cinema kills the very idea of identity. Today my mental image of myself is still formed by what I am at this moment. Imagine what will happen when the cinematograph splits my self-image into what I was at eight years old, at eighteen, at twenty-five! . . . What on earth will remain of my integrity if I am given free access to what I was at different stages of my life? . . . It's frightening.'

A century has passed. We could still look at Leonid Andreyev now, if the film still exists. Nor is the process over. Some believe it is only just beginning: Apichatpong Weerasethakul, the Buddhist writer and director of *Uncle Boonmee*, believes cinema is not yet a meditation, or in itself any form of enlightenment. What it may do, one day, is take us somewhere else: 'film is very crude, very primitive . . . the best cinema is the mind, if we can train our mind we can create a super-cinema.' That perhaps is where all this was leading, all along.

EPILOGUE

. . . .

There are those who believe that after a century and more film as a medium is finished, that it has exhausted all its artistic possibilities and is currently consuming its own tail before disappearing in an exhausted blur of self-reference. At the time of writing a film set in the silent era, without dialogue, has been acclaimed at the Cannes Film Festival and purchased for widespread distribution. Is this delayed vindication of the 'purist' notion of what cinema can do, what director René Clair, regretting the passing of silent film, recalled as the 'comfortable numbness that a trip to the land of pure images used to bestow upon us'? Or is it an acknowledgement of how much the relationship between viewer and film has changed over the century – that familiarity has maybe dulled our reactions and that film may not in the future transport and bewitch us to the extent it has done?

We are now subject to more images of greater complexity than ever before through all kinds of media. Moving pictures are no longer confined to cinemas: they may enliven or aggravate a journey on a bus or up an escalator. Television and YouTube put friends and neighbours where stars used to be. Almost anyone can make a film, but in practice relatively few, even the professionals, make ones that are enduringly good.

We are also regularly captured on home video or CCTV and the ownership of images has become an issue for filmmakers both in practice and as a theme. I was reminded of Kieślowski's *The Double Life of Veronique* not so long ago when an unknown correspondent sent photographs to the BBC of me sitting on a train, gazing out of the window, by the look of it in Eastern Europe. This was unnerving: I had travelled to Russia not long before – had I been captured by a stranger's camera? If so, why could I not recall the exact location? The woman was wearing jeans and a parka, which was plausible; it took some scrutiny before I concluded this doppelganger was not me (she had long painted fingernails) but maybe like Kieślowski's heroine, or Sam Worthington's Pandoran identity in *Avatar* or any of the subconscious adventurers in films like *The Matrix* or *Inception*, she is wandering still, living a looking-glass version of my life.

A recent spate of thrillers with intellectual pretensions seems emblematic of the duality of film in our lives, in that they aim to entertain while subverting our perceptions. There would certainly seem also to be a new contemplative quality to film: in apposition to the 3-D, enveloping sound show that is designed to pull audiences into the multiplex and IMAX, there are quiet, almost silent, meditations. Technology moves on and new developments will bring new ways of showing the world; directors including James Cameron and Peter Jackson have filmed at speeds faster than twenty-four frames per second. Will greater detail bring greater revelation?

It seems unlikely that these extremes – the eye-popping spectacle and the quiet contemplation – will be shown in the same venues or be seen by the same people. Current industry trends suggest that funding will be available for either very high- or low-budget pictures aimed respectively at young people and niche audiences, showing either at big venues or in cafés, cinema clubs or galleries, The mid-budget dramas that are more popular with the middle-aged audience, the baby-boom bulge and their younger and older siblings, may struggle to get into production or to be distributed in theatres. This would seem to condemn a generation to decades of downloads via their entertainment centres at home, or it might drive that kind of drama exclusively to television.

Yet a recent conversation with a Hollywood producer – a man whose films have taken $15 billion in receipts – suggests that the communal aspect of cinema-going remains a live issue. However sophisticated the entertainment at home, people, he maintains, will always want to get out of the house.

My children consider *The Lord of the Rings* trilogy as their bildungsroman; we can laugh about it now, but in time those films may well prove to be the ones they revert to in times of uncertainty. With another family we went to see each film as it came out – a winter ritual for three years. Against expectations, film continues to be one of the great communal experiences. Despite the much proclaimed atomisation of society, people demonstrate every day in groups of two, two hundred or two thousand in living rooms or cinema clubs, multiplexes or giant outdoor screenings that, when they can, they still want to see movies together and, best of all, argue about them afterwards.

We will have to resign ourselves to losing the beam from film projector to screen in a digital age. I regret that – the beam instilled something close to a religious formality to the act of watching, and the darkness between frames allowed our stimulated brains time and space to supply their own home movies to add to the version onscreen. Yet there are skilled and imaginative filmmakers still at work and more to come who will bring undreamt-of revolutions to the screen, if we still need a screen; we have increasing access to more than a century of masterpieces; and, in time, film's power to be crystal ball or time machine, therapy or analysis, consolation or revelation may only increase. There's little chance we'll relinquish our collective dreaming any time soon.

ACKNOWLEDGEMENTS

. . . .

The idea for *In Glorious Technicolor* came out of conversations with my long-time colleague Stephen Hughes, who was producing BBC Radio 4's *The Film Programme* at the time. We had both searched without much luck for writing on the way cinema intersects with what you might distinguish separately as life; to us it seemed an endlessly fascinating and important aspect of cinema's history.

This book would not exist without Stephen. His contribution runs through it and I am indebted to him for a good deal of the research, as well as countless invaluable discussions and brainstorms over the years. His imprint is on the best of it. Errors, omissions and the more bizarre idiosyncrasies are all mine.

Gratitude is due to the staff at the BFI Library who provided speedy access to all kinds of material, ably demonstrating the virtues of having all the resources on one site. The London Library proved yet again to be a deep mine of surprises.

Thanks also to the team at Chatto and Windus – editorial director Becky Hardie, Juliet Brooke, and the book's early champion, Jenny Uglow. I'm grateful once again for the support and insight of my agent, Clare Alexander.

At home, Rob, Bex and Elle have long been far from passive consumers of cinema, tolerating my insistence on a projector, but often arguing against everything else. Bex, I'm sorry I made you sit through *Celine and Julie Go Boating* (and I understood the rant about how, for you, it represented the worst in French cinema) but then again, you were touched by *Full Moon in Paris*. Elle, I love that at sixteen you could taste the bitterness of *The Graduate*'s ending; from Ingmar Bergman to Michael Bay, your analysis is always a revelation. Rob, no one's fooled by that pretence of sleeping – as a critic you take no prisoners. Thank you to all family, friends and fellow audiences (bar the talkers and texters) who make film the particular communion it is.

SELECT BIBLIOGRAPHY

Adorno, Theodor, and Max Horkheimer, *Dialectic of Enlightenment* (tr. John Cumming), Allen Lane, 1973

Agee, James, *Film Writing and Selected Journalism*, Literary Classics of the United States, 2005

Agel, Jerome, *The Making of Kubrick's* 2001: A Space Odyssey, New American Library, 1970

Barker, Jennifer M., *The Tactile Eye: Touch and the Cinematic Experience*, University of California Press, 2009

Barry, Iris, *Let's Go to the Pictures*, Chatto and Windus, 1926

Bazin, André, 'The Ontology of the Photographic Image' (tr. Hugh Gray), *Film Quarterly*, 1960

Bergson, Henri, *Laughter: An Essay on the Meaning of the Comic* (tr. Cloudesley Brereton and Fred Rothwell), Macmillan, 1911

Blumer, Herbert, *Movies and Conduct*, Macmillan, 1933

Bordwell, David, *The Way Hollywood Tells It: Story and Style in Modern Movies*, University of California Press, 2006

Bordwell, David, and Kristen Thompson, *Film Art: An Introduction*, McGraw-Hill (8th edition), 2008

Broadbent Friedman, Diane, A Matter of Life and Death: *The Brain Revealed by the Mind of Michael Powell*, Authorhouse, 2008

Brownlow, Kevin, *The Parade's Gone By,* Secker and Warburg, 1968

Brunetta, Gian Piero, *The History of Italian Cinema* (tr. Jeremy Parzen), Princeton University Press, 2009

Burkett, B.G., and Glenna Whitley, *Stolen Valor: How the Vietnam Generation was Robbed of its Heroes and its History*, Verity Press Publishers, 1998

Burnett, R.G., and E.D. Martell, *The Devil's Camera: Menace of a Film-Ridden World,* Epworth Press, 1932

Chion, Michel, *Film: A Sound Art*, Columbia University Press, 2009

Christie, Ian, *The Last Machine: Early Cinema and the Birth of the Modern World*, British Film Institute/BBC, 1995

Clair, René, *Cinema Yesterday and Today*, Dover, 1970

Clooney, Nick, *The Movies That Changed Us*, Atria Books, 2002

Cocteau, Jean, *The Art of Cinema* (tr. Robin Buss), Marion Boyars Publishers, 1992

Cousins, Mark, *The Story of Film*, Pavilion, 2004

Dewe Matthews, Tom, *Censored*, Chatto and Windus, 1994

Dika, Vera, *Games of Terror:* Halloween, Friday the Thirteenth *and the Films of the Stalker Cycle*, Fairleigh Dickinson University Press, 1990

Dyer, Richard, *Heavenly Bodies: Film Stars and Society*, Macmillan, 1986

Feeney, Mark, *Nixon at the Movies*, University of Chicago Press, 2004

Forman, H.J., *Our Movie-Made Children*, Macmillan, 1934

Franklin, John Hope, 'Birth of a Nation: Propaganda as History', *Massachussetts Review*, Autumn 1979

Herzog, Werner, *Herzog on Herzog* (ed. Paul Cronin), Faber and Faber, 2002

Hesley, John W., and Jan G. Hesley, *Rent Two Films and Let's Talk in the Morning*, John E. Wiley, 1998

Higashi, Sumiko, *Cecil B. DeMille and American Culture: The Silent Era*, University of California Press, 1994

Kaes, Anton, *Shell-Shock Cinema: Weimar Culture and the Wounds of War*, Princeton University Press, 2009

King, Stephen, *Danse Macabre*, Everest House, 1981

Kracauer, Siegfried, *From Caligari to Hitler: A Psychological History of German Film*, Princeton University Press, 1974

Kuhn, Annette, *An Everyday Magic: Cinema and Cultural Memory*, IB Tauris, 2002

Levy, Emanuel, *John Wayne: Prophet of the American Way of Life*, Scarecrow Press, 1988

Luckhurst, Roger, *The Trauma Question*, Routledge, 2008

Lumet, Sidney, *Making Movies*, Knopf, 1995

Lynch, David, *Catching the Big Fish: Meditation, Consciousness and Creativity*, Michael Joseph, 2006

Mamet, David, *Bambi vs. Godzilla: On the Nature, Purpose and Practice of the Movies*, Simon and Schuster, 2007

McCabe, Colin, *Godard: A Portrait of the Artist at 70*, Bloomsbury, 2003

McGinn, Colin, *The Power of Movies: How Screen and Mind Interact*, Vintage Books, 2007

McPherson, Edward, *Buster Keaton: Tempest in a Flat Hat*, Faber and Faber, 2005

Mirisch, Walter, *I Thought We Were Making Movies, Not History*, Wisconsin Film Studies, 2008

Mottram, Ron, *Danish Cinema before Dreyer*, Scarecrow Press, 1988

Moley, Raymond, *Are We Movie-Made?*, Macy-Masius, 1938

Munsterberg, Hugo, *The Photoplay: A Psychological Study*, Appleton, 1916

O'Connor, John E., and Peter C. Rollins, *Hollywood's West: The American*

Frontier in Film, Television and History, University Press of Kentucky, 2005

Orwell, George, *The Road to Wigan Pier*, Gollancz, 1937

Packard, Vance, *The Hidden Persuaders*, IG Publishing, 1957

Plantinga, Carl, *Moving Viewers: American Film and the Spectator's Experience*, University of California Press, 2009

Powdermaker, Hortense, *Hollywood: The Dream Factory*, Little, Brown, 1950

Pendergrast, Mark, *Victims of Memory: Sex Abuse Accusations and Shattered Lives*, John Reed, 1996

Richards, Jeffrey, *Visions of Yesterday*, Routledge & Kegan, 1973

Richards, Jeffrey, *The Age of the Dream Palace: Cinema and Society in Britain 1930–39*, Routledge, 1989

Richards, Jeffrey, and Dorothy Sheridan, *Mass Observation at the Movies*, Routledge & Kegan, 1987

Richie, Donald, *Japanese Cinema*, Oxford University Press, 2002

Riesman, David, *The Lonely Crowd: A Study of the Changing American Character*, Yale University Press, 1950

Robinson, Robert, *Eisenstein on the Audiovisual: The Montage of Music, Image and Sound in Cinema*, Tauris Academic Studies, 2009

Sartre, Jean-Paul, *Words* (tr. Irene Clephane), Penguin Modern Classics, 1964

Saviano, Roberto, *Gomorrah: Italy's Other Mafia*, Macmillan, 2008

Schaeffer, Dennis, et al, *Masters of Light: Conversations with Contemporary Cinematographers*, University of California Press, 1984

Schrader, Paul, and Kevin Jackson, *Schrader on Schrader*, Faber and Faber, 1990

Schrader, Paul, *Transcendental Style in Film*, University of California Press, 1972

Scorsese, Martin, *Scorsese on Scorsese* (eds Ian Christie and David Thompson), Faber and Faber, 1996

Sedgwick, John, *Popular Filmgoing in 1930s Britain*, University of Exeter Press, 2000

Shafer, Stephen C., *British Popular Films 1920–30*, Routledge, 1997

Slide, Anthony (ed.), *The Picture Dancing on a Screen: Poetry of the Cinema*, Vestal Press Limited, 1988

Slotkin, Richard, *Gunfighter Nation: The Myth of the Frontier in Twentieth Century America*, Atheneum, 1992

Smith, Murray, *Engaging Characters: Fiction, Emotion, and the Cinema*, Clarendon Press, 1995

Smith, Henry Nash, *Virgin Land: American West as Symbol and Myth*, Harvard University Press, 1950

Sprengnether, Madelon, *Crying at the Movies: A Film Memoir*, Saint Paul, 2002

Tarkovsky, Andrei, *Sculpting in Time: Reflections on Cinema* (tr. Kitty Hunter Blair), Bodley Head, 1986

Thompson, Kristen, *Exporting Entertainment: America in the World Film Market 1907–1934*, British Film Institute, 1985

Thorp, Margaret Farrand, *America at the Movies*, Yale University Press, 1940

Truffaut, François, *Hitchcock*, Simon and Schuster, 1968

Tsivian, Yuri, *Early Cinema in Russia and its Cultural Reception*, Routledge, 1994

Tyler, Parker, *Magic and Myth of the Movies*, Secker and Warburg, 1947

Weaver, James B., and Ronald C. Tamborini, *Horror Films: Current Research on Audience Preference and Reactions*, Routledge, 1996

Wharton, Edith, *Summer*, Macmillan, 1917

Whyte, William H., *The Organisation Man*, Simon and Schuster, 1956

Wills, Gary, *John Wayne: The Politics Of Celebrity*, Faber & Faber, 1997

Wolfenstein, Martha, and Nathan Leites, *Movies: A Psychological Study*, Free Press, 1950

Wood, Robin, and Richard Lippe (eds.), *The American Nightmare: Essays on the Horror Film*, Festival of Festivals, Toronto, 1979

Woolf, Virginia, 'The Movies and Reality', *The New Republic*, 4 August 1926

INDEX